GLASGOW'S DOCTOR

James Burn Russell (1837–1904)

GLASGOW'S DOCTOR
James Burn Russell, MOH, 1837–1904

Edna Robertson

TUCKWELL PRESS

First published in Great Britain in 1998 by
Tuckwell Press
The Mill House
Phantassie
East Linton
East Lothian EH40 3DG
Scotland

Copyright © Edna Robertson, 1998

ISBN 1 86232 055 1

The publishers acknowledge subsidy from the Scottish
Arts Council towards the publication of this volume

British Library Cataloguing in Publication Data
A catalogue record for this book is available
on request from the British Library

The right of Edna Robertson to be identified as the
author of this work has been asserted by her in accordance with the Copyright, Design and Patent Act 1988

Typeset by Carnegie Publishing, Lancaster
Printed and bound by Cromwell Press, Trowbridge, Wilts

*In memory of my friend Dorothy A. M. Geddes,
1936–1998, former Professor of Oral Biology at the
University of Glasgow and Dean of the Faculty
of Dental Surgery of the Royal College of Surgeons
of Edinburgh*

Contents

Illustrations

Plates

Russell with his grandmother and sister

Russell as a student at Glasgow University

Helen Fenton Davidson, Russell's wife

Russell's sister, Agnes

Councillor John Ure, pioneer of the public health movement
in Glasgow

Professor William Tennant Gairdner

Russell in middle age

Russell in his sixties

Councillor Robert Crawford

Councillor Samuel Chisholm

No. 80 High Street, Glasgow, 1860s

Nos 97 and 103 Saltmarket, Glasgow, 1860s

Russell investigating sewage pollution on a Clyde sludge boat

Russell at the International Hygiene Congress in Budapest, 1894

Foreword

James Burn Russell –
Glasgow's Medical Officer of Health
(1872–1898)

JAMES Burn Russell was Glasgow's first full-time Medical Officer of Health. I was its last. No one is more conscious than I am of his lasting importance and I am delighted that at last a book has been written about this remarkable man, one of the truly great figures of late Victorian Glasgow. He has long since been forgotten by the general public – but not by those working in Public Health in Glasgow. In the old Sanitary Chambers in Montrose Street he was almost venerated by successive generations. Even today a bronze bust of Russell, once prominently displayed in Montrose Street, presides over the Greater Glasgow Health Board's latest headquarters – having accompanied the Board in its various flittings. This seems to symbolise his long-lasting influence. His heroic struggle against the extremely poor housing and sanitary conditions of Glasgow was an inspiration to his successors. Even his method of recording statistics continued, in modified form, until the abolition of the office of Medical Officer of Health in 1974. The continuity of recording statistics meant that it was possible to study the waxing and waning of diseases over a period of nearly a century. I did such a study about measles and whooping cough showing how these diseases were being modified with improving social conditions. In like fashion it was possible to record the changing face of other areas of concern such as genito-urinary medicine over a long period.

The importance of walking about in one's district was always emphasised in the old Public Health Department. This was essential to get a feel of what was going on; to rely on the

Registrar General's 10-year census was always dangerous: the bulldozer could have been busy and the whole picture changed in the interval. The Sanitary Inspectors of old knew all about this and made a great contribution to the health of the city. With a bacteriologist colleague I inspected restaurant kitchens and public houses in the city to elicit facts about their cleanliness. These inspections were carried out in the early 1950s prior to the passing of the Food Hygiene Act. Russell's legacy was an inspiration to generations of Public Health Doctors, Health Visitors and Sanitary Inspectors in Glasgow and beyond.

T. Scott Wilson

Acknowledgements

I wish to thank James Burn Russell's descendants, particularly his granddaughter, Agnes Rodgers, and her son and daughter, Ian and Jenny, for their active co-operation and for providing access to valuable unpublished material. Alice Carey, whose husband belonged to another branch of the family, also provided information. Other facts about family history were supplied by Pat Bayliss, of Vernon, British Columbia, where Russell's son settled.

I am especially grateful to Brenda White, who led the way with research on Russell and sanitary administration in Glasgow when she was a member of the Department of Social and Economic History at Glasgow University, and who has been generous with her help and encouragement and with constructive comments on the typescript of this book. Dr T. Scott Wilson, Glasgow's last Medical Officer of Health, has also taken an interest in this project from the outset and offered valuable suggestions after reading the typescript.

Not least, I have to thank the Wellcome Unit for the History of Medicine at Glasgow University under their Director, Dr Johanna Geyer-Kordesch, for sustained help and encouragement and for cheerfully adopting a journalist as one of their honorary research associates. I have found this association extremely stimulating, and while many members of the department have been most helpful, special thanks are due to Dr Marguerite Dupree and Dr Fiona Macdonald, who scrutinised the typescript and made many suggestions which I have adopted. Dr Jonathan Andrews, who was a member of the unit at the time, gave help with the passages dealing with the Glasgow Royal Asylum at Gartnavel.

Dr Dermot Kennedy, Consultant at Ruchill Hospital, Glasgow, and historian of the hospital, cast a clinical eye over the typescript. Other expert help was given by Dr Iain Smith, Consultant at Gartnavel Royal Hospital, Glasgow, and Sam Galbraith, MP, now

Scottish Minister for Health and the Arts. Dr John McCaffrey, of Glasgow University's Department of Scottish History, gave extensive help on the political background. Acknowledgement is also due to Professor John Butt, of Strathclyde University, Brian Kelly, Director of Legal and Enforcement Services for Glasgow City Council, Dr John Womersley, Consultant in Public Health for Greater Glasgow Health Board, Dr S.D. Slater, Consultant at the Victoria Infirmary, Glasgow, Professor David B. Wilson, of Iowa University, Dr Myron Echenberg, of McGill University, Dr Mike Barfoot, of Edinburgh University Library, David Weston, of Glasgow University Library, Dianne Howieson, of the Scottish Law Commission, Barbara Mortimer, of Queen Margaret College, Edinburgh, Adam McNaughtan, Dr Elizabeth Mahoney, and Jane McAllister.

In addition, I would like to thank Professor Michael Moss, of Glasgow University Archives, Alistair Tough, of Greater Glasgow Health Board Archives, and the staffs of Glasgow City Archives, the Mitchell Library, the library of the Royal College of Physicians and Surgeons of Glasgow, Glasgow University Library, the Wellcome Institute Library, London, Cork County Library, and the indomitable *Herald* Library. And apologies as well as thanks to Stockport Central Library, where I inadvertently caused a bomb scare.

A number of friends, including some former *Herald* colleagues, gave professional help and advice, lent books, took photographs, and made suggestions (some more helpful than others!) for titles. They include Lesley Duncan and the late Dorothy Geddes, who both read the typescript chapter by chapter as it was being produced. Jean Reid helped with the index. Help was also given by Harry Reid, Betty Kirkpatrick, Mary Baxter, Anne McLaughlan, Charles Marwick, Helen Lillie, Janey Buchan, Neil Carmichael, A.W. Jarvie, Jeanne Brady, Isobel Risk, William Hunter, and my sister, Linda Chapman, our family's genealogist.

The frontispiece portrait of Russell was supplied by the Wellcome Institute Library, London, and William Gairdner's by the Royal College of Physicians and Surgeons of Glasgow. Maps are by Mike Shand, of Glasgow University Department of Geography and Topographic Science.

Preface

If grapes grew and ripened in the slums of Glasgow, or
the orange and myrtle were luxurious and plentiful as
daisies and thistles in the fields, people would say, 'it is a
miracle,' and yet we go confidently in search of delicacy,
refinement, and high-toned morality amid physical
circumstances which are equally inimical to those fine
growths and efflorescences of the moral nature of man.

James Burn Russell

THE tall, stooping, bearded man with his slightly Roman nose and blue-grey eyes was a familiar figure in some of the vilest areas of late-Victorian Glasgow. James Burn Russell, the city's first full-time Medical Officer of Health, was no desk-bound administrator. He was constantly out and about in the poorest parts of the city, knocking on the doors of damp and airless dens and ill-lit single ends, wading across backcourts green with slime, or striking matches to light his way up dark staircases.

He visited the old woodcutter, whose 'pale, shrivelled face' could be seen by the light of the paraffin lamp as he sat sorting sticks into bundles and tying them up with string. He called on the two old ladies who sat sewing in a garret which had no carpet but a well-scrubbed floor. He knocked on the door of the woman whom he thought of as Salvation Sal – a rugged-faced warehouse cleaner and reformed drunkard who lived with her distinctly unreformed husband in a dilapidated, earthen-floored tenement in a cul-de-sac farmed out to hawkers, beggars, and street walkers.[1]

Russell, who as a boy had been fascinated by the wilderness tales of Fenimore Cooper, thought of these worthies as backwoodsmen among the Red Indians of Glasgow's criminal sub-culture, 'moving out warily in the daylight, keeping close inside in the dark, with the storm of the drunken brawl bursting on their ears from the court beneath.' But he also came into contact with the 'Indians', the criminal types who were clearly distinguished in Russell's mind from the colonies of skilled workmen and labourers whose fondness for the bottle might sometimes land them in trouble. The really desperate characters, Russell noted, were to be found in the backlands – houses built in the backcourts of other houses – where watch was readily kept, defence easy, and attack difficult. Those tenants who were not obviously criminal were 'mysterious and enigmatic' but as medical officer Russell was trusted as no other official would have been. The sanitary official, he remarked, saw these people as no one else saw them: 'They receive him frankly. He takes no notice of the evidence of gruesome business that he sees about. His eyes are only for the leaking roof or the damp wall ... Information as to the comings and goings of people in those localities is difficult to get, but the sanitary man never tells the police.' Russell's unassuming manner must also have encouraged confidences.

His accounts of what he saw and heard offer incomparable insights into slum conditions in late-Victorian Glasgow. They also enabled him to enlist influential opinion in his crusade for sanitary and environmental reform. At a time when Scottish novelists had little interest in urban conditions Russell did more than anyone else of his time to open the eyes of the middle classes to the grim realities of slum life. This was one reason why Glasgow, which at the beginning of the Victorian era was judged to have the worst living conditions in the civilised world, was by the end of the period internationally renowned for its public health service.

Many people played a part in that remarkable change but Russell's name deserves to be remembered more than any other. Grapes were still not growing in the streets of Cowcaddens or Calton when he had finished his work, and he would not have claimed to have realised his ideal of making the city as healthy a place as the country. Conditions had deteriorated so drastically in the first part of the nineteenth century that the dramatic reduction in the death rate achieved in Russell's time merely brought it back to the level of a hundred years before. But Russell battled heroically against overwhelming problems and had every right to claim that during his quarter of a century as MOH, from 1872 to 1898, remarkable progress had been made 'in the development of Glasgow towards a clean and healthy life for all its citizens.'

As MOH at a time when health provision depended largely on local initiative he was very much part of the great flowering of municipal enterprise that made late nineteenth-century Glasgow an inspiration to other Scottish cities and even to some transatlantic ones. With his broad, environmentally conscious approach and his emphasis on preventive medicine he believed that 'every public park, and the flowers and music which attract people thither, every open space and children's playground, every cricket and football field, every gymnasium and drillground, is a precaution against Consumption.'[2] This sense of mission helped to make Russell the leading figure in Scottish public health by the end of the century: a presence in the land.

Other cities, of course, also made advances in these years, but Russell was fighting against exceptionally heavy odds, cutting Glasgow's death rate from 29 per 1000 to 21 per 1000 during a period when the city's population increased by some 200,000. As he remarked in 1886, 'Glasgow is devouring the population of Scotland even more rapidly than London that of England.' He was up against not only unimaginably atrocious housing conditions but also local resistance to reform and a general reluctance to recognise the causal link between destitution and disease. Russell challenged these attitudes with an energy and persistence unmatched elsewhere in Scotland. The late-Victorian period produced other Scottish medical officers of eminence and formidable ability – Henry Littlejohn of Edinburgh, Matthew Hay of Aberdeen, and John McVail of Stirlingshire. But unlike Littlejohn and Hay, who occupied university chairs of forensic medicine, Russell devoted all his working hours to grappling with the problems of urban life – 'To be MOH of Glasgow, it takes all of your time, and more,' he once remarked. In that respect he followed in the footsteps of the pioneering William Henry Duncan of Liverpool, the first MOH to be appointed in England, who was so committed to public health that he insisted that his post should be made full-time. Russell also resembled the great John Simon, London's first MOH before he moved on to the national stage, in combining scientific thinking and literary power to devastating effect.

As an arts student at Glasgow University Russell had won prizes for essays and verse composition. The commonplace book that he kept in his youth could well have been that of a future philologist, historian, or naturalist. His literary skills and range of interests served him well in his work as MOH. He presented his case with statistical thoroughness and scientific rigour – having been one of Kelvin's most promising students before starting his medical studies – but he knew how to bring the facts to life with a vivid turn of phrase. He described Glasgow as a semi-asphyxiated city and remarked that it was safer to fall asleep under a tree in Central Africa than under a lamp-post in the Briggait. As he once pointed out, the conventional phrases give an inadequate picture:

'We say "damp" when the hearth-stone never dries, when the joists are buried in earth and rotten, or the bits of old carpet or waxcloth spread on the planks to cover the holes are wet and mouldy ... We say "defective in light" when, in the longest and brightest summer day, the gas, or more usually a paraffin lamp is kept burning, and when often, in the extremity of poverty, there is no artificial light but a glimmer of red ashes ... We say "want of ventilation" when the house door opens off a court with a window beside it, and if you go to the innermost recess of the apartment the air seems to be a sort of residue of all the breath that has ever been breathed in it.'[3]

He lectured endlessly, often to small groups like Park Church Literary Society. Such audiences suited his reserved personality (friends spoke of his 'morbid fear of public speaking') but also enabled him to target listeners whose opinions counted. He shrewdly appealed to enlightened self-interest by arguing that neglect of public health would in the end cost the ratepayers more than positive measures, but he also appealed directly to the feelings of his listeners, inviting them to consider how they would cope with life in a single-end, and shocked them into an awareness of conditions in the slums. In one of his most in-fluential papers, 'The Children of the City,' he told his audience: 'Of all the children who die in Glasgow before they complete their fifth year, 32 per cent die in houses of one apartment; and not 2 per cent in houses of five apartments and upwards. There they die, and their little bodies are laid out on a table or on the dresser, so as to be somewhat out of the way of their brothers and sisters who play and eat in their ghastly company. One in every five of all who are born there never see the end of their first year.'[4]

Although a shy man, Russell frequently became embroiled in controversy: he fought pitched battles with the medical establishment and town councillors and upset the city's architects. He had his detractors at the time and has had his critics since. His public health regime has been criticised by some as authoritarian, but his instincts were anti-establishment and his writings leave no room for doubt that he was driven by compassion rather than a desire for social control.[5] Whatever his shortcomings, he was a man of ideals who saw that the slum clearance programme was no more than half a policy and insisted on tighter building regulations so that the new houses would not replicate the faults of the ones that had just been pulled down.

Why, then, less than a century after his death, is his name not better known in the city on which he made such a powerful impact? One reason is that although Russell was 'almost venerated' by succeeding generations of public health officials[6] this side of Glasgow's history was for long neglected and undervalued. This has since been remedied and Russell's greatness has been given scholarly recognition.[7] Sadly, though, his name, which a century ago was known in Budapest and Boston, is now unknown to the majority of Glaswegians.

Russell himself is to some extent responsible for this neglect. With an innate preference for obscurity he ignored calls for the publication of a collection of his work and turned down a knighthood. If fame had been the spur he would have chosen a more fashionable branch of medicine, or a more glamorous profession – perhaps by continuing his association with Kelvin.

Characteristically, he left no diaries for posterity, despite having been an incessant writer of papers and reports. Nor did he leave any family in Glasgow to help keep his memory alive. Little has been recorded about his married life. His wife died 20 years before him, which undoubtedly had much to do with

his increasing reclusiveness in later life. The records of Glasgow
Necropolis provided the clue to the strange and tragic circumstances of her death. The rest of the story emerged after I had
succeeded in tracing his granddaughter, Mrs Agnes Rodgers,
who was able to provide much original material, including a
journal kept by Russell during the Atlantic Cable expedition.
The trail that eventually led to Agnes Rodgers's door is
described at the end of the book. Unpublished correspondence
held in the Wellcome Institute Library yielded additional
information.

Russell's story illuminates some of the darker corners of
Glasgow's Victorian past, but he also has messages for our own
times. As a Victorian Liberal who did not believe in a state-
funded national health service, and who thought it was better
for people's souls to make charitable contributions than to pay
taxes, he does not slot neatly into present-day political debate.
Yet he was the enemy of mean-spiritedness and argued passion-
ately against ideologues like Herbert Spencer who insisted that
sanitation should be left to market forces. 'What can one man
wedged up in a crowd do to get fresh air, pure water, more
standing room, or to avoid his neighbour's disease?' he asked.
In his view there had to be co-operation, not only locally but
nationally and internationally.

As he put it: 'Self-interest enlists the most enlightened nations
in the promotion of the physical welfare of the poorest and most
wretched inhabitants of the remotest corners of the earth.'

Although Russell has a message for posterity he appears to
have had no interest in posterity's view of himself. With his
elusive personality he is good at escaping the clutches of the
biographer. There are gaps in the story; mysteries remain. The
trail of some of his foreign travels has gone cold. There are
minor as well as major puzzles. Among the letters which he
kept till the end of his life is, for example, the following scribbled
note which he must have been sent in his youth: 'My Dear Jim,
Be kind enough to look in upon me this evening: about half
past five if convenient: bring your Heroditus with you – nobody
is to know of your calling – I'll explain. P. McK.' The biggest
mystery is his personality, which defies analysis. This book is
therefore not so much a full-blown, definitive biography as an

attempt to show the influence of this singular man on Glasgow's social history, and some of the influences which helped to make him what he was. Incidentally, although he had come to be widely known as James Burn Russell by the end of his life, he always signed himself James B. Russell. The quotations at the beginning of each chapter are from his writings.

Chapter One

Broomielaw Launching

*The Clyde – a river which flows through the richest coal
and iron fields in the kingdom, and spreads its arms at its
junction with the sea as if to welcome the merchant ships
of the world.*

G LASGOW was changing rapidly when James Burn Russell
was born on May 5, 1837, a few weeks before Queen
Victoria ascended the throne. Before her long reign
ended the city would become the workshop of the world.[1]

Russell's background could not have been more closely connected to the city's rising fortunes. He was born in Robertson
Street, round the corner from the cranes, sheds, and busy quays
of the Broomielaw. Among the first sounds to reach his ears
must have been the shrill notes of the new steam whistles that
were introduced to the river steamers in the year of his birth.

His grandfather, James Russell, who also lived in Robertson
Street, was the steamboat harbourmaster. A hero of the Battle
of Waterloo, he had taken up this appointment in 1823 after
obtaining his discharge from the Army. The first steamboat
harbourmaster to be appointed by the Clyde Navigation Trust,
he combined his duties with those of captain of the river police.
This formidable man was to be probably the most powerful
influence on his grandson's life.

James Russell and his wife Margaret had three sons, who
grew up to be a missionary, a printer, and a barrister at the
English Bar. The middle son, David, the printer, was James
Burn Russell's father. Then 28 years old, he was a partner in
the small letterpress and stereotype firm of Aird and Russell in
Buchanan Court, off Argyle Street.[2] A few months later, with
financial help from his father, he acquired sole control of the
business when John Aird set off to become a missionary in
Jamaica. David Russell was once described as 'a letterpress
printer of the good old times, when the traditions of the Foulis

brothers were still green, and typography had yet something
of the character of a fine art.'

David Russell's father provided more than financial backing.
He and his wife obligingly moved farther along Robertson
Street, leaving their original house to be occupied by David and
his wife Agnes and the baby. The young couple had married in
the previous summer when Agnes Cassels was only nineteen –
eight years younger than her husband. She was the youngest
daughter of John Cassels, a grain merchant in Calton, the former
weavers' village which had become a working-class burgh and
had not yet been absorbed into Glasgow despite being only half
a mile east of Glasgow Cross. (In its brief life as an independent
burgh Calton, which boasted its own police force, pursued a
notably progressive line in sanitary matters.) Though not involved in public affairs the Cassels family, like the Russells, was
making its contribution to urban development. One of Agnes's
three brothers, Robert Cassels, was to become the founder of
the Glasgow Iron Works at Garngad. Another was a merchant
with a house in well-heeled Monteith Row on Glasgow Green.[3]

At the time of his son's birth David Russell may have reflected
on how the area around Robertson Street had changed since
his own boyhood days. He had been 14 years old when his father
became steamboat harbourmaster, a decade after Bell's *Comet*
had made the Clyde 'the nursery of steam navigation.' The
dredging of the river resulted in a tremendous increase in traffic
and by the mid-1830s sailing vessels from North America and
the West Indies were berthing regularly at the Broomielaw,
along with the rapidly growing number of coastal and river
steamers.

Unfortunately the quay space had not expanded with the river
traffic. The steamboat harbourmaster was constantly having to
listen to complaints from captains of coastal vessels who objected
to the preferential treatment given to the big ocean-going ships
in the scramble for berths. In the graphic language that his
grandson was later to use when calling for environmental reform, James Russell described his problems to the Clyde
Navigation trustees and argued forcefully that additional quay
space was 'indispensably necessary in order to accommodate the
rapid increase in trade.' A permanent berth for passenger ships,

he added, would be of particular benefit to women and invalids, to save them from having to clamber across the decks of cargo boats to reach dry land.[4]

There were other problems. By the time of Russell's birth the inhabitants of Robertson Street must have been acutely aware of the smells as well as the sounds of the river. Conditions in the Broomielaw had deteriorated since the days when the youngest of the three Russell brothers used to recite his school homework to his father in the shelter of the harbourmaster's hut on the quayside. The Clyde had become an open sewer, its filthy waters churned by the paddles of the river steamers. Dirt and sludge were accumulating in the street and in bad weather streaming down to the quays to make life even more difficult for foot passengers. The steamboat harbourmaster fired off a letter to his employers, urging them to arrange for the Clyde Navigation Trust scavengers to take over the cleaning of the street as well as the quays.

It was part of a much bigger problem. Glasgow was growing at breakneck speed during the Industrial Revolution. A human tide was rolling in from Ireland and the Highlands. The population had almost trebled since the start of the century to become more than a quarter of a million by the time of the young Russell's birth in 1837. Glasgow's textile age was soon to give way to the age of iron and engineering: already the furnace fires were casting their glow over the city. The first Clyde-built iron ships had been launched at Whiteinch.

Incomers in search of work swarmed into the medieval core of the city near the factories and mills of the east end. The working-class tenements were partitioned and sub-divided, and shoddy new dwellings sprang up in their backyards till the whole area became 'a compact mass of building intersected only by narrow wynds.' Other cities were growing in an unregulated way but what made Glasgow exceptional was the tremendous concentration of population in this relatively small area well to the east of its burgeoning new terraces of Blythswood.

The city was ill-equipped to cope with this relentless surge. Its rapid increase in wealth had come unexpectedly and development was more haphazard than that of Edinburgh. The urban area still included a number of independent burghs, an anachronism which meant that adminstration was parochial rather than municipal. Medical officers of health, sanitary inspectors, and permanent health boards were still unknown – in Glasgow as elsewhere – when the Victorian era opened. The city had several miles of sewers – a remnant of the tradition of civic intervention established in the eighteenth century – but also streets with open channels like elongated cesspools. In some areas human excrement was disposed of by sink-like contraptions outside the stair windows which were connected by wooden pipes to the stinking dunghills below. The muck accumulated till farmers arrived to buy it for their fields, a valued perquisite for the landlords. There was no public water supply: the Loch Katrine development was 20 years in the future. The Clyde, along with the ancient wells, was the source of much of the city's water supply, and the destination for most of its sewage.

Living conditions were particularly atrocious in the wynds and vennels around the High Street, the Saltmarket, and the Briggait (or Bridgegate). There were houses where cows and pigs lived with the family, dens where a whole family slept in one bed and several families slept under one roof, hovels with earthen floors, cellars regularly flooded by the Molendinar burn, common lodging houses where a score of people slept on straw on the floor of one room, dwellings without proper drainage or ventilation, backcourts with dunghills as high as the first-floor landing. A police officer was permanently posted at the entrance to the most notorious of these wynds. The area was described as an 'abode of crime' by Frederic Hill, writer on crime subjects, who visited Glasgow in the year of Russell's birth.[5]

The Assistant Commissioner on the Condition of the Handloom Weavers, J. C. Symons, picked his way through this filth and fetid squalor in the late 1830s. He reported that although he had seen appalling scenes of human degradation in England and abroad he had not believed, before visiting the wynds of Glasgow, 'that so large an amount of filth, crime, misery, and disease existed in one spot in any civilised country.' The Chief Constable of Glasgow, Captain Miller, who accompanied Symons on his rounds, used even more vivid language. He described the city as an accumulated mass of squalid wretchedness, a loathsome and pestilential place with houses not fit to

be pigsties and apartments filled with 'a promiscuous crowd of
men, women, and children all in the most revolting state of filth
and squalor.' A few years later the report of the Poor Law
Commissioners under Edwin Chadwick concurred with these
opinions.[6]

The scourge of Asiatic cholera, after an absence of two cen-
turies, returned to Glasgow five years before Russell was born.
Lesser outbreaks followed over the next few years, together
with epidemics of typhus and typhoid. Medical opinion was
divided as to the cause – the miasma rising from the drains and
dunghills, or contagion, or poverty leading to lowered vitality.
In so far as Scottish doctors were less inclined than English
ones to believe in the miasma theory the incentive for sanitary
reform was smaller. Meanwhile the popular belief that epidemics
were acts of God produced fatalism towards disease. There were
no preventive measures. When epidemics struck, a fever hospital
would be rapidly constructed, only to be just as rapidly dismantled when the emergency was over.

The connection between the environment and disease was not
lost on everyone. A few brave voices had been raised. A Glasgow
University professor had called for public water closets and
rigidly enforced measures 'to promote the general health.' But
the commercial and professional elite, relatively small in comparison with those of other Scottish cities, was more interested
in moral than in physical cleansing.[7] Glasgow would have to
wait another two decades for a sanitary movement.

The city, still heavily dependent on the textile industry, was
easily affected by movements in the trade cycle; and typhus
invariably accompanied a downturn.[8] An epidemic was raging
in the year of Russell's birth, a time of recession and high
unemployment. The cotton spinners were on strike and roamed
the city in half-starved bands. Among the handloom weavers
there was chronic distress as new factories continued to open.
The fever wards, like the houses, were overflowing. More than
5000 typhus cases were treated in the Infirmary in 1837. The
outbreak pushed mortality 60% above its normal level. Robertson Street was not in the worst part of town – it was nowhere
near as nasty as Pipehouse Close, Havannah Street, and other
notorious haunts around Glasgow Cross. But disease was

rampant, too, in the tenements near the Broomielaw and the adjacent burgh of Anderston. Highland immigrants, many of whom were seafaring people, were crowding in (a local doctor recorded that there were many houses in which English was not spoken). From a single tenement, in a street running from Argyle Street to the river, 60 typhus cases were sent to hospital by a local doctor in a single winter.

It was not an ideal environment in which to bring up children. But it was probably on account of the mother's health as much as the child's that not long after Russell's birth the family moved to a cottage (probably purchased by his grandfather) on the rural outskirts of Rutherglen, some three miles from Glasgow. Agnes Russell was suffering from consumption, a disease on which her son was one day to become an internationally recognised authority.

The country air failed to effect a cure. The young couple's second child, a girl, was born in the autumn of 1838, but Russell's mother died in the following summer, just a few weeks after his second birthday. She was buried in Rutherglen's Parish Church of St Mary's. The funeral cost ten shillings and the parish register records that there were four ushers. Agnes Russell was 22 years old when she died. It was the first in a series of tragedies in James Burn Russell's life.

Chapter Two

Waterloo Legacy

The opportunity of the child is the education of the adult.

AFTER his wife's death David Russell and the two children continued to live in the house in Rutherglen, where his parents joined them on his father's retiral several years later. Auburn Cottage stood about a quarter of a mile from the burgh in gently hilly country in the north-west corner of Rutherglen parish, near the public footpath to Cathcart. Its grounds were separated from the neighbouring properties by march stones, but there was a right of way to the old well in the garden. James Burn Russell's grandfather was proud of his house. He wanted it to remain in the family after his death as a memorial to 'the successful industry and moral rectitude' of himself and his wife. The wish was unfulfilled but the puritan work ethic behind it was thoroughly instilled in the young Russell.

There could hardly have been a greater contrast with the Broomielaw's urban clamour. Rutherglen had been a more important trading centre than Glasgow in late medieval times and before long would regain commercial significance; factories were spreading east from the city as rapidly as fashionable terraces were spreading westwards. But the Industrial Revolution had not yet made much of a mark on the ancient burgh, which still consisted of a broad main street with wynds on either side.[1] The surrounding countryside was 'beautifully diversified with a regular succession of hills and narrow dales'. From the top of Hundred Acre Hill, near Auburn Cottage, young James and his sister could look down on fields dotted with country houses and comfortable farm-steadings, with Cathkin Braes in the background. Speedwell, forget-me-nots, silverweed, and a profusion of other wild flowers bordered the footpath below.[2]

During his Auburn years Russell acquired a love of hill-walking and natural history which was to last his lifetime. Less expectedly, his rural upbringing may have contributed to his understanding of the problems of Glasgow slum-dwellers. One of his closest colleagues remarked that 'Dr Russell had the great advantage of being brought up in the country, thus mixing with, and knowing intimately from childhood all classes of persons, their customs, and their views of life, and in consequence had developed that sense of personal sympathy with mankind in general which as a rule can only be acquired in youth.' Town life, Russell's friend added, was so artificially segregated that the conditions of the poor were regarded as problems to be solved 'according to the type of mind of the thinker' rather than as 'matters pertaining to human life.' [3]

The countryside was Russell's playground. One local history records that he and his sister Agnes ('Aggy') used the ancient well near the cottage for games of 'dockies' – climbing on to the top ledge and jumping to the ground.[4] It seems unlikely, though, that they were among the band of local children who used to sell tins of water from the quarry well to thirsty promenaders from the city.

Many of these visitors had come to Rutherglen in search of something stronger. The owner of the property next to Auburn Cottage was a local celebrity popularly known as Bauldy Baird, who earned a living by turning the grounds of his cottage into a pleasure garden and serving 'fruits in their season' with curds and cream to Sunday strollers from Glasgow and courting couples arriving from the city by boat. His house was also 'notorious for its Sunday traffic in other things besides gooseberries,' for the enterprising Baird also dispensed Glenlivet. The Sunday walkers used to make a circuit of Rutherglen and Cathcart 'more frequently than was strictly necessary for health purposes with the result that the little exclusive garden in Bauldy's backyard became the most popular rendezvous in Rutherglen.' It was less popular with the Russells, who objected to the loud laughter from the next door garden. David Russell, James's father, took Bauldy Baird to court, alleging that his licence had been wrongly granted. After a fierce legal battle the licensing court put a stop to this Sunday trade. The Russells appear in a poor light in one contemporary account of the incident in which they are described as 'virtuous neighbours ... who were determined that there should be no more "cakes and

ale".' The writer's sympathies were clearly with Bauldy, who
soon 'found his occupation in a great measure gone, his garden
an unpeopled wilderness, and himself a standing jest for trium-
phant teetotallers.' [5]

James Burn Russell was himself to be a lifelong abstainer.
His father, however, was a waning influence. Not long after the
Bauldy Baird incident he left for Australia and became literary
editor of the *Sydney Morning Herald*. According to family tradition he left under a cloud, his relatives having disapproved of
a liaison that he had formed with a Russell cousin. It is also
possible that his printing business had fallen on hard times. The
firm, which never became one of the better known printing
businesses in the city, may have been vulnerable to the business
recession of 1847.

Russell was then in his early teens. For the second time, a
great gap had opened up in his life. Later, when he was 17, he
wrote about it in a poem to his father published in the *Glasgow
Citizen*, in which he lamented 'that lang-empty armchair.' [6] After
his father's departure he and his sister remained in Auburn
Cottage with their grandparents. There is every indication that
his grandfather in particular was a strong formative influence.
In later life one of Russell's colleagues remarked that he had
the vivid Celtic imagination of his grandmother, Margaret Macdonald Russell – a Glasgow Highlander born in the Gallowgate
– as well as the sterner virtues of his Lowland grandfather; but
it was with the latter that he was most often compared.[7] James
Russell was regarded as a 'man of sterling worth' and of 'high
ideals and strength of character.' A devout man, who was apt
to quote from the Book of Proverbs in letters to his sons, James
Russell was one of the oldest members of the congregation in
Glasgow founded by the famed Congregationalist preacher, Dr
Ralph Wardlaw, and used to take his young grandson to the
West George Street chapel to hear him preach.[8] Russell was to
remain an active Congregationalist all his life.

He and Agnes had a strict upbringing. The moral tone of the
household was conveyed by the birthday present that the two
children, at the age of six and five, gave to their grandmother:
a copy of the *Memorial of the Life of the Rev. J. Williams, Missionary
to Polynesia* (although Margaret Russell would have had a

personal as well as religious interest in the subject since her eldest son, Russell's Uncle James, was a missionary). As a former sergeant-major in the Scots Greys their grandfather was a practised disciplinarian: when he left the Army to become Glasgow's steamboat harbourmaster he had had, in the words of one of his contemporaries, 'to overcome the prejudices of nautical men to a mere landman, and to introduce order and discipline where there had been previously little of either.'[9] In later life, James Burn Russell used to tell his children how his grandfather, a self-educated man who had carried a dictionary in his kit at Waterloo, had once corrected his pronunciation when he was reading aloud, and when his advice was rejected said: 'James, pronounce the word correctly, or I'll knock you down.' The boy still refused, and was duly knocked down. The story illustrates not only the grandfather's strictness but also the grandson's stubbornness, a characteristic that he was certainly to display as a health administrator.[10]

Despite this clash of wills there was a strong affinity between Russell and his grandfather. In later life Russell used to gain reflected happiness by looking back on the summer visits to Monreith in Wigtonshire that he used to make with the old man.[11] James Russell was undoubtedly a caring and understanding grandparent, for he, too, had lost his parents early in life and spent his boyhood as a herd near Lanark. He had later become apprenticed as a mason in Glasgow, where relatives had a business in Dempster Street, near the quarry above the present George Square. Afterwards he used to point with pride to buildings in the Trongate in which he had had a hand, but becoming 'disgusted with his trade, and especially with the tyranny of the foreman', he enlisted in the Royal North British Dragoons, or Scots Greys, in 1798 and had been promoted to troop sergeant-major by the time of the Battle of Waterloo.[12]

His grandson heard of his exploits on the battlefield from an early age, most likely from his father, on whom they had made a deep impression. David Russell had been six years old when his father embarked for the Continent, but he later claimed to remember the talk of Bonaparte's return from Elba, and the din and preparation for war. Above all he remembered 'the sorrowful parting of my noble-looking, manly-hearted father, with our

dear mother and us ... the last wave of that good father's hand
– the tearful eyes with which, foresaken and alone, we sat on
the beach and saw the sails unfurled that were to waft our sole
earthly stay, protector, and support to a foreign shore, and to
the 'tented field,' perhaps never to return.' [13]

In the event Sergeant-Major Russell came through the battle
unscathed, though many of his comrades were killed and his
horse was shot. The Greys, shouting 'Scotland for Ever' as they
felled French soldiers with their sabres, were supposed to have
earned the admiration of Napoleon.[14] Sergeant-Major Russell
gave a vivid account of the fighting:

'My dear, since I wrote you last we have had a most bloody
battle with the French as was ever fought ... from about 11
o'clock till nearly dark, when the field was covered with the
dead and wounded in number scarcely to be numbered ... We
are now the weak Greys, out of 6 squadrons we now form only
about one. When night came on the Prussians came up and
attacked the French and put them totally to rout. We have been
pursuing them these 3 days and never have been able to come
up with them ...

'My dear, I would change the subject and inform you of myself.
I have lost all my things, this day I am getting a dead French-
man's shirt washed to put on. My horse was wounded and sent
into Brussels during the action and has lost my whole kit so I
am now as I stand. However, blessed be God, I am the spared
monument of his mercy for I never thought it was possible that
any man could escape.' [15]

The following January the regiment returned to England and
Sergeant-Major Russell's wife set off from Glasgow, where she
and her sons had been staying with their Dempster Street
relatives, to join him at Canterbury barracks. James Burn Russell
must often have heard from his father the story of their six-week
journey through the January snows in an old-fashioned stage
wagon with heavy wheels. Describing the account nearly 40
years on, in the sunshine of Woolloomooloo in New South
Wales, David Russell (who was never given to understatement)
said it chilled his blood even to think of it. As he told it, in a
letter to launch a Waterloo widows' and orphans' fund, the snow
was many feet deep and the frost was so severe that on one

occasion he and his mother and older brother had to be lifted numbed from the wagon when they halted at a roadside public house to change horses. His mother's old red cloak made the English landlady realise that they were a soldier's wife and children and she ushered them in for a hot breakfast in her kitchen.

At Canterbury a third son was born, but before long the family was on its travels again. In 1817 the regiment marched to Glasgow, but several other postings throughout the British Isles followed before James Russell returned to the city as steamboat harbourmaster so that his three boys could enjoy the advantages of a civilian education. Every year, though, he would celebrate the anniversary of the battle with two of his old troop mates by dining in the country and toasting the Duke of Wellington and all who fought under him and telling anecdotes of the battle. David Russell, who was sometimes allowed to accompany his father on these outings, years later recalled for his readers in the *Sydney Morning Herald* 'the big tears coursing down the cheeks of these hardy old warriors' as they toasted the fallen.[16]

The old soldier was perhaps less sentimental than his son on the subject of Waterloo. The story has come down through the generations that he joined the Army because his wife, Margaret Macdonald, refused to marry him unless he followed in the steps of her soldier father. It was his wish that his son David should 'avoid ornament' on his headstone and 'confine any inscription to my services as Harbourmaster.' David disobeyed on both counts. The old man, who lived to the age of 82, was buried not in the family lair that he had purchased in Rutherglen but in Glasgow Necropolis. The inscription, now too weathered to be read in full, describes him as 'a good soldier' and records that he fought with the Greys at Waterloo.

Chapter Three

John Street and Beyond

*Misery begets social unrest, and the heart of misery is
ill-health.*

D ESPITE his country upbringing Russell was exposed at
an early age to the grimness of urban life. As a pupil of
Glasgow High School in the late 1840s and early 1850s
he was familiar with the seamier side of Glasgow. The school
was then in John Street, close to George Square, which had
supplanted Glasgow Cross as the city centre. Banks and businesses were rapidly colonising this former middle-class suburb
as its residents migrated westwards to elegant new terraces. But
only a few hundred yards on the other side of the school lay the
pestilential slums that had spread along the medieval spine of
the city. Russell must have passed close to this area every day
on his way to and from John Street.

His schooldays coincided with a turbulent period in Glasgow's
history. During the 'hungry forties' the Irish potato famine
brought swarms of incomers. In the four months from December
1847 to the following March nearly 43,000 Irish people arrived
in the city, most of them destitute. Glasgow was the destination
for the very poorest migrants – the slightly less poor went to
Liverpool, while those who could afford it crossed the Atlantic.
The same year brought the worst typhus outbreak in the city's
history. On his way to school Russell may well have seen Irish
women holding up their sick and dying children to the gaze of
passers-by in the city centre.

Under these pressures the slums became even more pestilential and the slum-dwellers even more desperate. Thousands
died from typhus. As well-to-do Glaswegians moved west the
social fabric of the older city continued to deteriorate. One
observer remarked that 'domiciles which last century formed
the cosy retreats of city clergymen, physicians and merchants
are now often tenanted by pickpockets and prostitutes.'[1] Dr

Ralph Wardlaw, the pastor of the Congregational church attended by Russell's grandfather, estimated the latter at 1800 but some people claimed that the number was much higher.

These were years of social unrest and disorder in the streets. *The Glasgow Herald* referred to the 'off-scourings of our over-grown city' and reported that wrongdoers found it easy to escape through narrrow streets cluttered with carts and barrows and clogged with dungheaps.[2] Political agitation grew during the trade depression of the late 1840s. In 1848, the year of revolution in Europe, rallies of the unemployed in Glasgow Green were followed by rioting in the streets. Carts were overturned, shops were looted, and mobs marched through the city centre brand-ishing stolen rifles and bits of torn-down railing before order was restored at the cost of several lives by a cavalry charge in the High Street.

The High Street area was also among the parts of the city worst affected by the cholera epidemic that struck in the same year. The author of the official report on the outbreak noted that in such places 'all sanitary evils exist in perfection.' He added that the overcrowded conditions had brought typhus, and that 'wherever typhus has prevailed, there cholera now prevails, or has· done so recently.'[3]

The High School, uncomfortably close to this insalubrious area, was not itself the healthiest of places. The cramped building was poorly lit and ventilated, the playground too small. Exten-sive repairs were often necessary, as when the floor of the mathematics classroom gave way. Educationally, however, the school's reputation was high and Russell made the most of his time there. One of his teachers later wrote that his academic performance was distinguished, that 'no circumstance has occurred to mar the bright promise,' and that despite his shyness he was 'beloved and admired by all his class fellows.'[4]

The school had undergone great changes as a result of the growth of specialisation. The post of rector had been scrapped and each department operated more or less autonomously. Alex-ander Dorsey, the head of English in Russell's day, regarded his department as a school in its own right. More than 300 pupils enrolled, showing the popularity of Dorsey's innovating approach. With his unorthodox predilection for lecturing on subjects like 'the history of the earth,' rather than on the finer points of grammar, he must have made a significant contribution to Russell's notably liberal education.[5] But the most gifted and, almost certainly, most influential of Russell's teachers was the head of the mathematics department, James Bryce.

Bryce, born in Belfast of Scottish descent on his father's side, had won high honours in Greek and Latin at Glasgow University and was a noted amateur geologist. After teaching at Belfast Academy he took up his post at the High School in 1846, teaching geography as well as mathematics and voluntarily undertaking a class in natural history because he felt so strongly that it should be part of the syllabus.

Bryce was most impressed by Russell, not because he was a mathematical genius – he was only third equal in Bryce's class – but because of his originality, powers of observation and reasoning, his 'reflective powers of a high order,' and his ability to grasp a difficult subject and convey it in his own words. 'At an early period of our acquaintance,' Bryce later wrote, 'I began to cherish the hope that my young friend might have a bright and honourable career.' He praised his 'uprightness, truthfulness, manliness, high principle, and command of temper which cannot fail to give him great moral weight in any society amid which he may be placed.'[6]

These words were written in a testimonial (in which Bryce, incidentally, did not pass up the opportunity to mention that his pupil's liberal education had been 'judiciously conducted under the best teachers'). But the words came from the heart. Russell had become a friend of the Bryce family. James Bryce's son of the same name, who was later to become a legendary figure as a scholar, a member of Gladstone's Cabinet, and British Ambassador to the United States, was a schoolmate of Russell's and a friendly rival.

Their friendship, which was to be lifelong (if at times neglected), was founded on shared interests and intellectual energies. Both loved history, literature, nature, the solitude of the countryside, and the freedom of the hills. (Bryce, already a skilled mountaineer, was later to be a leading campaigner for right of access to the Scottish hills.[7]) They walked and talked together on Cathkin Braes, near Russell's home, and both had adolescent burdens to bear – Russell because his mother was dead and his father was on the other side of the world; Bryce because he suffered in his mid-teens from black depressions.[8]

Bryce, the future author of *The Holy Roman Empire* and *The American Commonwealth,* had the intellectual edge and regarded Russell as 'solid rather than swift, careful, exact, conscientious, with a winning gentleness of nature.'[9] Everything seemed to come easily to James Bryce. Having received an early education in Latin and Greek at home, he could learn a whole book of the *Iliad* by heart in a day. By the age of eight he was asking questions about the British constitution. At the age of 14 he 'felt that he had got all the benefit which it was possible for the High School to give him' and, too young to enter university, was sent for a year to Belfast Academy, where one of his uncles was headmaster, and where he learned among other things the rudiments of the Irish language. Other erudite uncles lurked in the background.[10]

Russell, with his self-taught grandfather, had a much less academic background, though his father's two brothers were graduates of Glasgow University. The older brother, James, was a Congregational minister who left to become a missionary in India a few weeks after Russell's birth. On home leave he seems to have been a good friend to his nephew – 'like a bright eye after sorrow,' Russell wrote in one of poems – before vanishing again 'like a vision in the night, of some far off Orient clime.'[11] At the age of 50 he visited his brother David in Australia – and left with a wife, who died only three years after their return to India.[12]

Russell saw more of his father's younger brother, John Archibald Russell, who had abandoned his plans for a Church career to study for the English Bar. A future QC and Professor of English Law at University College, London, he was already making a name for himself in the 1840s as an expert in commercial law. But every year he made time to visit his parents in Auburn Cottage, and to make a pilgrimage to the steamboat quay at the Broomielaw where long ago he had recited his school homework to his father. These visits no doubt provided added intellectual stiumulus to Russell, who by the time he left John Street in 1854 was amply equipped for the next stage in his education – an arts degree course at Glasgow University.

Chapter Four

Whetstones and Bushels of Peas

Oft the voice of wisdom finds
paths to reach unwilling minds
(from Russell's translation of a passage
in the 'Agamemnon' of Aeschylus)

W HEN Russell, at the age of 17, enrolled as an arts
student at Glasgow University, nobody suspected
that he was a doctor in the making. His literary
abilities were what attracted attention. He performed creditably
rather than brilliantly in his classes (eighth in first-year Latin,
fifth in Ethics) but shone at verse composition.[1] English was not
yet in the syllabus – it was introduced just after his graduation
– but there were other outlets for his writing talent. The Professor of Latin, William Ramsay, a terse and luminous lecturer
who was more interested in literary appreciation than grammar,
praised his graceful translations into English. The gentle and
courteous if slightly unkempt professor of Greek, Edmund Lushington, was more of a grammarian but at least had the literary
cachet of being married to Tennyson's sister.[2] Another influential
teacher was the Rev. Robert Buchanan, known to his students
as Logic Bob, who followed clerical fashion by wearing black
gloves while delivering his exquisitely polished lectures. In his
Logic and Rhetoric class Russell honed his dialectical skills by
writing Socratic dialogues. He won a prize, too, for the best
verse on the subject of 'Italy: A Sardinian Poet's Dream', and
with his friend James Bryce, back from Belfast and impressing
everyone with his brilliance, he shared first prize for a holiday
translation of Catullus (years later Bryce admitted that his
mother used to help him with these exercises).[3]

Glasgow University, then in its last years on the High Street
site, was not in one of its happier phases. Its government was
oligarchical and corrupt. Its seventeenth-century buildings, although still 'graceful and full of memories,' were in a state of

decay. The atmosphere was darkened by smoke and polluted with chemicals from the factories nearby. The city's worst slums – perhaps the worst in Europe – lay on its doorstep. Members of the Scottish Universities Commission in 1858 held their noses and reported that it was 'hardly possible to conceive a combination of circumstances less favourable to the bodily and mental well-being of the Youth attending a University.'[4]

Yet Russell's friend Bryce, who later went on to Oxford, thought Glasgow the more intellectually stimulating of the two. Nineteenth-century Scottish education was more democratic and less elitist than Oxford and Cambridge. There were no formal entrance requirements, prizes were awarded by the vote of the class, and many students never bothered to graduate. The appetite for learning was enormous. Students flocked to the classes of Ramsay and Lushington. 'Whenever we had a chance we would talk about our work, discussing the questions that came up, an incessant sharpening of wits upon one another's whetstones,' Bryce recalled. Some students found that the best place for this sharpening was one of the numerous High Street taverns, but Russell and Bryce and their friends were among the groups who wandered between classes on the grass behind the Hunterian Museum. 'Here I remember long arguments over freedom of the will and other metaphysical topics to which the Scottish mind was prone,' Bryce wrote later. 'The ambition of most of us would have been to be metaphysicians. That seemed the highest kind of mental exertion.'[5]

Russell's friends thought him 'of a naturally retiring disposition'[6] but he fought his fear of public speaking to become one of the Liberal Club's leading debaters. He campaigned in rectorial elections, when the quadrangles rang with political invective and arguments were backed up with 'bushels of peas and flour, policemen's rattles, huge bells, and all manner of unmusical and discordant instruments.'[7] Once he deserted the Liberal cause to campaign for the novelist and politician Sir Edward Bulwer Lytton, who was being promoted by the Conservatives as a literary candidate. He also read papers on a remarkable diversity of subjects to the Literary and Philosophical Society. His wide-ranging interests brought him into contact with a cross-section of the student body. Glasgow

students, though predominantly middle-class,[8] included youths
from a variety of social backgrounds. Some were having to work
their way through college: one of the stars of Logic Bob's class
spent much of the year as a blacksmith. There were also Non-
conformists from Wales and from England. Russell's
fellow-Liberals included a future Methodist minister, Radolphus
Abercrombie, who was regarded as by far the best speaker of
his day, with 'great power of sarcasm' and a copious vocabulary.
Their Conservative opponents included the brothers Norman
and John Macleod of the famous ecclesiastical dynasty and a
genial Gaelic-speaking Nova Scotian, George Grant, who later
became the principal of a university in Ontario. Outside politics
his friends included David Macrae, a jovial member of the Total
Abstinence Society who was to have a varied career as *Glasgow
Herald* leader writer, novelist, travel writer, and later United
Presbyterian minister in Greenock until he famously fell out
with the synod for dissenting from the doctrine of everlasting
torment. He was a founder of the Scottish Patriotic Association
and at a gathering at Bannockburn moved a formal protest
against the title adopted by the new King Edward VII.[9]

Like the majority of his fellow-students Russell lived at home.
Auburn Cottage seems to have been a happy household at that
time. Russell's grandparents, then in their 70s, remained in good
health. His sister Agnes was doing well at her own lessons and
was top of the class in grammar. Russell entertained the family
with stories of college but said little about his achievements. In
a letter to his father in Australia[10] his grandfather described
how the young man had amused them all with his account of
Professor Ramsay's comments on a student's translation; when
his grandmother trapped him by asking, 'Did the Professor say
anything about yours?' Russell was forced to concede that his
effort had been described as 'an elegant, correct, and graceful
translation.' His father was warned not to mention the matter
when writing home, 'for James does not like to hear anything
about himself.'

His private reading in these days amounted to a parallel
education. The commonplace book that he kept as a student
reveals the intensity of his interest in literature and language.[11] He delved deeply into early English poetry – Caedmon,

Langland, Chaucer – and wrote page upon page of notes on Anglo-Saxon grammar and syntax, with occasional references to Icelandic and Swedish. He read medieval French literature. He explored the derivations of words, cutting out newspaper articles on the subject, copying down Professor Ramsay's exposition on the changing meaning of 'parasite', and noting how often American slang expressions were simply antiquated English phrases. Ballads interested him as well, partly because of the insight they offered into social history. He wrote down the Scottish ballads recited by his grandparents' servant, Ann Howat, and tried his hand at vernacular verses in such homely contributions to the Glasgow University Album as 'Out at E'En' ('The bleeze frae the ingle lichts up the bit biggin ...') as well as offerings in standard English. He read about the history of neighbouring Cathcart and the Battle of Langside. He saved the articles on Australian natural history from the *Sydney Morning Heralds* sent by his father, savouring the esoteric information about sea elephants, fruit-eating bats, insectivorous marsupials, black wallabies, and flying squirrels. He walked with Bryce on Cathkin Braes, looking down over the distant smoky city as they chatted about metaphysics, botany, or their shared interest in Oliver Cromwell. 'The sweetness of his temper, and his power of drawing simple things, made him a charming companion, as the range of his attainments made him no less an instructive one, from whose talk one always went away the wiser,' Bryce noted.[12] But Russell's sweet temper did not stop him from writing and privately circulating a poem about the alleged plagiarisms of the Professor of Moral Philosophy, William Fleming, or from disparaging Disraeli in a nasty piece of doggerel during a rectorial election campaign.[13]

It was not surprising that although Russell's fellow-students were sure that he would attain high distinction, they 'could not foresee in what line his work would lie.'[14] His interests were even wider than those of Bryce, who was one day to be described as probably the most educated politician of his time. New avenues opened up when in the fourth and final year of his arts degree course he demonstrated that he was as adept at experimental electrolysis as at translations of Aeschylus.

The Scottish tradition of the 'democratic intellect' made such a combination perfectly possible. The Professor of Natural Philosophy, or physics, was the young William Thomson, later Lord Kelvin, who saw his subject in broad terms as an instrument for improving understanding as well as a key to material improvement. More of his brightest students went into the ministry than into any other profession (on meeting a former student who had become Professor of Biblical Criticism, Thomson remarked that he would now have time to write up his unfinished lab. notes).[15] An elementary knowledge of mathematics was all that was needed. Russell had taken mathematics in the previous year, under Thomson's friend, Professor Hugh Blackburn – admittedly not the most inspiring of teachers, and considered by some of his students to be less interesting than his artist wife, Jemima.

But if Blackburn gave Russell a solid grounding, Thomson's dynamic genius caught his imagination. Having been appointed to his chair at the age of 22, Thomson was then in his early 30s and well on the way to recognition as the outstanding scientist of his time. His lectures went straight over the heads of average students but the abler were stimulated by his unorthodox approach. He used no notes, declined to teach anything that could be found in textbooks, and moved rapidly from subject to subject. His thrust was practical, his lectures opportunistic – a thunderstorm was seen as a chance to gather data for investigation. 'He dispensed with the professorial gown after his introductory lecture and stood when lecturing, eager, alert, and animated like a runner waiting for the starting signal,' wrote one of Russell's student contemporaries. 'It was a strange sight to watch him as he became more and more eager in his exposition; a light seemed to play upon his forehead like an emanation.'[16]

A few years earlier Thomson had set up a research laboratory in the deserted wine cellar of an old professorial house, fending off the protests of the Professor of Moral Philosophy, who objected to the noise.[17] The laboratory, which was to become internationally known, has been seen as an important extension of the Scottish democratic tradition of student participation in class discussion. It was the first of its kind in any British university, and Russell, with the fortunate timing that marked

his whole career, was among the first students to work in it.
He was one of about a dozen carefully selected volunteers whom
Thomson gathered around him as unoffical research assistants.
This team worked not only with the professor but with his
private assistant, Donald McFarlane, who supervised the research. A patient and unassuming man, McFarlane was an
excellent teacher. He knew the contents of every recent scientific
paper in English, French or German and was also able to correct
Thomson's arithmetic. When the students asked him to supper
he used to relax and refer to the professor as 'Wullie.' [18] Russell
remained on friendly terms with him after leaving the natural
philosophy class.[19]

Thomson used to tell his students that he hoped that they
would remember the principles of natural philosophy whatever
their subsequent pursuits in life. His wish was certainly to be
fulfilled in the case of Russell, who in later life attributed his
scientific method and spirit to this early association.[20]

Chapter Five

A Sea Passage

*... a happiness so pure, that we can scarcely believe
it ever to have been ours.*

ONE other thing resulted from Russell's work for Thomson: the great adventure of his life. In the summer of 1858, just after his graduation, he was asked by Thomson to become his unpaid assistant on board the HMS *Agamemnon* on what turned out to be the first successful attempt to lay an Atlantic cable.

This put Russell, who had demonstrated his aptitude by winning a class prize for special investigations into electrolysis, briefly at the cutting edge of scientific progress. Sea cables had already been laid across the English Channel. Submarine telegraphy had come to be seen as the practical problem of the time. Important work on the subject was being done in Thomson's laboratory at Glasgow University, where it was the ambition of many students to become telegraph engineers. Ocean surveys had revealed a 'telegraph plateau' extending across the Atlantic and in 1857 the Atlantic Telegraph Company engaged Thomson's help in an attempt to lay a cable between Valencia Island in South-West Ireland and Trinity Bay in Newfoundland, which were already linked with the British and American telegraph networks respectively. The cable snapped at an early stage in the operation but by the spring of 1858 it had been resolved to make a second attempt. This time the cable-laying operation was to start in mid-Atlantic instead of on the coast; and Thomson, with his new marine galvanometer for testing and receiving signals, was to be much more actively involved.[1]

On May 6, the day after his twenty-first birthday, Russell set out from Auburn Cottage for Devonport to join HMS *Agamemnon*, a 3200-ton, twin-screw battleship which had been the flagship of Admiral Lyons at the bombardment of Sebastopol three years earlier. After successful trials in the Bay of Biscay the *Agamemnon* sailed from Plymouth on a June morning of mist and sunshine. A *Times* correspondent was on board to record the historic event, but Russell's own unpublished journal – written for his sister Agnes – provides an unsurpassed account of the expedition.[2] It is a superb piece of reporting, closely observed and vivid: whenever anything out of the ordinary happened on board the ship Russell rushed to the spot to gather material for his journal. He was interested in everything: navigation, marine life, the stories of his shipmates. The joy of living and a love of adventure radiate from the pages. It is clear that Russell experienced some of the most intensely happy moments of his life on this trip.

It was a hazardous undertaking. The first Cunarder had crossed the Atlantic less than 20 years before. In the best of summers the Atlantic winds reached gale force, and 1858 was not the best of summers. The *Agamemnon* was weighed down with 400 tons of cable in her hold. In the messroom when she sailed westwards was a Plymouth newspaper containing a letter from a naval lieutenant predicting that she would never return.

All was calm at first. The *Agamemnon* had to get up steam to go in search of wind. Russell basked in the sunshine and watched a shoal of porpoises passing like a flash of yellow light under the water. After dark he walked on the deck and thought of phantom ships and seas of flame as the ship with its huge ghostlike sails glided on slowly and a phosphorescent streak marked the waterline.

But on the third day out from Plymouth the sails rattled and cracked, the wind whistled through the rigging, and the ship rolled and pitched. At supper, Russell recorded for Aggy, there were 'fearful lurches' and 'a number of unfortunates would go whirling, chairs and all, followed by the breadbasket, and roars of laughter from their messmates.' To Russell's amusement one engineer held his grog aloft as he traversed the space between the table and the bulkheads.

Russell was elated. 'I feel quite jolly,' he reported in his journal. He found it great fun at breakfast next morning when the chairs were lashed to the table and knives and forks were being hunted all over the floor. Later he went on deck 'to enjoy the stormy scene', admire a flock of stormy petrels pursuing their prey along the surface of the waves, and reflect on the freedom and excitement of life at sea. 'When one stands on the deck and feels the good ship mounting a great swell bows-up, then bounding down the other side stern-up, it imparts electricity to the spirits, just as if one were taking a hedge on a good hunter,' he wrote in his journal.

After a brief lull the storm returned with exceptional ferocity. 'The scene was alarming and beyond my power to describe,' Russell admitted, relating how windows were smashed as 'the sea came gushing in like a torrent.' He didn't exaggerate. A recent biographical study of Kelvin records that 'the *Agamemnon* came close to foundering and taking William Thomson with her.'[3] The electrical testing room was flooded and Russell, dressed in his best clothes since it was Sunday, took off his shoes and socks, rolled up his trousers, and lent a hand in securing the instruments – only to be knocked over by some heavy lead weights which broke away from the clockwork. Soon afterwards he was ready for action again when the cargo of coal broke loose from its bunker, crashed across the deck, and barricaded two men inside the messroom. 'Watching for a favourable time in the motion of the ship I crawled on all fours between the coal bags and the beams and managed to wriggle in at the door,' Russell recorded for Aggy, adding that the two trapped men were 'very glad to be piloted out over the coalbags.'

The earlier mood of hilarity had been blown away in the gale. The ship's surgeon bustled about and the injured were led past, 'some pale as death and tottering with faintness.' The scene gave Russell, who two days before had thought of his grandfather on Waterloo Day, an idea of what a military engagement must be like. The sick suffered along with the wounded. Anderson, a junior member of the electrical staff who had become Russell's shipboard friend, 'stood holding on beside the mainmast looking rather blue' and the *Times* correspondent 'sat upon a stool on deck, in a corner near the wheel ... huddled up over head and ears in a rug, afraid to look the storm in the face.' After surveying the scenes of misery Russell cheerfully gulped down a plate of Irish stew as he stood with his legs planted firmly apart on the tilting deck. He watched the rolling waves and amused himself by calculating when the ship would give an extra lurch: 'As she ducked towards a coming wave, it would tower like a hill of water above the bulwarks, as if it must go right over us. But it would catch the ship in the waist, jerking her violently over into the trough, where there was scarcely any water to resist a complete immersion. Then the mast would bend, the yards fall over, and the shrouds flap as if the whole rigging were coming away.' At night, preferring to walk the decks rather than lie in his drenched cabin, he encountered Thomson, who arranged for him to sleep in the captain's sitting room. After being pitched repeatedly from the sofa, he lay on the floor wrapped in Thomson's plaid with his arms twined round the sofa leg. The journal conveys no hint of fear, but Russell must have been uneasy when he overheard Captain Moriarty remark: 'The ship is not sea-worthy. She is laden beyond her tonnage.' He must have been as thankful as anyone when the crashing waves eventually subsided and the sea became smooth as a pond.

Some of those on board the *Agamemnon* vowed never to go to sea again, but Russell's enjoyment of shipboard life was undiminished. He particularly enjoyed the gatherings after supper when two of the sailors entertained the company with their fiddles and others joined in singing and dancing. 'There is something curious about the effect of music on me, I know not whether peculiar or no,' Russell wrote in his journal. Whenever he appeared at one of these concerts one of the fiddlers would play 'The Bluebells of Scotland' or 'Ye Banks and Braes', which gratified Russell and reinforced his belief that 'our melodies are more pathetic and suited for the popular heart than those of any other nation.'

His shipmates must have wondered at first what to make of the tall, shy Scot scribbling notes in the messroom every evening. He was a deeply serious youth, meditative, religious and high-minded, but with an unsophisticated love of fun – and an inability at times to suppress his laughter. He could be hot-tempered in debate. 'I would never do for a lawyer in respect of coolness of argument,' he confessed after a political row with some of the ship's engineers. But his messroom comrades seemed to regard him with affection. They called him Lord John (after

Lord John Russell, who had been Prime Minister several years before), borrowed from his stack of Waverley novels, and read his journal, sometimes spilling grog over it. Whenever there was disagreement about some historical fact, 'Lord John' was consulted. He in turn found the ship's engineers intelligent and well read and enjoyed their tales of service in the Black Sea and the Baltic. He walked on the poop deck with Mr Clements, the senior assistant engineer, and heard about his exploits off China during the Crimean War.

He gave reading and spelling lessons to his shipboard servant, worried about the sailors' diet – particularly the 'very black, suspicious-looking garbage' that passed for meat – and was upset when two sailors accused of theft had their hair cropped as punishment. 'I saw it done and felt the degradation more than the men did,' wrote the future sanitarian. 'I'd rather see a man hung.' But a session with a hair-cutting marine left the back of his own head closely cropped with 'hair sticking out like stubble on a harvest field.'

In mid-Atlantic the *Agamemnon* had its rendezvous with the *Niagara*, and the splicing of the cable, which Russell compared with a marriage ceremony, took place. Once the splice box was submerged and the paying-out wheels set in motion Russell went to the electrical room where signals were being sent to the *Niagara*. Thomson 'panted with excitement' but when the ships were only six miles apart a fault occurred as the result of the fouling of the cable on board the *Niagara*, and the splicing procedure had to be gone through again. This time the cable broke after 80 miles had been laid and a third attempt was made. Russell, who took his turn at keeping watch in the electrical room, thought how thin and insignificant the cable looked when it disappeared in the wake of the ship but how the whole operation bordered on the marvellous. 'If we succeed we shall certainly oust the seven wonders of the world, and reduce their number to one.' But after 114 miles the cable broke again. At Thomson's insistence the *Agamemnon* returned yet again to mid-Atlantic in an attempt to make contact with the *Niagara*. It was a pointless and unpopular move. Provisions were running very low. 'Hard nail,' or pigskin with some of the bristles still sticking out of it, was often on the menu. Russell found it 'not

at all bad' but there were times when he remembered his sister's
more delicate concoctions. In mid-Atlantic a fog descended. The
sight of the *Agamemnon's* sentries looming mysteriously out of
the white mist put Russell in a melancholy mood. 'There is
something about this scene which strikes me as analogous to
the mystery of life – mystery before, mystery behind – all we
certainly have within the grasp of our understanding is the
"now", and even this is often clothed in doubt,' he wrote in the
journal.

Finally the *Agamemnon* headed for Queenstown (now Cobh,
the harbour for Cork) in south-west Ireland for fuel and provisions. These were idyllic days for Russell. He and Anderson
shared a room in the local hotel with an inebriated Killarney
farmer. Their roommate was assisted to bed in the early hours
by a waiter who mistook Russell's snorts of suppressed laughter
for snoring. On a pleasant July day he set off with Anderson
and two others for the lakes of Killarney. On the steamer from
Cobh to Cork they passed fine mansions with lawns, a village
'garlanded with foliage', and through the leaves a mossy sum-
merhouse with statues on pedestals. Russell found time to note
that the local girls in their long black mantles and neat caps
'look very pleasing with their braided hair and faces always
smiling.' From Cork they travelled at top speed in a horse cab
to Blarney, winning a race with a milk cart drawn by a donkey
and driven by a girl. Russell, of course, insisted on kissing the
Blarney Stone, which meant hanging down from the ledge high
on the castle wall. 'I took off my coat and cap and gave it a
hearty smack, while Anderson held my feet,' he reported in the
journal. The group continued to Killarney by train, joking and
laughing so uncontrollably that Russell was sure that the old
lady in the corner seat thought they were vulgar young men.
In Killarney they stayed in an old-fashioned boarding house
which reminded Russell of the house where he had stayed on
Wigtonshire holidays. The visit to the lakes is unrecorded in
his journal – the only gap in five months – but Russell later
described it in idyllic terms in a magazine article:

'My recollections of these pleasant days are like one of those
glimmerings of the happiness of our childhood, which often flash
on memory's backward eye – a happiness so pure, that we can

scarce believe it ever to have been ours ... We pass the Purple Mountain and descend across the mouth of the Black Valley, whose recesses lead the vision into dreariness and gloom. Those girls will follow us, lightly tripping over the heather, with their whisky and goat's milk, their Irish "blarney," and their Irish eyes. We row together down the Lakes; we look into their clear waters and see the inverted foliage of the mountain sides gorgeously draping and festooning imaginary halls and bowers, we land on a fairy island, and spread our repast in the shadow of the arbutus. Again onward, shouting and singing to raise the distant mountain echoes.' [+]

Two days later they were on board the *Agamemnon* again and making for the mid-Atlantic in brilliant sunshine. The sea, wrote Russell, sparkled as if powdered with stars. The weather remained fine for the rendezvous with the Niagara. The splicing operation was performed and the *Agamemnon* headed for Ireland while paying out the cable. Russell was constantly at work in the electrical room, although on one occasion Thomson relieved him at his post so that he could watch an exceptionally fine shoal of porpoises. Thomson's nervous excitability is graphically portrayed in the journal. Once, when a serious fault developed, Russell summoned him to the electrical testing room. 'He came in a fearful state of excitement,' wrote Russell. 'His hand shook so much that he could scarcely adjust his eyeglass. The veins on his forehead were swollen and his face was deadly pale.' Russell was glad when the emergency was over, 'not for my own sake, though I was anxious, but for the sake of Thomson especially. He is not the man for such a trial. Coolness is everything.'

Finally, after a near-collision with an American three-masted schooner, the *Agamemnon* approached Ireland. Thomson joined Russell and Anderson in the electrical room 'in a state of enjoyment so great as almost to create absence of mind' and congratulated them on having been part of the expedition, whose success he now regarded as assured. 'I really could scarce keep my seat for joy,' wrote Russell. 'I felt 'like a hen on a hot girdle.'' It was a joyful time for him. During one of last watches in the electrical room he heard the fiddlers playing nearby and felt 'quite ravished with delight' at the sweetness of the music, the fineness of the evening, and the motion of the ship. He thought of gondolas, guitars, and moonlit waves, of Cleopatra's barge with its sails of silk.

The marines fired a salute and sailors cheered farewell from the mizzen rigging when Thomson and the electrical staff left the *Agamemnon* at Valencia Island and headed for the shore in the cable boat. The reception committee included the owner of the island, the Knight of Kerry, who advanced at full speed in a gunboat, but was upset in the water during the scuffle for the honour of pulling the cable boat ashore. A 'bevy of ladies' gave it a token haul – just enough, Russell noted, to tar their gloves.

Offices were set up in the nearby slate quarry and soon Thomson sent the first current from shore to shore. The first current from America was received five minutes later. 'Thus was the grandest undertaking of the century crowned with success,' wrote Russell. That evening bonfires were lit and jigs were danced to the sound of fiddle music. 'I was much interested with the innocency of the proceeding,' observed Russell rather loftily, noting how the Irish girls danced with their faces modestly muffled up in their shawls and mantles. Soon, though, his own modesty was evident when a young man led his partner forward and asked Russell if he would dance with her. 'Nothing could have given me greater pleasure but I am much too elephantine in my motion,' he confessed to his journal. He was less inhibited when some of the boys began flinging burning peats at each other. 'I felt so much humour for frolic boiling up within,' he wrote afterwards, 'that as the most innocent way of expressing it I joined and fired away until my hands were scorched – the peats flying through the air like rockets or live shells.'

On his way to the telegraph station one morning soon afterwards Russell met an old woman who exclaimed: 'Happy news, Sur! There's a message from Newfoundland.' Thomson, skipping about in delight, sent out to the hotel for porter for everyone, and pulled corks like (Russell thought) Vulcan at the feast of the gods. A few days later a message from Queen Victoria for President Buchanan was removed from its Foreign Office envelope and transmitted to Newfoundland. President Buchanan reciprocated. His pious message, describing the cable as an instrument of divine providence, was then relayed from Valencia Island via Dublin, Carlisle, and Manchester to London in seven and a half minutes. Russell found it remarkable that the first half of the message had been received while the clerk was still transmitting the latter part. Soon Thomson, in what Russell described as 'a paroxysm of telegraphing', was transmitting bits of American news to *The Times* and cabling London for items from the European capitals to send in return. ('News today. News today from America!' he said while clapping his hands in an ecstasy of enjoyment.) The clerks were up all night sending messages and Russell was getting only four hours of sleep.

For a while Valencia Island became, as he put it, a great electric heart sending its quick pulsations to the uttermost parts of the earth. He was witnessing what was then regarded as the greatest event of the century. *The Times* claimed that there had been nothing comparable since Columbus discovered America. It was widely believed that instant communication would further not only trade and commerce but civilisation and peace, even religion. Kipling was later to write:

Here in the womb of the world – here on the tie-ribs of
    earth
Words, and the words of men, flicker and flutter and beat –
Warning, sorrow, and gain, salutation and mirth –
For a Power troubles the Still that has neither voice nor
    feet.

Russell wrote in his journal of the cable 'knitting the limbs of empire into one gigantic frame' with London as the seat of supreme intellect. For him as for others the cable reinforced confidence in human progress, particularly British progress:[5] he wrote in his diary of the 'dim grandeur of the future.' He himself had actively contributed to the achievement. Thomson trusted him and gave him responsibility. After the initial failures of the cable Thomson had wanted to return home while Russell remained with the expedition, but to Russell's relief was persuaded to change his mind. When Thomson left Valencia Island to attend the Lord Mayor's banquet in Dublin it was Russell who was left in charge of the instruments and of the professor's affairs. He thought it a great responsibility but soon was cheerfully improvising an improvement to the observatory for the galvanometer with the help of 'a bit of zinc and sixpence with paper moistened with saliva between.'

But things had begun to go badly wrong. Eventually, in early October, after more than 700 messages had been transmitted, the cable ceased to function. Recriminations began. Company directors began to arrive on the scene. Whitehouse, the company electrician, was made the scapegoat, although the cause of failure was complex. Thomson, initially at least, defended Whitehouse, and Russell followed his lead: he even wrote to *The Times* to refute the accusations of Cyrus Field, the head of the company. But aboard the *Agamemnon* it was Thomson who was the chief target of criticism. During the expedition he had been, on Russell's evidence, the object of much more grumbling than has hitherto been realised. He was mocked behind his back. 'It is sickening to me to hear such poor creatures taking their fun out of a man like Thomson,' wrote Russell. 'Even the workmen in their vulgar way are constantly making a fool of him.'

He found the atmosphere intolerable. Until then he had enjoyed himself on Valencia Island – swimming in his free time, observing the local customs, watching the cormorants as he rowed out on a sunny morning to inspect part of the cable, and singing (or growling, which was the most he could manage) so loudly during an evening stroll with some of his comrades that the local people opened their doors to find the cause of the uproar. But now he felt 'more and more disgusted and eager to get out of this.' First, however, the failure of the cable had to be investigated. It was dispiriting work. Thomson himself was bored with what he described as the pathology of faults. Later, at a banquet given in his honour in Glasgow, he was to reassert confidence by declaring: 'What has been done can be done again. The loss of a position gained is an event unknown in the history of man's struggle with the forces of inanimate Nature.' [6]

Success would finally come to Thomson in 1866, but Russell was to have no part in that enterprise. Even before he left Ireland his thoughts were turning to the new university session and the start of his medical studies. He left Valencia Island at the end of September, at the same time as Thomson. Toasts were drunk in his honour in the mess and at one in the morning he was escorted to his lodgings by a crowd who sang 'Auld Lang Syne' twice over very noisily on the doorstep. The demonstration of affection pleased him for he had found it 'no easy matter seeing they were all for Whitehouse to uphold Thomson's name and maintain friendly relations with all.' He was up packing till 3 a.m. and after breakfast set out for Dublin by rail and coach by way of Tralee, Limerick, and Athlone. After seeing round the city he caught an overnight steamer for Greenock. He travelled by train to Glasgow and by cab to Rutherglen, reaching Auburn Cottage in time to join the others at breakfast.

'I shall never forget these six months,' he concluded his journal. 'I have lived more in that time than in all the preceding years. But now it is all over, and it seems like a dream, for memory dwells close upon the shadowy boundaries of dreamland.'

Chapter Six

A Democratic Intellect

*Upon my word, I believe England has more to learn from
us than we from her, in University matters.*

Medicine was held in low esteem in the strongly commercial atmosphere of mid-nineteenth-century Glasgow. 'The social status of the profession is ...
immeasurably below the proper standard,' wrote an anonymous
contributor to the *Glasgow Medical Journal*.[1] The thrusting new
science of submarine telegraphy had a much more glamorous
image. A more ambitious young man might have seen the Atlantic Cable expedition as an exciting career opportunity but Russell
had been, in his own words, motivated 'only from attachment
to Dr Thomson and a wish to see "summat".' By the end of his
arts course he had decided to become a doctor, perhaps in reaction
to the suffering and destitution on the doorstep of the university.
The decision had been made before he set off on the Atlantic
Cable expedition, and he saw no reason to alter it. It is easy to
imagine a hint of exasperation in Thomson's tone when, during
a shipboard conversation, he said to Russell: 'You are determined
to go on next session with your medical studies?'[2]

Glasgow University medical school, with 10 professors and
some 300 students, was not at its brightest and best when
Russell began his studies in the autumn of 1858. Edinburgh's
medical faculty had a much more distinguished line-up. Glasgow's reputation had declined since the Enlightenment although
before long, thanks to Lister and Macewen, it would make an
even bigger impact on the world than it had done under William
Cullen and Joseph Black. Something of the Enlightenment spirit
still lingered in Russell's day – the broad approach associated
with Cullen's search for a general theory of disease which could
be linked with speculations about the nature of life. The medical
faculty, whatever its shortcomings, was still imbued with the
same philosophical spirit to which Russell had been exposed as

an arts student. When he began his medical studies this tradition was coming under sharp attack from the 'assimilators' who wanted Scotland to emulate the more specialist approach of Oxford and Cambridge. An educational crisis had been precipitated by the poor performance of Scottish candidates in the Indian Civil Service examinations, and the underlying question, as some have interpreted it, was whether Scotland's cultural autonomy could be preserved at a time of increasing economic and political dependence. The Scottish Universities Act of 1858, while not surrendering to the assimilators, undermined traditional values seriously enough to have been seen by some as a cultural turning-point. Meanwhile, other academic reforms resulted from the Medical Act of the same year, which regulated the profession more tightly.[3]

But change came slowly. Many of the old traditions persisted.[4] The new Bachelor of Medicine degree, resulting in modest changes to the four-year curriculum, was introduced too late for Russell, who was one of the last students to graduate with the old MD degree along with his CM (Master of Surgery). He was very much a product of the old Scottish tradition, and its stout defender against the onslaughts of the 'assimilators'. In a letter to his friend James Bryce, by then at Oxford, he deplored the narrowness of English philosophy teaching, which he regarded as 'conservatism and classicism gone mad.' He added: 'I should very much like to have a set-to between one of Buchanan's leading seniors or middlemen and one of your heavyweights – any odds on the Scotchman ... Upon my word, I believe England has more to learn from us than we from her, in University matters.'[5]

But if the medical faculty was strong in philosophy, it was perhaps weak in the teaching of practical medicine. Missing from the syllabus, moreover, was anything in the nature of public health. Two decades earlier Professor Robert Cowan had included lectures on medical police in his course on medical jurisprudence but his successor, Henry Rainy, a venerable Highlander with an air of aristocratic distinction, was interested only in forensic medicine. Even there his practical contribution was limited: Edinburgh held sway in forensic medicine, with the Madeleine Smith trial in 1857 being no exception.[6] The

Edinburgh syllabus, in contrast with Glasgow's, included lectures on medical police, which may help to explain why Russell apparently toyed with the idea of enrolling there instead of at Glasgow. At any rate he sent away for the statutes for its MD degree and even did some of his studying there (conceivably at extra-mural lectures given by the future medical officer of Edinburgh, Henry Littlejohn).[7]

Still, the Glasgow medical faculty was evidently a more harmonious body than its Edinburgh equivalent — a 'band of brothers' compared with the 'quarrelsome giants' in the east.[8] Prominent among them was Allen Thomson, Professor of Anatomy, a man of quiet authority who once quelled a snowball riot simply by appealing to the students to stop. It was Thomson who was later put in charge of the arrangements for the removal of the university from the High Street to Gilmorehill (already being planned in Russell's student days). The Professor of Materia Medica was John Easton, inventor of the health-giving Easton's Syrup and a man of much learning who 'sometimes wandered to matters not quite relevant to his main subject, as for instance whether a particular vowel was long or short in some Latin word.' Easton had a high opinion of Russell and once commented that in addition to his natural talents he had 'a diligence in the acquisition of knowledge as vigorous and untiring as if diligence were all he had to depend upon for success in the journey of life.' The young man also attracted the favourable attention of Andrew Buchanan, Professor of Physiology, who was credited with being the first person to give a clear account of the nature of coagulation of the blood. Buchanan was a notable figure in the quadrangles, while his coachman, his brougham, and his old white horse were a familiar sight in the city streets. Other members of the Medical Faculty at that time included a shy American, Darwin Rogers, who was Professor of Natural History, and John Pagan, of the Chair of Midwifery, who had an exceptional gift of intuitive diagnosis.[9]

It is remarkable that Russell, having helped William Thomson to lay the Atlantic Cable, was now to come into contact with Joseph Lister when he was pioneering antiseptic surgery. It was in the third year of his course that Russell became a member of Lister's first surgery class in Glasgow. Then only 33, Lister had already established a reputation as a scientific thinker at Edinburgh University. His introductory lecture, in the autumn of 1860, would not have been readily forgotten by anyone who attended it. Lister, who had had the lecture theatre redecorated at his own expense, was heard in perfect silence by the students, who also paid him the equally unusual compliment of removing their hats. His lectures were models of clarity, delivered with infectious enthusiasm in a musical voice, and 'through all his teaching there ran a golden thread of high moral earnestness.' [10] With his gentle manner and notable patience, he must have seemed to Russell a very different mentor from the excitable William Thomson. On becoming Professor of Surgery at Glasgow University he was pleased to find the best students 'nice, intelligent, earnest fellows,' [11] and was particularly impressed by Russell's 'superior abilities' and 'literary culture.' [12] When the class presented Lister with an address of appreciation at the end of his first session, Russell was selected to read it (he had also, Lister guessed, probably written it). Years afterwards Lister was to recall the incident, remarking that the good opinion of Russell's comrades was a sign that he would distinguish himself in later life. He marked Russell down for 'a bright career of usefulness.' [13]

Although Russell had been determined to study medicine, he did not apply himself single-mindedly to the task. Maintaining his link with William Thomson, he combined the first year of his medical studies with a postgraduate class in natural philosophy, winning the university silver medal for his essay on 'Vital Dynamics.' In the same session he wrote a study of 'The Nationality of our Early Poetical Literature,' having gathered the material in the British Museum during a holiday spent with his barrister uncle in London.[14] He addressed the Literary Society on topics ranging from submarine telegraphy to Anglo-Saxon literature, wrote up his Atlantic Cable adventures for the *West of Scotland Magazine* and the *Sydney Morning Herald* (the paper on which his father still worked),[15] and encouraged by these successes went on to become a contributor to *Recreative Science*, a popular journal published in Stoke Newington.[16] Life at sea had also whetted his sense of adventure, and in the following summer he and a friend volunteered to ascend in a balloon to make meteorological readings for the British Association – an offer that was politely declined by the B. A.'s 'Balloon Committee.' [17] He also turned out regularly for the University Volunteers. Its rank and file also included William Thomson, who used to determine the velocity of a bullet by firing his rifle at a pendulum in the classroom, then leaping to the board to start the calculations before the smoke had cleared.[18] Russell was disappointed when Thomson was elected a captain of the City Rifle Guard. 'I am sorry we lose so zealous and notable a private, for his enthusiasm was unbounded,' he wrote to Bryce. 'Besides, he is not suited for a captain, either as to time or temperament.' [19]

Towards the end of his second year, after delivering a paper to the Literary Society on 'Illustrations of Pagan and Early Life in England from Anglo-Saxon Poetry', Russell was forced to admit that his outside interests were taking up too much of his time. 'I suppose this must be my farewell to such activities,' he wrote to James Bryce in Oxford, confessing that he was glad that the end of session was in sight – 'I never had such work, and yet I have been neglecting my Medical classes.' [20]

The resolution was soon broken. In the following session an essay on 'The Probable Influence of Western Civilisation on the Social, Political, and Moral Condition of China' won him the rector's prize of £25 to add to his first-class certificates in Materia Medica, the Practice of Medicine, and Surgery. He also remained a Liberal Club stalwart and was a leader of the somewhat fraught campaign to elect Lord Palmerston rector. Palmerston – denounced by Bryce, in a letter to Russell, as 'an old adventurer and a sham' [21] – upset his backers by telegraphing on the eve of poll to say that if elected he would not accept office. It was too late to withdraw his name. He was duly elected, but when Russell wrote to him later on the subject of his forthcoming inaugural address he received the following snub from Downing Street: 'I am desired by Lord Palmerston to thank you for your communication ... but to say that he has no inaugural address to make.' It is not surprising that the eventual address was described by one of those present as 'perhaps the worst ever delivered on such an occasion.' [22] Palmerston was all too obviously totally unprepared. By the time he concluded his ramblings Russell may well have been in agreement with Bryce's judgment.

Despite these distractions Russell managed to take a high place in all his classes. A more serious threat to his studies came in the final year of his course when enteric fever – then a life-threatening disease, which he probably caught in the wards of Glasgow Royal Infirmary – kept him away from college and unable for a while even to write.[23] Thomson, who was himself hopping about on a stick after a fall on the ice at Largs, made frequent inquiries about his progress.[24] 'Anything to delay your MD?' teased Bryce in a letter in which he also suggested Mommsen's *History of Rome* as suitable reading for convalescence.[25] Russell, however, did graduate that year. At the age of 25 he then launched himself upon his medical career as resident in the Royal Infirmary.

Chapter Seven

To the Poorhouse

*It has happened to me, from time to time, in the course of
my life, to have some learned friend shrug his shoulders
and drop the hint that my official work, the ultimate
object of which is the conservation of life, somehow was
opposed to the laws of the universe.*

R USSELL was a houseman at the Royal Infirmary during
the decade when it became known as the birthplace of
antiseptic surgery. It was in the early 1860s that Joseph
Lister, deeply upset by the disease-ridden conditions and high
mortality rate in the infirmary's new surgical block, determined
to grapple with the problem of infection. The breakthrough did
not come until 1865 with the application of Pasteur's germ theory
of disease but already, during Russell's brief spell at the infirmary, Lister had begun to experiment with the use of carbolic
acid. An American doctor who visited the Lister wards said that
the experience was 'like suddenly stepping out through a door
from an old era to a new one.'

Russell, too, stepped through this door. He was a resident
house surgeon for a spell before becoming a house physician.
As a student he had been awarded a first-class certificate in
Lister's class, and had assisted him in the wards, and now, as
a houseman, he worked for the eminent William Lyon, who said
that he had never had an abler assistant in his 20 years at the
Royal. He also worked for the cantankerous James Morton, who
was one of the leading denigrators of antiseptic surgery.[1] This
must have been an uncomfortable position for Russell, who was
deeply influenced by Lister's battle against infection. Lister was
later described as one of the foremost sanitarians of his day
because of the value he attached to cleanliness,[2] and this was
the nature of his influence on Russell. As the young man saw
it, Lister had demonstrated that prevention was better than
cure, and the same principle had to be applied to medicine.[3] This

was the line of attack that Russell planned. He had no great desire to be part of the surgical revolution, any more than he had been seduced by the glamour of submarine telegraphy. He had already set his mind on a career in public health. The decision appears to have been made during his illness in the year of his graduation,[4] but the seeds must have been planted earlier. All through his school and college days he had been exposed to the urban blight around the High Street. The area was still festering as rankly as ever during his years as a medical student, when its foul dens and 'fever nurseries' were strikingly described by 'Shadow,' the pseudonym of Alexander Brown (who like Russell's father was a letterpress printer).[5]

Russell was setting out on an unmapped path.[6] When he left university in 1862 there was still no public health framework in Glasgow,[7] although change was on the way: the Glasgow Police Act of that year authorised the appointment of a Medical Officer of Health, and in 1863 William T. Gairdner, the recently appointed Professor of the Practice of Medicine at Glasgow University, was selected for the part-time post.

The appointment was of huge significance for Russell. Gairdner brought with him to Glasgow a deep interest in public health matters, acquired during his years as pathologist at Edinburgh Royal Infirmary and lecturer at Edinburgh University. In 1861 he had lectured on 'Public Health in Relation to Air and Water' to a mixed audience of students and 'persons otherwise interested in the subject of Public Health.' Although Russell had graduated by the time Gairdner arrived at Glasgow University, he eagerly enrolled in his class. His resolve to enter public health was reinforced by the experience. Gairdner was to have a profound influence on Russell's career, and was to be his lifelong friend.

Then in his late 30s, Gairdner was a 'prince of clinicians and most erudite of physicians.'[8] Years after his death it was still being remarked that 'no man of the Glasgow school for the past two generations exercised such a wide influence and directed so many minds along scientific paths of medicine.'[9] Old G, as his students called him, was concerned to give philosophical insight into the phenomena of disease rather than simply to teach facts. He exhorted his students to 'add to the most ardent love of truth the cultivation of those gentle humanities which enable you to enter into the feelings and to soothe the sufferings of others.' [10] Like Lister, he developed bedside teaching, often becoming so absorbed in this task that he could be seen with his students scampering down the hill from the Infirmary to the college so as to be in time for his own lecture. Although he could be scathing on occasion he was noted for the sweetness of his nature, and he shared Russell's literary interests. He had written poetry as a young man and was 'widely versed in the literature of many languages, intimately acquainted with the drama of modern Europe, deeply interested in politics, both ancient and modern, and quite an expert on matters ecclesiastical, even beyond the domains of Christianity. ...' [11] He had some of the innocent eccentricities of the archetypal absent-minded professor, having once told a colleague about his daughter's engagement without realising that he was speaking to her fiancé. His propensity for getting on the wrong train was a trial to guards, porters, and other railway attendants as well as to his colleagues. 'Guid God! Is this you again?' said one dismayed porter when the professor alighted at the wrong station for the second time in two hours. [12]

With Gairdner's example to encourage him, Russell seized an early opportunity to take his first step towards a career in public health. Typhus fever, always present in mid-nineteenth-century Glasgow, was at a particularly high level after the downturn in trade in the late 1850s. In 1863, when it was breaking out into one of its periodic epidemics, Gairdner put pressure on the City Poorhouse to open fever wards, since the Royal Infirmary was restricting admission to patients with subscribers' lines. [13] The extra accommodation was duly provided and in 1863 Russell was appointed assistant medical officer of the Poorhouse, with responsibility for the new fever wards. He took up his post not long after a two-month spell at the celebrated Rotundo maternity hospital in Dublin, where he had charge of 'numerous cases of labour, some of which were of special difficulty.' [14]

The Infirmary work had been hard – 'No time for aught but medicine?' wrote James Bryce – but not as testing as what was to follow. The new post was hardly glamorous. The City Poorhouse, or Town's Hospital as it was originally called, had been founded in the early eighteenth century as a charitable refuge for the sick and the destitute but had passed into parochial hands after the 1845 reform of the Scottish Poor Law and was overseen at national level by the new Board of Supervision.[15] It had moved from its original site near the Clyde to the former premises of the Royal Lunatic Asylum in Parliamentary Road, a part of town which had become densely populated and smoke-polluted by the 1860s. The building itself, though imposing – the dome over the great central staircase was a city landmark – had become overcrowded and insanitary and the new fever wards had been hurriedly improvised from the schoolrooms and children's dormitories – not an ideal arrangement.[16] The status of the medical assistants had also deteriorated. At one time the Poor Law medical service had included some of the city's medical elite but by Russell's time the posts were left largely to young graduates like himself and to the minimally qualified who were glad of the chance of secure, salaried employment.[17]

Russell could have found more attractive openings. He made a good impression on those around him. Not long after he started work in the City Poorhouse his grandfather received a letter from William Mackenzie, probably the most renowned and influential eye surgeon in Britain at the time, who had performed a minor operation on the young Russell. 'Where is your grandson, the doctor, and what is he doing?' Mackenzie wanted to know, for his assistant was about to go on leave and he thought that Russell might welcome the chance of serving in his place in the Bath Street practice.[18]

At the City Poorhouse Russell led a more hard-pressed existence than he might have done as Mackenzie's assistant. Although not primarily a medical institution, the poorhouse treated some 5000 people annually in its hospital.[19] Rather chillingly the medical superintendant, Dr Alex Robertson, once argued that it should become a teaching hospital because 'where there is such an immense mass of disease, with a large mortality, there must be an excellent field of clinical and pathological research.'[20] Because of the stringent economies practised by Poor Law institutions the treatment was not always of the best. Robertson once remarked that he didn't consider himself justified in ordering the more expensive apparatus and appliances employed in many general hospitals.[21]

The work was hazardous as well as demanding. Fever doctors and nurses were at high risk of infection. At the Royal Infirmary, for example, 'many of the officers and servants of the house were attacked' during the typhus epidemic of 1864–65.[22] Russell was among those who caught the fever at the City Poorhouse,[23] suffering the intense headaches and delirium that characterise the disease – though in compensation acquiring a considerable professional asset: immunity from further attacks. Despite the difficulties of his situation he made full use of his brief spell at the Poorhouse. Already he was displaying the thoroughness and the analytical approach that marked his later career. His interest in nutrition (diet was a vital part of the treatment for typhus) led him to seek Robertson's permission to study the accounts of the provisioning department. He also embarked on a survey of 300 typhus cases treated in the hospital, a study as notable for its sociological as for its clinical content.[24] Russell recorded the addresses of the patients, usually in the Saltmarket and similarly run-down areas. He recorded their occupations, noting the large number whose work brought them into contact with the typhus poison – which he described as just as specific as the poison of a rattlesnake. Although it was not yet known that the fever was spread by infected lice, Russell – like other fever doctors of the time – was clearly aware of its connection with 'personal and general filthiness', including dirty clothing, and he noted that shoemakers accounted for a fifth of adult male cases. Typhus patients, he found, were generally well enough nourished, but were so dirty that it was difficult to make a diagnosis before they had been given a bath to expose any skin rash. 'The skin is to such people virtually lost as an organ,' he wrote. 'Coated with the accumulated excretions of years, its functions must be either in abeyance, or seriously crippled.'[25] He saw that slum conditions made this inevitable: 'It is quite impossible that necessary ablutions could be performed in a small room in which ten or a dozen people of both sexes reside. Dirtiness begins, therefore, as a sin of circumstance.' He advocated tackling the problem of overcrowding and also building free baths and wash-houses, pointing out that 'in no city could this more easily be done than in Glasgow, with its bountiful Loch Katrine and its central river.' The words presaged Glasgow's great era of municipal enterprise.

The typhus epidemic raged on. More than 2000 cases were reported in Glasgow in the first half of 1865, with more than 500 deaths. Russell watched sympathetically as Gairdner, in his new MOH role, visited the epidemic black spots and struggled to bring the outbreak under control with pitiful resources. 'The Medical Officer and his pigmy staff found themselves immersed in a rapidly rising flood of Typhus,' he noted grimly. 'As usual nothing had been done to prepare for the evil day, still less to avert it.'[26] He backed Gairdner's pleas for the provision of a new municipal fever hospital. With the Poorhouse authorities giving notice that they would no longer admit patients other than paupers, the Board of Police – acting under the new powers granted to it under the legislation of 1862 – resolved to look for temporary accommodation. Plans to convert a disused mill in Anderston (not far from Russell's birthplace) were dropped in the face of ferocious local opposition, and reluctantly it was decided that there was no alternative to building a new hospital. A site was purchased off Parliamentary Road, on the other side of Dobbies Loan from the City Poorhouse, and building work began amid deep snow in the winter of 1864–65. In April a pavilion hospital consisting of wooden sheds on brick foundations opened its doors to the first patients.[27] It was the first municipal fever hospital in Scotland (previous temporary hospitals had been funded from other sources) and was to prove more durable than the Town Council originally intended.

Russell, with a salary of £240, was made its first medical superintendant and resident physician. His post at the City Poorhouse had lost much of its purpose with the closure of its fever wards in 1864, and he had applied for the job of house surgeon and superintendant of the lunatic asylum at Barnhill Poorhouse near Springburn.[28] Either the application was – fortuitously – unsuccessful or he backtracked on learning of the fever hospital opportunity. Before saying goodbye to the Town's Hospital he was placed in sole medical charge of the entire institution for a fortnight during Robertson's absence. It was good preparation for what was to follow.

Chapter Eight

Fever Pitch

*It is a conviction established in my mind by observation,
and daily strengthening with experience, that success in
the treatment of continued fever can be gained only by
faithful, minute and intelligent attention from hour to
hour on the part of the nurse, and to a certain extent also
on the part of the medical attendant.*

RUSSELL was only 27 when he became superintendent of
the City of Glasgow Fever Hospital, more often known
as Parliamentary Road or Kennedy Street Hospital. He
had graduated less than three years before. Gairdner's influence
had been crucial: he had told the magistrates' committee of
Glasgow Police Board that the post should be filled by someone
of 'discretion and judgment' who had extensive experience of
treating fever cases and had had the disease himself. He then
recommended Russell.[1] In later years Gairdner was pleased to
be able to claim that he 'may be said to have had in some degree
the credit of introducing Dr Russell into public life.'[2]

Russell had remarkable freedom of action in his new post.
The hospital was an experimental venture. The details of
management had to be thought out from scratch.[3] It was left
to Russell to do most of the thinking. The municipal authorities
had no experience of hospital management and for the first year
or so took little active interest. Gairdner was a guiding influence
but as a part-time MOH he had other things on his mind – his
professorial duties as well as his attempts to put public health
on a proper footing. Taking up his post in the spring of 1865,
Russell felt like the commander of some remote administrative
outpost.[4]

With no medical staff to help him he personally recorded his
observations of each patient in the ward journals at least twice
daily. He checked the housekeeping accounts, concerning himself
with the price of potatoes and the cost of hay for the horse that

drew the fever ambulance.[5] With the matron he made a weekly
inspection tour of the nurses' dormitories and issued bulletins
on what he saw – 'The room occupied by Mrs B., M.A., and
J.H. is in a very discreditable condition. ...'[6] Despite these daily
pressures he set about writing a series of strategy papers on
hospital management, encompassing everything from nutrition
to nursing, which proved of lasting influence.

Nursing was a particularly urgent problem. It caused him
'more anxiety and vexation than could well be described.' The
influence of Florence Nightingale, who had done so much to
introduce modern nursing methods during the Crimean War,
had yet to be fully felt. Of the 35 nurses engaged during his
first year 18 had, by the end of the year, been dismissed for
drinking, five for inefficiency, four for dishonesty, one for 'ill-
using patients,' and one for bad temper. Russell was pained
when some who had seemed trustworthy neglected to give
patients their alcoholic stimulant, or drank it themselves. The
popular idea that nurses, like washerwomen, were inseparable
from drink was all too true, he remarked: 'Slatternly widows,
runaway wives, servants out of place, women bankrupt of fame
and fortune, from whatever causes, fall back upon hospital
nursing.' It was, he wrote, the last resort of female adversity,
and a fever hospital was particularly unattractive to 'respectable
women' because few had the immunity conferred by the illness.
It was no wonder that the matron, Miss Jane Gibson, told him
that her friends remarked: 'Surely your character is lost, or you
would not be in a place like this?'

People thought Russell naive to imagine that things might
be different. He sensed their amusement that he had not learned
that 'drink and dishonesty were essential properties of a nurse.'
What was needed, he insisted, was proper training, decent pay
and pensions, a professional organisation, and 'firm and kind
moral supervision.' He was deeply impressed by the handful of
good nurses who stood out from 'the succession of waifs and
strays' who flitted in and out of the hospital. Often at midnight
he stood silently watching the scenes of delirium and sometimes
violence in a male ward and 'wondered at the courage a woman
must have to pass the long hours of a night watch alone in such
company, and still more at the rarer gentleness where such

courage exists, which must combine with and soften its manifestations.' When three nurses died of typhus during the
hospital's first year he praised their heroism – one of them had
literally dropped at her post – and arranged for a hospital burial
ground to be provided at Sighthill. Convinced that even a fever
hospital could raise its nursing standards, he deliberately
recruited women with no previous hospital experience, raised
pay from 25s to 30s, placed a copy of Florence Nightingale's
manual in the hands of each nurse, assembled a small library
for them, and charged one of the better nurses with instructing
the others. These changes put Parliamentary Road ahead of
many better-known hospitals. Florence Nightingale's work in
the Crimea did not have a real impact on the UK itself for 15
years. Guy's Hospital, for example, did not reform its nursing
system till 1871.[7] Russell argued that if the general hospitals
were to introduce reforms it would not be long before surgeons
began to demand something more than a tidy woman with a
white apron. There would then be no more sneers, he said, at
the idea of teaching nurses anatomy. He had known a patient
bleed to death because the nurse, not knowing how to deal with
a haemorrhage, ran for help instead.[8]

Recruitment problems persisted but in a few years Russell
was expressing satisfaction with the improvement in standards.
This emphasis on nursing was bound up with his whole approach
to treatment. Experience had taught him that a typhus patient
with a good nurse and a poor doctor had a better chance than
one with a bad nurse and an indifferent doctor. Rather than
'drenching' the fever patient with drugs he believed that the
physician's job was limited to 'intelligent and minute observation' to enable 'the support of the vital energies in their natural
tendency through disease to health.'[9] His clinical approach was
as meticulous as his methods of hospital management. It was
not for nothing that, as a student, he had marked a passage in
a speech given by Sir Edward Bulwer Lytton, the novelist and
politician: 'I am no believer in genius without labour; but I do
believe that labour, judiciously and continuously applied,
becomes genius in itself.'[10]

Nutrition was an important part of this approach. For typhus
patients this mainly meant bolstering 'the vital energies' with

beef tea and sweet milk, even when they were crying out for porridge and tea. (During a visit to the London Fever Hospital Russell watched patients enjoy custard pudding but 'abandoned with chagrin' the attempt to administer this to his own gastric fever patients, who merely stirred it about with their spoons.[11]) Fresh air, he believed, was also of great importance: he thought it fortunate that the hospital layout allowed easy access to the grounds and believed that this explained why the average stay of patients was shorter than it had been for those under his care at the Town's Hospital. Walking sticks were provided for convalescents and the feeble were carried out to the airing ground. The hospital itself was so well ventilated that it was considered safe to allow typhus patients to be visited by close relatives.[12]

This controversial policy, which brought protests from within the medical profession, was introduced at Gairdner's instigation; and Russell was also following Gairdner's lead when he reduced the amount of alcoholic stimulation (the orthodox line of treatment at that time) given to typhus patients. Yet this policy was in tune with Russell's own way of thinking (not to mention his teetotalism) and he implemented it in characteristic style by an extensive clinical study which he reported to the *Glasgow Medical Journal*.[13] This challenged the idea that alcohol provided nourishment as well as stimulation, drew attention to the dangers of excessive doses, and emphasised the importance of careful observation of individual patients.

At a time when many hospitals still resorted to bleeding and leeching to 'reduce' the fever, this approach put Russell at the forefront of moves towards a less interventionist treatment, a trend that was to become firmly established in the following decade.[14] The policy paid off. Russell's own statistics showed that the hospital's typhus mortality rate was lower than those of the London Fever Hospital, the headquarters of interventionist treatment, and Dundee Royal Infirmary. He knew better than to take this crude league table at face value, realising that age was a critical factor. On further analysis he was puzzled to find that his own hospital had the worst record as far as the youngest age group was concerned, until on even more minute examination he concluded that this was because of its particularly high proportion of suckling infants who had been infected by their mothers' milk.[15]

The hospital, although under-utilised for the first few years of its history, was becoming known to the city's poor. Although supposedly only a temporary expedient, it was fulfilling an obvious need. Gairdner had given Russell power to admit patients at his own discretion without reference to the district medical officers.[16] Many were admitted after turning up at police offices but others simply arrived at the hospital gates, including children in their parents' arms. The place provided a refuge for those who were unable to obtain lines of admission to the Infirmary from its subscribers yet did not qualify as paupers or were unwilling to be classified as such. Russell was sympathetic to these cases. He was hostile to what he described as a 'system of pauper manufacture' and thought it should be ended for social as well as sanitary reasons.[17] He noticed a particularly high mortality rate among the older paupers and maintained that it was 'the dissipation and abandoned life which are so generally the basis of pauperism, and not the effects of poverty pure and simple, which render typhus more dangerous to paupers.' He had often noticed that half-fed and emaciated patients, provided they were not debauched, withstood typhus better than the better fed.[18]

By the time the Glasgow Police Act came up for review in 1866 the hospital's value had become recognised and a clause was inserted to put it on a permanent footing. Glasgow was the first local authority to commit itself to permanent hospital care although its lead was swiftly followed after the 1867 Scottish Public Health Act empowered other authorities to do the same.

Russell's reputation was growing along with that of the hospital. He was given credit for making it fully operational 'in an incredibly short space of time.' By the end of the first year at his post he had, according to Gairdner, 'won the confidence of all.'[19] When a cholera epidemic threatened the city in 1865–6 it was natural that he should be put in charge of the emergency hospital arrangements as part of the elaborate defensive measures planned by Gairdner. The Parliamentary Road hospital was cleared and held in reserve for cholera patients and plans were made to provide six new district hospitals radiating round the most densely populated part of the city. Russell was responsible for equipping and furnishing them. He planned a service of cabs to ensure 'punctual and frequent communication between headquarters and the various districts.' He drew up a six-shift nursing system, with 12-hour rest periods, to limit exposure to infection. When the epidemic reached Liverpool he visited the fever hospital there and tried to emulate it by recruiting an emergency nursing corps. Hundreds of women responded to his newspaper advertisements but almost all were found to be 'useless by reason of age and other infirmities, or, if able-bodied, useless by reason of sundry vices.' The upshot of this expensive campaign was an emergency band of four nurses to meet the needs of a cholera epidemic. Russell admitted that the exercise had been a hopeless failure.[20]

It turned out not to matter. Instead of an epidemic there was a minor outbreak. Loch Katrine water, which had reached the city at the end of the 1859, held the disease in check. Gairdner's extensive preparations, which included the recruitment of a 3000-strong interdenominational body of church members to do house-to-house visits with information and advice, looked out of proportion to the threat, but he claimed that things would have been worse without the precautions because the water supply did not reach all households. He had also to take account of the public fear generated by this dread disease. Its relentless progress from Egypt through Western Europe and then to London and Liverpool had been watched in Glasgow with what Gairdner described as 'a vast and indefinite sense of possible disaster.'[21] The city had suffered badly in the epidemics of 1832 and 1848, and the 1854 epidemic, in which Glasgow accounted for 4000 deaths out of a Scottish total of 6000, was still fresh in the memory.

This time there were only 66 cases in the city and only one of the proposed new district hospitals, Greendyke Hospital on Glasgow Green, was completed and utilised. The Parliamentary Road hospital admitted 11 cholera sufferers, of whom only two survived despite careful treatment with cold water, ice, friction, and hot bottles – not to mention a constant spray of carbolic solution ejected from gas-evaporating stands.[22] There were also numerous sufferers from choleraic diarrhoea and several who pretended to be ill for the sake of a bed for the night and a hot breakfast – such as the healthy-looking girl with her young child who spent 'two comfortable days' in the hospital. The first cholera patient was a seaman who had arrived from Arisaig via the Crinan Canal, but more typical cases came from the 'very lowest and most disreputable class' and from a variety of over-crowded areas. Russell mapped the disease with his usual care and discovered an 'epidemic tendency' only in the New Vennel, near the university, which accounted for almost half the admissions to Parliamentary Road and Greendyke. He visited the lane with Gairdner and found that 'their abodes were filthy to a degree; their habits drunken and dissolute.' In one house they saw the body of a boy lying on loose straw from which his father had just been removed to die in hospital and a 'little precocious girl keeping an unconcerned watch over her dead brother.' Gairdner's 'kindly remonstrance' to a woman whom they encountered amid the filth outside the house met with a stream of abuse, 'and a friendly advice from a workman hard-by, to hold our tongues and take ourselves off as quickly as possible.'[23]

On another occasion Russell visited the notorious Havannah Lane in the same locality to attend a patient who lived in an unlit, unheated hole without bedclothes. The man refused to be taken to hospital and when Russell returned later to the house with the van that had come to remove the man's body to the hospital morgue, he found the coffin guarded by the patient's wife, furious with drink, her sleeves rolled up ready for violent resistance. Russell tried to reason with her but in the end called for a priest who was able to persuade the unfortunate woman to change her mind.[24]

There was little time for anything but work. 'How you stand it all is more than I can understand,' wrote James Bryce. 'Hard work is hard work, but when a man does not even get his sleep, what is he to do?'[25] Russell had at least joined Glasgow Philosophical Society and must also have lifted his head from the cholera outbreak for long enough to follow William Thomson's renewed and finally successful attempts to lay an Atlantic cable. Life at Parliamentary Road was very different from the one that he would have led if he had followed in Thomson's footsteps. 'These beautiful days they have delicious sunshine, delicious even when reflected from the walls of a fever hospital,' he wrote in a poignant letter to Bryce. The recent past had brought sadness. His grandmother had died in 1863 and his grandfather, who had rapidly become more infirm after his wife's death, in the following year, at the age of 82. Russell confessed to Bryce that he found the summer sunshine 'painfully suggestive of former delights not now to be had .... What jolly times were these when I used to go with my poor grandfather to Wigtown.' Although not believing that he had really been happier in those days, he acknowledged that 'there were in my life those elements which are not now but of which I feel the want,' and which still gave reflected happiness.

'The harder ingredients seem to appear more prominently as we get older,' added Russell, who had recently had his twenty-eighth birthday. 'Our lives become more valuable, our pleasures become deeper, more intellectual and moral, less emotional.' [26] But soon there were to be important changes in both his private and his professional life.

Chapter Nine

Bath Street and Belvidere

One generation is economical, but only at the expense of another.

I N the early autumn of 1868, when he was 31 years old, Russell married Helen Fenton Davidson, a 26-year-old Edinburgh nurse. It was a time when young middle-class women in the city were being encouraged by the new Edinburgh Society for the Training of Sick Nurses to follow in the footsteps of Florence Nightingale.[1] Although there is no record of whether Helen Davidson worked in a hospital or as a district nurse, Russell doubtless detected in her that combination of courage and gentleness that he had noted when he stood silently watching the scenes in the wards of the Fever Hospital at midnight. As a student he had copied a sentimental passage from *John Halifax, Gentleman* about the life of a nursemaid – 'deafened with ever-sounding rills of laughter all day, and lying down at night with a soft, sleepy thing breathing at her side.' His comment had been that 'there is perhaps more of a woman's heart in the ... passage than in any I ever read before.'[2] But such idylls were not to be the stuff of his married life despite the high expectation of friends who remarked on the 'happy, serious faces' of the young couple.

'You don't know how truly good she will be to and for you,' wrote Dr John Brown, a close friend of the Davidson family, in a letter to Russell after the engagement.[3] Brown, an amiable Edinburgh practitioner whose patients had difficulty in distinguishing between his professional and social calls, might have been the original link between the two young people (a more obvious possibility was that they met when Russell visited Edinburgh as a student). Like Russell, he had a close connection with William Thomson, whose wife was related to Brown's stepmother. As a literary doctor – the author of *Rab and his Friends* and other popular books – he had something in common with the young man, for whom he had a high regard. Their friendship was to outlive Russell's marriage.

The wedding took place at the Davidsons' house in Saxe-Coburg Place. The ceremony was performed by the bride's father, the Rev. Peter Davidson, minister of Queen Street United Presbyterian Church and author of such works as *The Pentateuch Vindicated from the Objections and Misrepresentations of Bishop Colenso.* Earlier, when he was minister of another Edinburgh congregation, 'his fidelity to the standard of Christian character told seriously on the communion roll.' But by the time of his daughter's marriage he had gained recognition. St Andrews University had conferred an honorary degree upon him, and the *North British Review* had described his published lectures as luminous, lofty, and 'marked by a manly eloquence.'[4]

The family was formidably clerical. Three of Helen Davidson's brothers became ministers and her maternal grandfather, Alexander Young of Logiealmond, in Perthshire, had been such a powerful preacher that worshippers forded rivers and crossed muddy fields to hear him. Her uncle, the Rev. John Young of Newburgh, assisted her father at the wedding service.

On their return to Glasgow the Russells settled in the long, curving terrace at the west end of Bath Street on the edge of the fashionable Blythswood district, which by then had become almost a medical colony. Earlier in the year Russell had obtained permission from the municipal authorities to live outside the hospital, remaining in control of its affairs but delegating some of his medical duties to a resident physician. In his letter to the Police Board he made no mention of his forthcoming marriage but said that he felt the time had come to enter private practice.[5] Some of his obituaries state that he actually did so for a brief period but there is no evidence of this and indeed Gairdner, perhaps to refute such suggestions, stated categorically that 'he never engaged in anything like private practice.'[6]

His time for such pursuits must in any case have been limited. He visited the Fever Hospital every morning and evening, retaining charge of the two wards for the oldest patients and as far as possible seeing each one of them every day. These were busy times at Parliamentary Road. With typhus once again on the increase the hospital, which had been only partly occupied for the first few years of its existence, was now fully stretched. In the early spring of 1869 the typhus mortality rate in the hospital rose alarmingly, as did the general death rate in the city. There was fierce controversy about the causes but Russell was in no doubt that deteriorating living conditions were the main reason. During the preceding year he had noticed in his patients 'traces of long-continued underfeeding and general destitution, such as I at least have not previously recognised.' [7] Overcrowding, he added, was worse than it had been for some time. He was struck by the bitter expressions in the faces of some of the patients with whom he discussed this problem. In addition enteric fever, associated with poor drainage, was on the increase in Glasgow, and before the end of 1869 an epidemic of relapsing fever was sweeping north from London.

The state of the city's health was becoming a matter of public controversy and Gairdner, as MOH, was the target of much criticism. Russell found himself participating in this debate not only in his role as public health administrator but also as editor of the *Glasgow Medical Journal*, a position that he had taken over in 1868. The journal, started in 1828, had been rescued from imminent closure by a number of medical men who formed the Glasgow and West of Scotland Medical Association to guarantee continued publication for five years. Russell's name never appeared on the title page but he was the journal's 'dominant spirit as well as the active editor.' He also did the proof-reading and was a prolific contributor on subjects ranging from the distribution of enteric fever to smallpox vaccination. With William Gairdner also among its most prominent contributors the *Journal* was strongly slanted towards public health in this period, though Russell tried hard to extract articles from other members of the university medical faculty. He also encouraged general practitioners to contribute on the grounds that 'the great bulk of the disease which exists in a country is treated where it arises, and is seen by no eye save that of the private practitioner.' Dr Alex Robertson, Russell's old chief at the City Poorhouse, also wrote regularly for the journal, but not all the contributors were cronies. Dr Andrew Fergus, a town councillor with strong views on sanitation, wrote an eloquent denunciation of water closets in which he argued that the streets were honeycombed with gigantic laboratories for the production of disease.[8]

The journal flourished and won international plaudits during the six years of Russell's editorship but was given a rough ride by its rival, the *Glasgow Medical Examiner*. This publication, the mouthpiece of a group who had broken away from the Faculty of Physicians and Surgeons of Glasgow, regularly ridiculed such prominent medical figures as Lister with his 'much puffed carbolic acid treatment' and was often egged on by its readers. 'Yet a little time and the gaudy temples of quackery shall fall,' wrote one correspondent. The *Examiner*, nicknamed 'Mustard Plaster', was against everything progressive but had a special loathing for the public health movement. It pilloried the 'extreme sanitarians' with their 'whitewash, disinfectants, and deodorisers,' and with brains that were 'a pandemonium of effluvial ideas.' Gairdner was mocked as 'our successful sanitary functionary' and Russell, as editor of the *GMJ* as well as a member of the Faculty, was no doubt considered doubly deserving of this treatment. His writing style was denounced as turgid and platitudinous and it was strongly implied that he and Gairdner formed a mutual admiration society and that they unfairly claimed credit for pioneering work on the reduction of alcoholic stimulation in typhus whereas in reality they were 'only following after lights who have gone before them.' As for the journal: 'We are certainly sorry for it, but we are forced to the conclusion that *Glasgow Medical Journal*, like the poetry of Tennyson, must be either profoundly wise or profoundly stupid, or like the above-received articles, very transcendental.'[9]

Russell, though, had other problems on his mind. Relapsing fever, having apparently been introduced by Polish immigrants to Whitechapel, was spreading rapidly through the country – frequently carried by tramps, who had time to cover considerable distances between the primary attack of the illness and the relapse some seven to nine days later. 'Relapsing fever haunts the dirty and the destitute,' Russell noted. 'All that sedimentary population which settles down from year to year into the slums of our cities seemed to be stirred up and brought to the surface in our hospitals.' The first victims to arrive in the fever hospital were five hollow-cheeked, miserably clad members of a Gorbals family. Russell visited the house and found a gaunt and sallow woman 'so insufficiently clad that she held about her person during my visit what seemed to be a bedcover.' There was not a stick of furniture in the house and the only bedding was a bag of straw, on which an infant was sleeping under a ragged towel.[10]

Although direct mortality during this outbreak was only 3% the disease was, Russell noted, painful and distressing and the cause of much misery. By early 1870 it had assumed epidemic proportions in Glasgow and was outrunning the available hospital space despite recent extensions to Parliamentary Road. Russell joined Gairdner in campaigning for additional accommodation. The Town Council, thanks to a ratepayers' rebellion against sanitary improvement, was not in a mood to be sympathetic. Its relations with Gairdner had become extremely strained. But Russell, like his mentor, was prepared to be outspoken. The shortage of beds, he wrote in the *GMJ*, resulted 'entirely from the supineness of the Board of Police ... The circumstances are so urgent that they will at last provide temporary wards, but, we fear, cannot retrieve the results of the home treatment which has necessarily been adopted for some time.'[11] He also injected a note of controversy into the annual report of the fever hospital. 'It seems to me that the hospital treatment of fever in Glasgow has hitherto been carried out on principles which have been in every respect erroneous,' he declared. The enormous expenditure on emergency measures meant, he argued, that one generation was being economical at the expense of the next. It was as if the fire brigade was dismantled between fires, so that half the city might be burned before it was reassembled.[12] 'We surely do not require to see the disease actually ravishing the people before we can be convinced that it is necessary to spend money in providing accommodation for its victims,' he pleaded.

A potent argument deployed by Russell was that municipal hospitals served the general interest by ensuring that patients remained isolated until they had passed the infectious stage, whereas other hospitals owed a duty to the individual patient only. As he put it, 'the principle of treating infectious disease at common expense for the common good should be extended.'[13]

Under the pressure of relapsing fever this argument finally prevailed. The Police Board instigated a search for a suitable site for a new permanent fever hospital and eventually settled on Belvidere Mansion and its 32-acre estate, two miles east of Glasgow Cross between London Road and the Clyde.

Russell, having discarded his residential responsibilites at the Parliamentary Road hospital, was well placed to take overall command at Belvidere as well. He was appointed superintendent and placed in charge of equipping and furnishing the new buildings. This was done under tremendous pressure. Relapsing fever was spreading so rapidly that wooden buildings 'of the most temporary kind' were run up with astonishing speed. The contractors entered the stubble field on November 22, 1870, and the first pavilion was ready to receive patients before Christmas, despite heavy snowfalls and such severe frost that sometimes the wood had to be thawed with salt. There was not even time to make wrought-iron bedsteads; wooden ones, of the type used during the typhus epidemic that had accompanied the Irish potato famine, were substituted.[14] Russell remarked that although the hospital was meant to be permanent its first buildings were much more makeshift in material and workmanship than Parliamentary Road, which was originally intended to be temporary. Nevertheless this marked the beginning of a great success story. Belvidere was later described as 'the largest fever hospital out of London and the finest in the three kingdoms.'

The surroundings could hardly have been finer. 'I believe,' declared Russell, 'that there has never been such a noble provision made by any community for its stricken poor.' Convalescents could wander in the walled garden of the mansion or on the slopes of one of the three valleys running down to the River Clyde. 'In summer,' Russell remarked, 'it is one of the most pleasant sights to see the children rolling about on the grassy slopes of the glens, and the seats, placed here and there, occupied by people who for the first time in the lives of so many are tasting of the sweets of Nature.' Close to the southern horizon lay the wooded slopes of the Cathkin Hills, where he himself had so often walked.[15]

There was little time to admire the view. Relapsing fever made heavy demands on the new hospital,[16] typhus was still on

the rampage, and a smallpox epidemic threatened. In the event
the smallpox outbreak was trivial compared with Edinburgh's,
thanks to the Sanitary Department's 'persistent and thorough'
hunting-down of contacts and enforcement of preventive
measures. Doorstep vaccination was provided and isolation enforced by warrant when necessary. Russell, having so recently
denounced his own city's deficiencies, could now boast that 'the
history of smallpox in Glasgow illustrates admirably the advantage and ultimate economy of an apparently superabundant
hospital accommodation in a large community.' [17]

Between the two hospitals Russell now had responsibility for
more than 4000 patients a year. Under his command were some
promising young doctors. Joseph Coats, later to become Glasgow University's first professor of pathology, was a resident
assistant at Parliamentary Road and helped Russell to make
better use of the science of thermometry. The young William
Macewen was the first resident medical officer at Belvidere,
although he soon concluded that infectious disease was too
narrow a subject for his taste.[18] But Russell himself continued
to play an active medical role. On the strength of his work
during the relapsing fever epidemic he sucessfully applied for a
salary increase in 1870, and although a similar request was
turned down the following year he was awarded a £100 bonus
in view of 'the great labour devolved upon Dr Russell during
the last nine months.'

He was now in the front line of the public health movement.
The first decade of his career could hardly have provided a
better preparation for his life's work as Medical Officer of Health
for Glasgow. When, in 1872, the post became vacant, he was
the obvious candidate – although not a universally popular one.
The circumstances of his appointment were controversial, as
would be so much else about his long tenure of the post.

Chapter Ten

Rude Awakening

*To sanitation belongs the task of showing how men may
live in cities and be healthy.*

WILLIAM Gairdner used to say that his chief service to
Glasgow was 'to have discovered Dr Russell and
placed him in the track of my succession.'[1] But Gairdner's own achievements were impressive for a part-time Medical
Officer of Health operating on unknown and often unfriendly
territory. Little preliminary spadework had been done when he
took up his post in 1863. Despite its strong medical tradition
Scotland was a late starter in the public health movement. Although Edwin Chadwick had called in 1842 for medical officers
to be appointed throughout the land, urban Scotland had been
slower to respond than the progressive minority of English cities.
Liverpool appointed an MOH in 1847 whereas Edinburgh led
the way in Scotland in 1862, the year before Gairdner's appointment.

There was no clear lead from London: Westminster legislation
often proved inoperable in Scotland because it was not drafted
to take account of its separate legal system or distinctive needs.[2]
The 1848 Public Health Act, which facilitated the appointment
of MOHs, did not extend across the Border because the Scottish
medical establishment objected to the idea of being controlled
by a board of health in London rather than by a Scottish board
'conversant with the laws of Scotland.' It was not until 1867
that public health legislation was passed for Scotland, which
meanwhile had to make do with local police acts and minor
legislation – an unsatisfactory position in view of the confused
state of Scottish local government at that time.[3] The problems
of industrialisation were simply on too massive a scale for the
sense of civic responsibility that had developed in the eighteenth
century. Moreover in commercially minded Glasgow the proper-
tied classes, encouraged by fashionable *laissez-faire* doctrine,

ignored the wider needs of the community. It was not surprising
that Gairdner's first reports on the state of the city's health
bore a sad resemblance to those of the district police surgeons
20 years before. The same disease-ridden streets and wynds
were described, even the same tenements.

A certain amount of sanitary work had been carried out under
a series of local police acts.[4] In Scotland the term 'police' had
the wider sense of 'polity', covering such functions as scavenging, street lighting, and fire-fighting as well as public order.[5]
The landmark Glasgow Police Act of 1800 recognised street
cleaning as a public duty to be financed from public funds. It
established a Police Board of elected commissioners with rating
powers, which maintained a separate identity from the Town
Council even after it became entirely manned by councillors in
the 1840s. Initially more representative than the oligarchic
Town Council, it grew into a significant civic institution with
some potential for controlling the urban environment. The
commissioners, however, were reluctant to make full use of their
sanitary powers, particularly when this would have brought
them into conflict with property owners. Influenced by the
evangelical values of Dr Thomas Chalmers, the future leader of
the Free Church of Scotland, the board became more interested
in public morality than in public health. The civic elite packed
the pews of St John's Parish Church to hear Chalmers preach
that the Church, not the State, should retain responsibility for
the welfare of the poor.[6]

This message, which seriously delayed reform of the mean
and grudging Scottish Poor Law, was challenged by reformers
under the leadership of Professor William P. Alison of Edinburgh, whose main energies were devoted to this campaign
rather than to the cause of sanitary reform. Yet the case did
not go by default, even in Glasgow. Throughout the first half
of the nineteenth century brave voices were raised in opposition
to the prevailing ethos. It is clear from Russell's own account
of that period that he valued their efforts and was influenced
by their example. These medical men, he noted, 'drew from the
bitter experience of their time lessons which it took the municipality long years to learn.'[7] Among them was Robert Graham,
Professor of Botany at Glasgow University, one of the strong

Scottish supporters of the Continental idea of a 'medical police' as guardians of public health for the state. During the typhus epidemic of 1819 Graham walked through filthy wynds and alleys, just as Russell was to do half a century later, and concluded that wide streets should be driven through 'these depositories of wretchedness' and that the police should compel the removal of dunghills.[8] Two decades later Robert Cowan, whose family had produced seven generations of academic and medical men, was appointed to a new chair of Medical Jurisprudence and Medical Police at Glasgow University (one of a number of innovations reluctantly made by the university to pre-empt Government interference). Cowan, who for a while was associated with Chadwick in statistical work, argued that 'a few thousand pounds, judiciously expended in opening up the districts most densely populated,' would be less than the price of neglect.[9] His early death in 1841, only two years after his appointment, was a blow to the cause of reform. Progress remained fitful – an inspector of cleansing was appointed with a wide remit, but with no staff. Only during epidemics did the authorities stir themselves to establish boards of health and take other emergency measures. As Russell remarked, the scavenger sallied forth with his broom, the limewasher with his brush, and when it was all over 'the hospitals were pulled down, the doctors, nurses, and fumigators who had not been buried were paid off.'[10] There was no permanent body to cope with the chronic problems of ill health.

It was not until the 1850s that the need for reform became more widely accepted. In Russell's phrase this was a period of awakening. A number of developments brought the public health question into sharper focus. The boundaries extension of 1846, bringing Anderston, Calton, and Gorbals into the fold, prepared the way for a more municipal, less parochial, style of administration. The spur to action was provided by the dreaded cholera, which was feared far more than the familiar scourge of typhus because it struck with terrible swiftness and was no respecter of persons. After the 1848 epidemic the Dean of Guild Court made more use of its powers to order the demolition of insanitary buildings, and the epidemic of 1853–4 not only cleared the way for the Loch Katrine water supply after years of controversy but gave a boost to sanitary reform. New Scottish legislation introduced a medical element into nuisance removal by requiring parochial doctors to certify that a health hazard existed. In Glasgow a 'Committee on Nuisances' was set up by the Town Council in 1857 – the first acknowledgement that public health was a function of municipal government. It was this committee, under the chairmanship of Councillor John Ure, that urged the appointment of a Medical Officer of Health for the city.

Ure was one of the heroes of Glasgow's public health movement. For nearly 40 years he worked devotedly in this cause. He was a grain merchant with a house in Helensburgh and a passion for yachting, but as a youth in the Briggait he had explored the slums nearby and resolved to work to improve conditions. Becoming a town councillor at an early age, he pursued his aims systematically.[11] His allies included the Chartist activist James Moir and a future Lord Provost, James Watson, who called boldly for reforming legislation at a meeting of the Social Science Association in Glasgow in 1860. In the face of strong opposition Ure drew up a scheme for sanitary improvement and led a delegation to the principal towns of the UK which reported that Glasgow lagged behind England in such matters. The result was the Glasgow Police Act of 1862 which, although a tentative piece of legislation, provided for the establishment of a permanent sanitary committee and the appointment of a Medical Officer of Health with power 'to adopt special sanitary measures, with the view of preventing the occurrences of epidemics and contagious disease.' This was a logical consequence of the new nuisance law, since parochial doctors were not up to the task of deciding what constituted a danger to public health.

John Ure led the search for a suitable candidate. This was no easy task in Glasgow in the 1860s, but he was impressed when he came across the public health lectures given by Gairdner in his Edinburgh days. Ure and Councillor Nathaniel Dunlop went to hear Gairdner address a meeting on infectious diseases and 'came to the conclusion that the man for the work had appeared as if specially sent.'[12] Gairdner took up his part-time post in January, 1863.

His resources were meagre. As his assistants he had the five part-time district police surgeons. The non-medical staff consisted of a sanitary officer with a desk in the Central Police Office in Albion Street and the help of three police officers selected for special sanitary duty. Before long two shops in College Street were fitted up as a sanitary office. The operation remained precarious until the Public Health (Scotland) Act of 1867 paved the way for a permanent sanitary department able to set about its business 'undisturbed by a perpetually impending dissolution.'[13]

Despite these difficulties, and the rising flood of typhus, Gairdner laid the foundations for the future. He brought a scientific spirit to urban sanitation. Aware of the need to gather statistical data, he provided detailed fortnightly reports on 24 divisions of the city (an unpopular move with the municipal authorities because of the stark contrasts that this exposed). Chemists were engaged to analyse water supplies, a municipal washhouse was opened for the disinfection of bedding and clothing, and five women sanitary inspectors were hired to give house-to-house instruction in hygiene. Gairdner also won the battle to establish municipal fever hospitals, identified bad housing as the root cause of much ill health, and provided the final impetus to the setting up of the City Improvement Trust in 1866 to clear congested slum properties and rehouse the inhabitants. The backlash against the 'improvement tax' levied on occupiers in the designated areas was so effectively exploited by opponents of the civic leadership that Lord Provost John Blackie, who was closely identified with the scheme, lost his seat in the municipal elections. 'So shallow at times are the thoughts of the multitude,' commented Russell.[14]

Gairdner's own position was undermined. Questions were asked about the department's spending (which had escalated with the building of Belvidere Hospital) and about the high death rate (boosted by the typhus epidemic). The *North British Daily Mail* ran a series of highly critical articles. The cynics on the *Glasgow Medical Examiner* stirred up trouble by suggesting that there was no great harm in a little overcrowding – all Glasgow needed was better scavenging and some soup kitchens.[15] The Sanitary Committee (as the Committee on Nuisances had become) was deeply divided. The cantankerous Councillor Malcolm McEwan, a tobacco baron with a clever and sarcastic tongue, clashed repeatedly with John Ure. McEwan openly questioned whether Gairdner was worth his salary and was once accused by Ure of lacking common decency. 'I beg your pardon,' retorted McEwan. 'That was a rather gross way of speaking.' [16]

A delegation was sent to Bristol, where the mortality rate had recently declined (probably because a typhus epidemic had run its course), and its report resulted in an important administrative shake-up. The sanitary, cleansing, and fever hospital committees were merged into a more powerful Health Committee and a centralised sanitary office was opened in Montrose Street to administer all three branches of the service. The sanitary staff was considerably expanded – but unfortunately for Gairdner it was placed under the control not of the medical officer but of a newly appointed Chief Sanitary Inspector. Gairdner was particularly incensed at the promotion, arranged behind his back, of one of the district police surgeons (James Dunlop, who was also a professor at the Andersonian University) to an influential new post as assistant medical officer.[17] A subsequent investigation into the costs of the department resulted in the decision to replace Gairdner and his five part-time medical assistants with a full-time medical officer. Since the saving was marginal, it was clear that the aim was to get rid of Gairdner. McEwan would have liked to abolish the post as well but was visiting his tobacco plantation in Louisiana during the critical decision-making.

Not perhaps the most tactful of men, Gairdner finally antagonised even the loyal John Ure by claiming publicly that the committee had 'evil' intentions towards the medical staff – an accusation which Ure described as an 'unfounded and most ungenerous presumption.'[18] The Town Council approved the recommendation to rescind Gairdner's appointment.

The medical world was outraged. The affair became a *cause célèbre*. The *Lancet* thought Glasgow could 'scarcely fail to suffer with losing the services of such a staff and such a leader.' The *Medical Press and Circular* deplored 'a blunder almost unexampled in sanitary movements.' In an editorial almost certainly written by Russell the *Glasgow Medical Journal* commented acidly that Councillor McEwan was 'quite disposed to improve the medical staff out of existence.'[19]

Despite this off-putting publicity there were 45 applicants for

the new post. Many of them were graduates of Scottish universities but only one besides Russell was based in Scotland, the
police surgeon in the Anderston district of Glasgow. The short
leet of four included the medical officers of Carlisle and Salford,
and the final choice was between Russell and Dr Edmund Syson
of Salford (a man of about Russell's own age, whose subsequent
career was not particularly distinguished). The special sub-committee responsible for the selection unanimously recommended
Russell as 'a tried and efficient officer.'[20] Medical opinion in
Glasgow was solidly behind him, with 20 leading doctors sig-
ning a testimonial which Ure read to the health committee (as
the sanitary committee had become in the course of municipal
streamlining). The *British Medical Journal* reported that Russell
had convinced everyone that he was 'possessed of no mean
administrative ability.'

He had not convinced the health committee. At least one
bailie would have preferred the post to have been filled by a
sanitary engineer, but the main opposition to Russell came from
McEwan, who was hostile to any ally of Gairdner's. McEwan
said that when he had instigated the investigation into the
sanitary department he 'thought it would have yielded better
fruits.' He dared to add that he was surprised that Gairdner, a
man of high standing in his profession, had been 'displaced' by
one of his subordinates. He said that Glasgow, with its high
death rate, should have one of the best medical officers in the
country – one recruited from England, where sanitary science
was a specialist subject.[21] Coming from the arch-enemy of the
sanitary movement, this must have stunned the councillors.
McEwan was reminded that he had been responsible for the
economy drive and one councillor argued that if the city wanted
a better man it should be offering more than £600 a year.
McEwan neverthless managed to delay ratification of the appointment, causing the *BMJ* to comment: 'We hardly envy the
continual state of expectancy in which the candidate so recommended must have to exist during the long period in which the
matter has been under consideration.'[22] Russell's Uncle John,
the barrister, made much the same point in a letter in which
he remarked that there were many slips between cup and lip,
'particularly in appointments by corporations.'[23]

Finally, in November, 1872, the appointment was unanimously approved. Gairdner then declined the offer of a consultancy at £100 a year, which he said would have given the impression of divided responsibilities.[24] Russell, who had been under Gairdner's wing from the beginning of his public health career, was now in full charge. His life's work was about to begin.

Chapter Eleven

Doors of the Poor: the 1870s

*It is easy to prove, if any proof were needed, that death is
knocking loudest on the doors of the poor.*

G LASGOW was flourishing when Russell took up his post
in the closing weeks of 1872. A 'tidal wave of prosperity'
had been flowing for several years. More than 100 iron
steamers were being hammered out in the yards. The first horse-
drawn trams were rattling through the streets. The population,
a little more than half a million, had about doubled since Russell's
birth.[1]

A start had been made to slum clearance. The City Improvement Trust, whose creation had caused such a furore in
Gairdner's day, was acquiring and demolishing property, widening old streets and laying out new ones. The dungsteads had
disappeared from the backcourts and municipal cleansing
workers had replaced commercial manure collectors. New tenements had water closets in place of privies. But areas like the
Saltmarket and Bridgegate remained desperately overcrowded
and disease-ridden. The wynds and closes still contained the
'accumulated mass of squalid wretchedness' described by Glasgow's chief constable during Russell's boyhood. The staircases
were used as public urinals. Although the worst of 'the fever
years' were over, deaths from lung disease were still rising. The
infant mortality statistics were appalling.

As he contemplated this scene from the Sanitary Office in
Montrose Street, Russell may have felt a little beleaguered.
Glasgow's social problems were on the scale of Liverpool's and
Manchester's – among Scottish cities only Dundee was com-
parable – yet Russell had neither the statutory powers of an
English MoH nor even clear authority within the Sanitary
Department. His position, as the first full-time MoH in Scot-
land, was ambivalent and ill-defined. He had no medical staff
at his command – Gairdner had at least enjoyed the help of

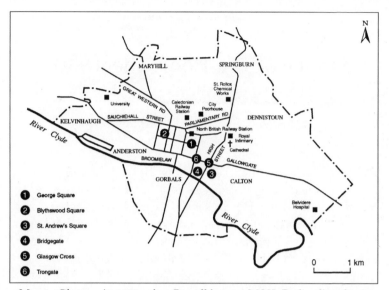

Map 1. Glasgow in 1872, when Russell became MOH. Broken line shows boundary.

the five district surgeons but as full-time MOH Russell was expected to manage on his own. Nor did he have authority over the sanitary staff. During the municipal intrigues of Gairdner's day the sanitary inspectorate had been built up at the expense of medical influence. The 45 inspectors were placed under the direct command of a Chief Sanitary Inspector with a wide remit which included common lodging houses, the enforcement of regulations against overcrowding, and nuisance removal − although the medical officer had to certify that the nuisance was a health hazard. The inspectorate swarmed over the city, making thousands of home visits every week in search of infectious disease, inspecting bakehouses and grocery stores, seizing and destroying large quantities of suspect sausages, rotten apples, or 'putrid herrings'. The sanitary inspectors could also call upon the cleansing department − the third division of the sanitary operation, also with its own administration and chief inspector − for fumigation and clothes washing or the emptying of ashpits.[2]

Russell's position was undermined by ambiguities in Scottish public health legislation. Whereas English MOHs were over-

A cartoon of Ruseell in 1876, soon after his appointment as MOH.

lords of their sanitary departments, the Scottish Public Health Act of 1867 confused the issue by naming the chief sanitary inspector (CSI) before the medical officer, giving the impression that the former was the more important official.[3] Later the Board of Supervision, who as administrators of the Poor Law were the central body in Scottish health matters, ruled that each officer was independent of the other, a confusing system of dual control that lasted for Russell's whole career as MOH. His starting salary of £600, on the other hand, was almost double that of the Chief Sanitary Inspector, Kenneth Macleod, and there is no doubt that John Ure and the other councillors responsible for his appointment intended him to be in overall command. Many people assumed that this was indeed the case, but Macleod had other ideas. He had been his own boss for two years before Russell came on the scene and had no intention of being shouldered into second place. A former sanitary inspector of Dunoon whose interest in medical matters had led him to attend classes at Anderson's College, Macleod was a 'somewhat self-assertive man' who in the words of one member of the Health Committee 'took things upon him that would more properly have been done by the medical superintendent.' [4]

With the two men producing separate fortnightly reports, based on different administrative divisions of the city, friction was inevitable – what one councillor described as 'more or less of jarring.' Years afterwards John Ure said that he would have intervened on Russell's behalf if he had realised how things stood, but both Russell and Macleod seem to have decided to thole each other, with Russell's allies maintaining that his conciliatory disposition saved the situation.

His strategy was to work with, and through, Macleod's inspectorate, particularly the epidemic inspectors who were the detectives of infectious diseases and who were responsible for reporting cases to the MOH although the CSI was their ultimate boss. Russell was in constant communication with these men, who traversed the city on foot to make perhaps 20,000 home visits a month. When hospital seemed indicated they walked to the nearest police station to telegraph Russell, who would wire the gateman at the fever hospital for a horse-drawn ambulance. The epidemic inspectors also arranged for home nursing in accordance with Russell's orders, and for the disinfection of houses or neighbourhoods. Their memorandum books, submitted individually to Russell every evening, provided material for his reports and statistics. [5] As he later wrote: 'I may say that I have always kept the epidemic inspectors in direct personal relations with me, and though working through men in whose selection I had no say, and who owned another master, I am satisfied that no part of the work of the department has been more consistently and successfully carried out.' [6]

Russell enjoyed his work with these men. At the end of his career he was to look back nostalgically to those pioneering times. It was long before the days of compulsory notification of

infectious diseases and he relished the detective work involved
in tracking down cases – the visits to the observant old woman
who kept a little shop at the close-mouth and knew all the
births, marriages, and deaths of the backlands; the hints dropped
by policemen; the neighbours who comforted the wife of a fever
sufferer but to save their own skins took the first opportunity
to tell 'the Sanitary' that there was a case of 'spotted typhus'
upstairs. Inspectors spied on the movements of doctors from a
distance, and raced to keep up when they took to broughams.
One of them developed an outstanding talent for detective work
– 'he has the nose of a sleuth-hound when put upon the track,'
said Russell admiringly. Sometimes a warrant had to be obtained
for the removal of the reluctant patient and the police were
warned to be on hand. Russell would then 'go in with the
fighting men of our staff' to carry the patient through an
unfriendly mob to the fever van. Once, when a Gallowgate door
was barred, he bent the law by sending an inspector up a ladder
to enter by a window. The inspector was then promptly set
upon by the patient's brother.[7]

As well as extending his influence over the inspectors, Russell
built up their prestige and expanded their role. He put these
medically unqualified former artisans through a short course on
smallpox revaccination (the primary vaccination in infancy failed
to give lasting protection). There was much popular resistance
to secondary vaccination, which unlike infant vaccination was
not legally compulsory, but the inspectors used surprise tactics
by raising the matter the minute they entered an infected house.
According to Russell, 'arms were bared and the thing was done
before they had time to think about it.'[8]

It was not surprising that people imagined that Russell ruled
the Sanitary Department. He was the source of most of its
initatives. Macleod could not match his moral authority, eloquence or analytical powers and had less influence on leading
members of the Health Committee and on public opinion. Russell
also made an important advance towards his ideal of an integrated local health administration in 1879 when disinfection and
fumigation operations were transferred from the cleansing staff
to the sanitary inspectorate.[9] This effectively marginalised the
Cleansing Inspector, John Young, who was left in charge of

little more than the municipal manure but nevertheless showed such ability that he was later appointed the first manager of the municipalised tramways.

From the beginning Russell pushed out the boundaries of his work. It was an irony of his position that infectious disease was waning by the time he became MOH, thanks both to rising living standards and sanitary improvements. Mortality from typhus had peaked in 1865 and other infectious diseases were being brought under control with the help of the municipal fever hospitals, the house-to-house visitations of the new sanitary inspectorate, and the washing and disinfection services introduced by Gairdner. Pulmonary disease was the main scourge of the city. As Russell noted in 1875, 'The class of disease which is directly under the control of this department, the infectious, furnishes absolutely a small proportion of the total deaths and relatively a declining number.' [10] The exception was childhood infections, which contributed to an appallingly high death rate among the under-fives. This had aroused comparatively little anxiety because, as Russell grimly noted, 'it was typhus that slew the breadwinners.' Children's diseases had, he thought, attracted too little attention during the heroic age of epidemics, but now that the dust and smoke of the main battle had cleared he intended to redirect the attack. [11]

Russell refused, however, to be stampeded. In his first weeks as MOH he turned aside a councillor's request for an immediate inquiry to establish why 45% of deaths in 1872 were of children under the age of five, an age group that accounted for only 14% of the city's population. [12] 'Haste to obtain results only leads to vexatious fallacies,' Russell declared. Like Gairdner he believed that there had to be a solid statistical basis for action. He began to amass the evidence. [13] From the middle of 1873 every death from infectious or pulmonary disease was recorded on a 'death card' which gave particulars about the size of the house and the position of the WC (if any) and jawbox or sink. Using the City Chamberlain's annual housing returns, he arranged the city's 24 sanitary districts in four groups according to their living conditions, and produced tables and graphs showing the comparative figures for death rates and the principal causes of death, relating these to age and population density (see graph on page following).[14] Soon he introduced more variables – house sizes; number of occupants per room; number of occupants in relation to cubic space; birth rates and illegitimacy rates. He analysed local variations in sub-divisions more elaborate than those of any other urban community in the country, their pattern made plain by the use of logarithmic graph paper – a significant innovation. He compared the death rates and housing patterns with those of the other Scottish cities and large towns. In his monthly reports he compared Glasgow not only with Liverpool and Manchester but with St Petersburg, Paris, Boston, and Philadelphia – an invitation to the third city of the Empire to think internationally in public health as well as in commerce.

This was ground-breaking work. Dr William Farr, the English Registrar General and architect of health statistics south of the Border, was greatly impressed and in 1875 wrote to congratulate Russell.[15] *The Glasgow Herald* declared that there was 'probably no city in the kingdom where so much information of the highest importance to those who care for the public health is regularly tabulated, and interpreted in a large and philosophical spirit.' There was enough solid fact and sound inference, the paper added, to set an entire social science association up in business.[16]

Russell's purpose was much less academic. The tables were an effective way of pointing up anomalies which he saw daily with his own eyes. His work took him into every corner of the city – to the new terraces and crescents of the West End as well as to dark and sour-smelling closes in the Saltmarket. He saw the sick children of wealthy parents tossing in feather beds enclosed by damask curtains – and heard the echoing voices and running footsteps of the children of the poor as they played in gloomy lobbies and dark staircases. Once, entering an East End tenement, he found the body of a six-year-old boy laid out on the only bed of a house occupied by his fireman father, his mother, and two younger children. The boy had died of smallpox the day before.[17] In another house boasting only one bed he found several children on the straw-covered floor 'shut up more like a litter of pigs than like human beings.'[18] He was far from insulated even in his own office. The destitute sick beat a path to his door. He examined them himself, sent out for milk and

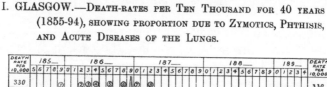

I. GLASGOW.—Death-rates per Ten Thousand for 40 years (1855-94), showing proportion due to Zymotics, Phthisis, and Acute Diseases of the Lungs.

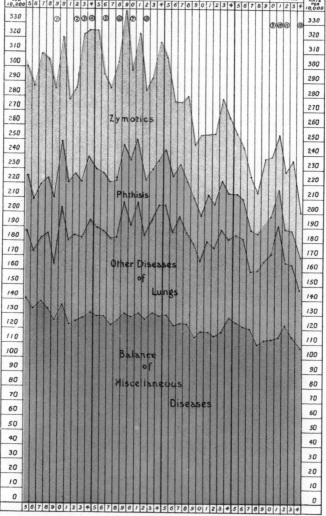

(1) Loch Katrine Water turned on. (2) Police Act (1862). (3) First Medical Officer of Health appointed. (4) First Municipal Fever Hospital. (5) Police Act (1866). City Improvements Act. (6) Cleansing Act (1866). (7) Sanitary Department organized. (8) Scotch Education Act. (9) Police (Amendment) Act. Notification Act adopted. (10) The City of Glasgow Act. (11) Building Regulations Act. (12) First Sewage Purification Work opened.

An example of Russell's innovative graphs, highlighting trends in death rates from infectious diseases, tuberculosis and other lung diseases.

brandy, and arranged for their admission to hospital. Not all
were local. An intoxicated woman tramp, found to have smallpox, had recently arrived from Portobello.

His statistics [19] remorselessly demonstrated the precise nature
of the connection between living conditions and disease. They
showed the critical role of population density. Inhabitants of
rural Scotland, Russell calculated, enjoyed an average of 16 acres
per person compared with eight yards per person in Glasgow.
The death rate of the first was 17 per 1000 and of the second
30 per 1000. 'We choke and hustle each other out of existence,'
he commented. The statistics also showed that the four places
with the highest death rates – Glasgow, Paisley, Greenock, and
Dundee – were also the most overcrowded, in terms not only
of population per acre but of the number of persons per room.
A quarter of the population of Glasgow lived in one-room
houses, compared with 14% in Aberdeen, which Russell considered a social fact of great importance. 'Not only are the
inhabitants of Glasgow more crowded upon the soil than in any
other Scotch town, but they are the most crowded in their
houses,' he wrote. He contrasted Glasgow with Edinburgh,
where the death rate was significantly lower. In Edinburgh only
17% of the population lived in one-room houses – and 27% lived
in houses of five or more rooms as opposed to 8.5% in Glasgow.
'It is impossible to exaggerate the difference in the physical,
moral, and social circumstances of the populations of Glasgow
and Edinburgh,' Russell concluded. He propounded his 'standard
of occupancy' – the smaller the house, the greater the number
of occupants per room.

No less striking were the disparities among the four groups
into which he divided Glasgow. The first, and most salubrious,
area included the fashionable Blythswood district in which he
himself lived; the second consisted of fast-growing working-class
suburbs like Maryhill and Springburn; the third, immediately
inside the previous ring, included Anderston and other former
suburban villages of old Glasgow as well as recent extensions
like Cowcaddens; and the fourth and worst included the closes
and wynds in the densely packed central area. These categories
allowed Russell to produce a dramatic health profile of the city
showing enormous discrepancies between the death rates of the

first and last group and a particularly marked difference in mortality from pulmonary disease. The disparities were greatest among the elderly and the very young. Infant mortality was horrifyingly high in all groups but Russell's statistics showed that mortality for babies under one in the unhealthiest group was nearly double that of the healthiest group, while the gap was even greater for children between one and five. The figures – 275 per 1000 compared with 140 per 1000 in the case of the under-ones – were somewhat distorted by flawed housing data, but the trend was clear. The children of the poor were not only more susceptible to lung disease, the biggest killer in all social categories, but suffered from nutritional disorders and a general unhealthiness which made them succumb more easily to child-hood infections. The answer, Russell believed, lay in improved housing and better sanitation but the statistics also reinforced his belief that children from the poorest districts should be removed to hospital or isolated when infectious disease was diagnosed.

This was no easy task in Glasgow of the 1870s. Although scarlet fever had claimed more lives than typhus during the previous 20 years, public opinion was complacent. People had finally been shaken out of their apathy and fatalism towards epidemics, Russell noted, but not towards the infectious diseases of childhood. 'The great obstacle in their preventive treatment,' he remarked, 'is the fact that they do affect children chiefly.' [20] One of the difficulties was that the first symptoms of measles and whooping cough were deceptively mild, so that parents were often reluctant to part with their children. Measles was treated with contempt and whooping cough, although in Rus-sell's opinion perhaps the most unremittingly fatal of all infectious diseases in Glasgow, caused similar problems.[21] 'There is probably no infectious disease so difficult to check by sanitary means because the symptoms so much resemble the common cold and leave the child free to walk about,' he lamented, adding that it was nevertheless a fatal disease among children with weak lungs and low vitality.

There was no respite. Adult infections ebbed and flowed but every year brought childhood infections in some form, varying from one part of the country to another or localised even in one area of the city. Russell's first year as MOH brought a particularly vicious outbreak of scarlet fever which lasted into 1874, while measles was also on the upsurge. In the autumn of 1873 he began 'to enforce removal of cases of scarlet fever wherever it can with propriety be done, most particularly in those parts of the city where epidemics of all kinds spread rapidly.' A fortnight later he reported that 34 out of 122 known cases had been despatched to Belvidere, many of them under warrant. He quietly persisted until more than 80% of known cases were removed to hospital without recourse to warrants – a policy which Russell described as unique to Glasgow. The secret, he claimed, was to have a well-managed hospital with a reputation for kindly treatment, to be understanding about the mothers' determination to cling to their children, and to demonstrate 'the firmness of reason and not of mere despotism.' Mothers were admitted along with children under five and in some cases were allowed to keep an eye on a whole family in the ward – a practice which was often 'a sore trial to the temper of nurses and a strain on hospital discipline' but which helped to disarm criticism. By the end of the 1870s the medical profession had come to expect that children's infectious diseases would be treated in hospital. Pressure on Belvidere was so great that part of its new smallpox unit had to be utilised for this purpose.[22]

There was an exception. In 1872 Glasgow had become the first local authority to attempt to treat measles cases in hospital. By 1877, however, only 159 patients had been removed to Belvidere, and this during a period when 1300 Glaswegian children died of the disease.[23] Parents, said Russell, thought measles as natural as teething, and he sympathised with their reluctance to part with their children. Eventually he abandoned the idea of hospitalisation as a community measure and instead targeted patients who would benefit individually, such as the children of tramps and lodging-house denizens. In other cases he put the emphasis on washing and disinfection, general sanitary supervision, and isolation, paying particular attention to schools. The Scottish Education Act of 1872, which made education compulsory up to the age of 13, greatly extended the school population just about the time that Russell took up his post, but also made sanitary intervention more feasible. Russell secured the new Glasgow School Board's agreement that child- ren from infected homes would not return to their classes without a certificate from the MOH. Some teachers grumbled, and urged parents to pay no attention, but Russell bombarded the board and head teachers with notices of infectious diseases. He visited schools, sometimes noticing a tell-tale rash on a pupil's face.[24]

His campaign against child and infant mortality was fought on many fronts. Believing that the mother was the domestic sanitary inspector, he saw to it that everyone registering the birth of a child received a leaflet on child management explaining the advantages of fresh air and warning that babies should not become accustomed to being rocked to sleep.[25] The message was reinforced by the Sanitary Department's team of women inspec- tors, while every death registered became the subject of a special inquiry. Leaflets explaining the law on infectious diseases were distributed, as were hints on the prevention of scarlet fever, including a warning against social contacts during an outbreak – 'much mischief is done by parents gossiping in each other's houses, or even making sympathetic visits.' In an attempt to reduce the death rate from infant diarrhoea Russell warned mothers to take heed of 'the summer stinks' in the closes and courts and pay extra attention to cleanliness in hot weather.[26] Since milk was often the source of this trouble he denounced 'the evil influence of artificial feeding.' In a series of public lectures he gave advice to wealthy parents as well as the poor – take down the curtains in the sick room, lift the carpets, clean the floor daily, have simple furniture. Why, he wondered, couldn't designers of houses with billiard rooms and smoking rooms add a hospital room at the top of the house?[27] After requests for help from 'persons in the highest social position' he arranged for the purchase of a hot-air chamber for disinfect- ing feather beds and mattresses and warned upholsterers that it was illegal for them to attempt this work.

But it was the vulnerable children in one-room and two-room houses who concerned him most. The stark fact was that at one stage in the bitter winter of 1874–5, with its lethal freezing fogs, 30% of the children who died from scarlet fever lived in one-room houses, 51% in two-room houses, 15% in three-room houses, and 4% in houses of more than three rooms.[28] A few months later when an outbreak of measles occurred on the North side of the city the children of Springburn and Maryhill were affected but Russell reported to the Health Committee that it was among the debilitated children of Cowcaddens that nearly all the fatal cases had occurred.[29] He drew attention to the huge numbers of children in such areas who died without apparently having been seen by a doctor. Altogether more than 30% of deaths in Glasgow were uncertified by a medical practitioner, which Russell described as a social scandal, but the number of uncertificated child deaths was far higher than those of adults, higher still in the case of children from poor areas, even higher among illegitimate children, and highest of all among illegitimate babies under one year old. Well over half of the illegitimate children in Bridgegate and the Wynds died without evidence of medical attention. In a report which was sent to the Lord Advocate and other authorities Russell argued that additional facilities for investigating and subsequently certifying such cases should be provided throughout Scotland. Throughout the decade the number of uncertificated deaths in Glasgow declined significantly, though less on account of Russell's campaign than because of a change in the law. From 1876 friendly societies were required to demand death certificates before making payment on the death of a child who had been insured – but, as Russell noted, often the certificates were simply an expression of the opinion of a doctor called in to view the body.[30]

Some of these deaths were highly suspicious. 'Child life has so little intrinsic value in the eyes of a considerable proportion of our urban population that the petty gain accruing from a Friendly Society on its termination is enough to offset any desire for prolongation,' Russell wrote in the *Glasgow Medical Journal*. Recalling Rousseau's confession that the inheritance of a pair of trousers on a friend's death considerably interfered with his grief, Russell commented that there were too many parents and commercial guardians of infants who had 'all the cupidity and none of the candour of the French philosopher.'[31] He declared that legislation was due and meanwhile did his best to track down as many cases of childhood illness as possible, once

severely censuring a sanitary inspector for neglecting to report
two cases of fever. He began to campaign for compulsory notification of infectious diseases and meanwhile sent stamped
addressed envelopes to general practitioners to encourage them
to make voluntary reports. The response was feeble but some
doctors were sufficiently impressed to report local outbreaks of
scarlet fever and enteric fever, which Russell strongly suspected
were sometimes caused by infected milk supplies.[32]

Russell went to amazing lengths to trace the origin of these
milk epidemics. His first exercise in detection was in the semi-
rural suburb of Parkhead where enteric fever broke out just
after he had taken up his post. He personally investigated all
the cases and found a dairyman's family among them. Following
this clue, he discovered that many of the other patients had
been supplied by the same dairyman, and after matching nine
milk suppliers with customers in five streets was able to demonstrate that this dairy was the source of the infection and that
the woman who milked the cows nursed the sick children.
Russell's investigation was so meticulous that he knew who took
milk with their porridge and who took syrup.[33]

It was the first of many such inquiries. Russell and the
inspectors used to travel by train and gig through thundery
weather to inspect some waterlogged steading in Ayrshire or
ramshackle Stirlingshire farmyard. Farmers looked amazed at
their arrival, and farmers' wives 'thought the Glasgow folk had
gone mad.' Russell would examine the drainage, establish the
relative positions of the byres and the middenstead, discover
perhaps that the pig sty was only inches from the water supply,
or that a dairymaid with enteric fever was sleeping in a garret
above the milk shed. Once he found chamber pots being emptied
into a channel in the byre. When three epidemics of enteric
fever occurred in widely separated parts of the city he discovered
that their milk supplies, though arriving by different channels,
were all fed from the same source. A later mystery was solved
by the discovery that the same measuring tins were used for
sweet and skimmed milk, and by some elaborate calculations
about distribution routes and journey times.[34]

These investigations resulted in a series of epidemiological studies which did a lot to establish the connection between infection and milk. They convinced Russell that 'the headquarters of enteric fever are in our small farms and villages' and that the 'neglected nastiness' of rural areas was a threat to the cities. He pointed out that the local epidemics in Glasgow had been derived from excremental pollution miles away: the town had nothing more to do with their origins 'than the thistledown which is borne into its streets from the country meadows.' [35] The fact was that rural local government (run by the parochial boards) was too weak and ill-organised to tackle sanitary reform and was often totally uninterested in the subject. Russell had many unrewarding exchanges with local sanitary inspectors. Once his inquiry was answered with the words: 'I am not aware of such a farm ... but there is a farmer lost two or three children, but I don't recollect the name of the farm at present.' [36] Another example once quoted by Russell was: 'I met Drumtochty yesterday at the kirk, and he said they were all well, excepting bits of colds.' Russell concluded that 'the power which shall move the dry bones of rural sanitary authorities must come from within the towns.' He arraigned the ineffectual Board of Supervision, which as the administrator of the Poor Law was the central health body for Scotland.[37] The board, an 'absurd executive' in Russell's view, then issued a circular urgently reminding rural authorities of their statutory obligations, and when this was ignored Russell put pressure on local authorities to appoint medical officers. He scored a notable success with Mearns, in Renfrewshire, despite the opposition of a member of the parochial board who argued for inaction on the grounds that 'we ought to do as other people do, and no harm will befall us.' [38]

He also persuaded Glasgow Town Council to appoint dairy inspectors to the sanitary staff to keep a watch on producers, middlemen, and city milkshops. In 1878 a daily inspection of dairies was launched to determine what improvements could be made either by persuasion or the force of law.[39] Russell was particularly concerned about families living in backshops or even in the shop itself. In just a fortnight in 1875 he learned of four milkshops with concealed cases of enteric fever nursed by the person attending the shop. 'Apart altogether from the risk of spreading specific disease, the idea of a woman attending a

helpless patient, and hurriedly running to answer the shop bell
and measure out milk, or handle and deliver bread, butter, etc.,
is very disgusting,' he told the Health Committee.[40] Once he
found eight people, including two children with enteric fever,
living in the back shop and a lodger in a shakedown in the front
shop. Excrement was carried through another shop to the midden. Russell warned owners that their living quarters must have
separate entrances or their shops would be closed.

Since the existing law was inadequate he pressed for reform,
as usual paving the way by arousing public feeling. With John
Ure, who was still chairman of the Health Committee, he drew
up plans to legislate for a local system of registration and
inspection.[41] This was unanimously backed at a public meeting
and a committee of citizens was set up to lobby for action.
Russell went to London to tackle the Lord Advocate on the
subject and eventually the proposals were included in a wider
and highly controversial piece of legislation, the Burgh Police
Bill, which was subsequently abandoned. The irony was that
the clauses relating to the milk trade were adopted in various
English local acts and then in the Infectious Diseases Prevention
Act, which applied only to England. Glasgow didn't have the
benefit of the measures until its Police Bill was amended in
1890. Meanwhile, a Privy Council order made under existing
legislation made it illegal for anyone in contact (much legal
argument was to turn on the definition of that word) with an
infectious case to milk cows. On the strength of this Russell
reported a farm at Baldernock, Stirlingshire, to the county
authorities although there was no evidence that it supplied milk
to Glasgow. Some people thought that he was over-reaching
himself. The city, complained one councillor, had already given
offence to the authorities of Renfrewshire, and now they were
'carrying the war into the county of Stirling.'[42]

As well as the law Russell used commercial leverage by
pointing out that contaminated milk was bad for business. As
he put it, 'the hand of the customer in Glasgow was laid upon
the factor, the landlord, and the authority; sanitation came to
be associated in their minds with self-interest.' One milk dealer
was so impressed by this argument that he arranged for his
dairy and the farms supplying it to be inspected at his own

expense – the certificate, signed by a posse of doctors, was then displayed in the Sanitary Chambers.[43] The Privy Council order brought a rush of applications from milk dealers who wished to be registered under its voluntary scheme.[44] Hundreds of inspections were made and improvements ordered. After a particularly severe outbreak of enteric fever the dairy inspectors went on a three-day sweep of the country from Balfron to Biggar to track down cases. Soon afterwards Glasgow adopted by-laws to forbid shops being used as sleeping premises or to be in direct communication with living quarters.

The milk epidemics showed how Glasgow had to reach far beyond its own boundaries to protect its interests. Smallpox brought similar problems. Russell detailed an inspector to meet the Forth and Clyde Canal trackboat from Kilsyth during an outbreak there in 1876. It was established that the infection had been spread by train when passengers recalled the bitter lamentations of a woman who was carrying home a bundle of her dead son's clothes from Kilsyth. Russell fumed about the risks to which Glasgow was exposed by the existence of such an 'ill-regulated, sanitarily neglected place.'[45] But he was even angrier with London, which he said was putting the rest of the country at risk by failing to isolate smallpox cases in hospital – nearly 50% of deaths there were at home, compared with scarcely 20% in Glasgow, which enforced hospitalisation for smallpox more sternly than for other infectious diseases. 'Such maladministration of sanitary affairs in the capital of the country is little short of a national calamity,' he thundered.

The trouble was that the medical officers of the London burghs were in disagreement as to whether smallpox hospitals became centres for infection, and there was strong middle-class opposition to plans for new ones. Russell, on the other hand, had decided as early as 1873 that the Parliamentary Road Hospital was responsible for propagating smallpox in the northern district and had taken immediate steps to provide an isolation unit in the grounds of Belvidere Hospital. A similar policy of building on riverbank sites was eventually to be adopted in London on the recommendation of a commission appointed in 1881.[46]

Like London, Glasgow had high exposure to smallpox as a

port city – a passenger just off a vessel from Canada, a ship's
steward arrived from New York, a sailor who had come from
Calcutta, were typical importers of the disease. The only clue
to the source of one case in the centre of the city was neighbours'
accounts of a sailor with an eruption on his face who had lodged
in the same close. A major difficulty with this disease was the
number of mild cases who remained mobile. Russell told of a
young woman who went to the theatre 'hoping by the use of a
thick veil to avoid observation.' [47] There was also the professional
athlete who, after smallpox had been diagnosed, proceeded to
Shawfield recreation ground instead of to hospital, then visited
his parents in a three-room house occupied by 11 people – a
case which resulted in a prosecution. [48] Russell was never content
until he had found the source of the infection. An isolated case
in the West End baffled him until he noticed a newspaper report
of an outbreak in Grangemouth and established that the patient
had just spent some days there.

Smallpox was then the one disease that could be prevented
by vaccination, which had been compulsory in Scotland since
1864, but responsibility for enforcement belonged to the parochial authorities and not the Sanitary Department. Russell
nevertheless took the initiative and launched a vaccination drive
by urging the Poor Law inspectors to take a more systematic
approach. Lists of vaccination defaulters were passed to Russell,
who set the epidemic inspectors on their trail. About a quarter
were tracked down and the 6% who turned out to be unvaccinated rather than merely uncertified were immunised by doctors;
the proportion of unvaccinated infants was quickly reduced to
2% (considerably lower than the London rate). [49] By instructing
the epidemic inspectors to perform vital secondary vaccinations
on willing subjects over the age of 10 Russell was again seizing
the initiative for the Sanitary Department. This was a delicate
task because of the unwillingness of many people to be vaccinated if there was no immediate danger of infection. Even when
danger loomed they often changed their minds before the deed
could be done. Russell was anxious to avoid the delay involved
in summoning a doctor to perform the vaccination. In his
experience people put their heads together in the interval, with
'consequent consolidation of all prejudices and old wives' fables,

so that scarcely anybody would submit.' The epidemic inspectors, who carried a stock of lymph about with them, were able to swoop more swiftly but still needed, in Russell's words, 'the scent of the pointer, the wisdom of the serpent, and the common-sense of human-kind.' To counter people's fears of losing work because of sore arms a small disability allowance was sometimes paid and where serious local inflammation occurred – usually from 'drink, rough usage, and dirt' – the patients were sent to one of the municipal reception-houses 'where they get free lodgings and food and are kept in bed and sober.' [50] Russell also proposed that all inmates of poorhouses, prisons, and hospitals should be inspected and as far as possible revaccinated. A public vaccinator, Dr Neil Carmichael, was appointed in 1873, and accompanied Russell to a model lodging house near Glasgow Green. Many of the lodgers had no vaccination marks on their arms but only two would submit to the procedure. The others ridiculed the suggestion 'in language of no moderate kind.' [51] The eventual solution, suggested by a lodging house proprietor, was to offer volunteers a night's free lodging – an incentive that was later more systematically adopted.

Despite these initiatives Russell remained unhappy about the involvement of the parochial boards in smallpox vaccination. 'One of the most important of all health functions is, in burghs, the only one which is left to parochial boards,' he complained in a report which was sent to the Board of Supervision. But at least the city gained the monopoly of the treatment of infectious diseases when the Royal Infirmary decided in 1876 that all cases of fever other than typhoid should be referred to the local authority hospitals. This development was doubly welcome to Russell, who had fallen out with the infirmary managers over their decision to stop supplying him with the names and addresses of patients with infectious diseases. Russell accused them of preventing the Sanitary Department from disinfecting the houses of these patients. He claimed that 'the public interest, which your managers are anxious to serve, will therefore be seriously injured.' The infirmary replied scathingly that 'the managers, who are not unacquainted with public affairs, and have seen in the newspapers that the returns hitherto sent have been used to create prejudice against the Royal Infirmary ...

will require some further evidence that the public interest demands them.'

The disagreement was further embittered by Russell's criticisms of the infirmary's waste disposal arrangements. His accusations were scornfully denied. 'It will no doubt surprise you to learn,' wrote the infirmary manager, 'that none of the excreta of the infirmary patients, which your medical officer says is so fertile in producing fever, passes into the public sewer.' The manager met the Health Committee who listened 'as a matter of courtesy' to what he had to say but concluded that this had so little to do with the point at issue that there was no need for any response. The infirmary later backed down and provided the names and addresses (except those of patients from outside the city) but its subsequent decision to abandon the treatment of fever patients was hailed by Russell as overdue recognition of the inefficiency of trying to treat infectious diseases from private charity rather than from the sanitary rates.[52]

In his view it was a significant step towards a unified command. He wished it could have been matched by greater territorial unity. With the suburbs growing faster than the city, a quarter of the conurbation was controlled by nine independent burghs. This distorted the statistics, prevented uniform building regulations,[53] impeded river purification, and generally made life difficult for a medical administrator. 'Houses are cut in two, streets are cut across, and everywhere you pass by a step into another jurisdiction,' Russell complained.[54] Once, questioning a dealer about the destination of his milk supplies, Russell was told: 'It gangs out o' your jurisdiction a'thegither – awa' Paisley Road way.' Yet the Royal Infirmary's decision to stop treating fever patients gave the city responsibilities outside its boundaries. Since more than half the infirmary's cases came from the suburbs and the surrounding country, the city was soon flooded with applications from these areas for accommodation in the fever hospital and for disinfection services. This gave Russell a useful lever. He agreed on condition that the local authorities took steps to provide their own hospital accommodation under the permissive powers of the Public Health (Scotland) Act of 1867.[55] Rutherglen, home of his youth, was warned that its patients would not be accepted in Glasgow unless it improved

its own primitive sanitary arrangements. Local authorities as
distant as Blantyre were excoriated for similar shortcomings.[56]
In this way Russell stirred the social consciences of communities
outside the municipality,[57] with the result that by the end of the
decade several rural hospitals had been constructed and two
suburban hospitals built by Glasgow's neighbouring burghs.
The burghs had also begun to co-operate with Glasgow over
outbreaks of enteric fever and plans for river purification.

The 1870s, when Russell was fighting both to establish his
authority within the city and to extend the city's influence over
its hinterland, were possibly the most difficult years of his career.
For Glasgow it was a time of extraordinary dislocation. The
middle class was migrating to the terraces of the West End
and the villas of Pollokshields. Workers and artisans were
moving out to Woodside or other parts of what Russell called
the New Glasgow, leaving their cast-off homes to the former
slum dwellers of central Glasgow who were being dispersed by
the operations of the railway companies and the demolition work
of the City Improvement Trust. The trust's aims were ambitious.
Central areas housing nearly 50,000 people had been scheduled
for a wholesale redevelopment which contrasted with the piece-
meal approach adopted by Edinburgh. A delegation, including
Gairdner, had gone to Paris in the 1860s and been impressed
by its new boulevards, its open spaces, its evidence that sanitary
progress could enhance civic amenity.[58] During the first half of
the 1870s more than 15,000 people were displaced from dilapidated property in the scheduled areas, with the MOH being
consulted about priorities. The death rate declined with the
population density. The authorities boasted of a fall in the crime
rate. Edwin Chadwick, attending the Social Science Congress
in Glasgow in 1874, was full of praise.[59] An English journalist
covering the same event spent a Saturday night in the wynds
and closes and found them much improved since his previous
visit some years before – although he still started back in fear
at glimpses of faces etched with vice and crime.[60]
But the trust, despite being a municipal enterprise, failed to
accept full social responsibility for rehousing the thousands who
had been displaced. It established model lodging houses in the

city centre and pioneered two model working-class estates at
Oatlands and Overnewton, but otherwise the building was left
to private developers. Most of it took place in outlying districts,
with the redevelopment area being devoted to commerce, but
when Russell launched a follow-up survey he managed to trace
about two-thirds of the displaced people to their new homes.
He was reasonably happy with the immediate results.[61] Fewer
people (40% compared with 49%) lived in one-room houses; the
rooms were more spacious than in their former homes; the
ashpits and privies were less offensive, and more of the houses
had WCs. The further people lived from the city centre the
better, in Russell's view; after a visit to London he declared
himself unimpressed with seven-storey working-class flats
erected by the metropolitan authorities in Farringdon Road.[62]
He didn't question the propriety of Glasgow's building work
being left to private enterprise, and if the rents were higher
than before that didn't worry him: people, he thought, could
afford the extra, and more money spent on housing meant less
spent on whisky.

Yet unlike many of his contemporaries he saw that the old
problems would re-emerge unless the municipal authorities had
full power to apply the sanitary lessons of the past. He wanted
new local building legislation to prevent large houses being
'made down' or subdivided, and to stop the abuses accompanying
'hollow square' building – tenements erected round a square
which then became built up in such a complicated way that
Russell referred to them as Chinese puzzles.[63] 'We confess we
have let slip a golden opportunity of erecting a model city,' he
declared at the British Medical Association conference in Shef-
field in 1876.[64] On one occasion he went as far as to say publicly
that if he were asked whether Glasgow had gone about the
renovation in the way most likely to produce the best results,
'I should distinctly say, No.'

The matter soon became academic. The building boom ended
with the depression of the second half of the 1870s. The unemployed were put to work in the parks and docks at a ha'penny
a day (double for married men) or organised into snow-clearing
squads with out-of-work clerks as timekeepers. Soup was ladled
out in the night asylum and, since the Scottish Poor Law made

no provision for the able-bodied unemployed, the five district sanitary inspectors began to carry tickets to give financial relief to 'necessitous cases' found on their rounds.[65] In 1878 the City of Glasgow Bank failure paralysed the business of the city. The demand for land fell and the Improvement Trust could not sell the remaining acres under its schedule. It would be fully a decade before it resumed operations. Meanwhile the trust attempted instead to patch up the properties that it had compulsorily acquired for demolition. Before long it became the city's biggest slum landlord.

All that Russell could do in the circumstances was to try to ameliorate the effects of bad housing. Even within the framework of the existing legislation he found scope for action. Although influenced by William Farr, he disputed his claim that there was an invariable mathematical relationship between mortality and population density. Better sanitation, argued Russell, would bring down the death rate even when the density remained constant; indeed the 'great mass of sanitary work' consisted of the enforcement of provisions aimed at moderating the effects of overcrowding.[66] Limiting the spread of typhus was a high priority. Although 1869 had seen the last of the epidemics, mortality was again rising by the mid-70s. The lodging house population, which had been swollen by the Improvement Trust's demolition work, was particularly at risk. One typhus nest in the Saltmarket yielded case after case and planted infection in other houses on the same stair until Russell ordered it to be closed.[67] Sometimes the infection was spread more widely by servants from infected houses who were in the habit of sleeping in their clothes – a common practice according to Russell. He gained startling insights into how people lived – the house in which 35 pawn tickets were found in a drawer; the one in which 707 dirty garments were found in cupboards and under beds; the many houses where typhus in children went unrecognised among so many other illnesses.[68]

He struggled to reduce overcrowding by the ticketing system that had been started in Gairdner's day – the fixing of metal plates on the doors of small houses to show the maximum number of persons legally permitted for the cubic space. Sanitary inspectors carrying lanterns swooped without warning in the middle of the night, counting people as they lay in their beds, or under them, or on the floor, and finding others in cupboards or even on the roof. Some landlords removed the tickets from the doors. Often the occupants kept a jump ahead of the inspectors, and even when guilty parties were brought to court the fines were usually only half-a-crown. Russell fully identified himself with this unpopular procedure, which he was convinced had deterrent value, and which he saw as the main defence against typhus. He wanted it to be extended to larger properties and to the houses to which displaced slum dwellers had moved, and instructed the sanitary inspectors to trace them to their new homes.[69]

He was conscious of the authoritarian thrust of this policy, which he described as 'repressive,' but considered it justified by what he described as the social evil of overcrowding. The 1871 census had shown that almost a quarter of all households in Glasgow included lodgers, and that almost half of these families lived in two-room houses and a fifth in single-ends most of which were 'made down' from larger houses – a recipe for bad ventilation and lighting, dark lobbies, and crowded stairs. Russell thought that while discretion should be exercised in the case of families who had simply outgrown their homes, no mercy should be shown towards people (mainly Irish) who took strangers into houses already overcrowded with their legitimate occupants. Strict surveillance, he argued, was necessary for these households, which consisted of unskilled workers and the criminal class and 'not the working classes as we see them pouring from our shipbuilding yards and engine works.' He wanted the magistrates to impose punitive fines and urged the Town Council to defy the landlords by raising the standard of occupancy for ticketed houses from 300 cubic feet per person to 400 cubic feet – something that was not done until the 1890s.[70]

His support for ticketing was part of a wider battle against rapacious landlords and unprincipled factors. 'There are unfortunately landlords in Glasgow who will expose their tenants, particularly of the poorer sort, to any amount of discomfort and risk without hesitation, if a few shillings can be saved or even delayed,' he wrote. To speed up prosecutions he asked the water commissioners to notify him when cutting off tenants' water supplies because the landlord had neglected to have leaking pipes repaired; the tenants themselves were afraid to complain openly although anonymous messages sometimes reached the Sanitary Department.[71] Russell also declared war against proprietors who let new houses before they were habitable – when the plaster was still wet, the windows were unhung, privies were non-existent, and the backyard was an earth pit into which tenants threw their refuse from the stair window. Not suprisingly many of these people were found to be suffering from severe attacks of bronchitis or rheumatic fever. Russell reported numerous cases to the fiscal but the fines were small; the real remedy, he thought, lay in certification before occupation and summary proceedings for contravention.[72]

Proprietors also came under attack for substandard properties. These had been tolerated by the authorities during the housing scarcity of the early 1870s, but after personally inspecting a number of these houses near Bothwell Street Russell notified the owners that continued occupation would be illegal under the Scottish Public Health Act of 1867, which had established the principle that houses injurious to health should in the last resort be closed.[73] He told the Town Council that now that there was surplus housing it had a duty to reinspect and abolish all such properties. He felt particularly strongly about underground houses, which had supposedly been outlawed by the Scottish Public Health Act. Statutory notices were sent to the owners of these dank cellars – some with their ceilings a foot below ground level – but there was a serious setback for this policy in 1877 when a sheriff asked a leading architect to recommend modifications for one of these dwellings instead of ordering it to be closed.[74]

This was not the only failed prosecution, but there were some notable successes. In a case against the owner of a made-down house with an unlit and airless lobby Russell was able to make use of the English Public Health Act, which unlike its Scottish equivalent required consent to be given for the structural subdivision of a house. This legislation was cited to show that the legal action was reasonable and justifiable. Sheriff W. C. Spens – a leading supporter of sanitary reform – accepted the argument and the owner (who earned Russell's contempt by attempting to claim compensation) was compelled to make alterations to the lobby. Critics objected that the house itself was the source of the poison but Russell's action was hailed by the Scottish public health movement as 'a successful stroke to the growing evil involved in the making down of large houses into single apartments.' [75]

Russell found some cause for satisfaction as the 1870s ended. The general death rate had declined from 29.6 per 1000 in the opening year of the decade to 24.6 in the last, with most of the improvement having taken place in the late 1870s. [76] The continuing decline in infectious diseases accounted for almost two-thirds of this improvement, which was experienced in all parts of the city. Russell was particularly encouraged at the diminished death rate among children under five and particularly the drop in the deaths of infants under one year from 160 per 1000 when he took up his post to 130 per 1000 in the closing year of the decade. [77] But the figures were deceptive. Exceptionally fine weather in 1879 had contributed to a sudden drop in the death rate of infants under one but the improvement would not be sustained in the years ahead: progress would be impeded by the lack of compulsory notification of infectious diseases, particularly important in the case of measles, whose persistently lethal effect on the poorer children was also associated with malnutrition and poverty.

Even the fall in the general death rate failed to match Russell's expectations. His annual estimates, based on a flawed assumption about the average number of inhabitants per house, had to be revised upwards when the 1881 census showed that the population of Glasgow had grown much less in the 1870s than had been supposed. It had the lowest urban growth rate in the kingdom, 4% over the decade, and latterly had become almost static thanks to the flood-tide to the suburbs, the falling birth rate, and the departure of the floating population which was attracted to Glasgow only during periods of prosperity. Russell was cast down by the discovery of this miscalculation, which he feared would provide ammunition for the anti-sanitarians. [78] He also acknowledged that the 'black spot in the death roll' was lung disease, which was almost as lethal as at the beginning of the decade and accounted for more than a third of total deaths.

But even the revised death rate (24.6 per 1000 compared with the estimated 23) compared favourably with those of other large industrial cities in the UK [79] and the Continent, and while Glasgow remained the unhealthiest as well as most densely populated large town in Scotland, its improvement was faster than average during the second half of the 1870s.[80] The crude statistics take no account of shifts in age structure, yet it may be worth recording that the reduced death rate compared with that of the previous decade translated into the saving of some 10,000 lives.[81]

Not everyone was impressed. The opponents of reform were still in full cry. Councillor Malcolm McEwan, who had made life so difficult for Gairdner, ridiculed slum clearance as 'missionary work of stone and lime' and observed that if they put a dog in a palace it was still a dog.[82] Councillor James Martin, a former weaver with a populist style of rhetoric, thought the improved mortality was the work of an unseen hand rather than of the Sanitary Department. He said it was 'bosh' for certain parties to be 'always bouncing on about the low death rate.'[83]

There were also accusations of authoritarianism – and not only in connection with ticketing. Russell was the target for widespread criticism over what became known as 'the dog crusade.' After several deaths from suspected rabies a proclamation was issued to enforce the muzzling of dogs and there followed a mass round-up of the unmuzzled and the uncollared. More than 1000 were destroyed, leading to protests about the 'indiscriminate butchery of faithful, loving companions.' The legality of the proclamation was questioned, as well as the wisdom of issuing an edict which might cause public hysteria. Part of the trouble was that the police went far beyond their remit, even attempting to round up a working dog which was herding sheep in the cattle market.[84]

Russell's opponents also distrusted him as a 'theorist'. But concern for the plight of individuals shines from his reports. While inspecting a particularly atrocious farm, for example, he sympathised with the woman in charge, who seemed 'exhausted and bewildered with her difficulties.' He sympathised with the carter who was reluctant to be quarantined with a mild case of smallpox. Russell 'went with him to his master, got him released of his horse and arranged for his place being kept open, and he went to hospital quite satisfied.' Individual suffering also inspired a passionate attack on the shortcomings of the Scottish Poor Law. Russell was outraged by the treatment of two destitute women who made their way to his Montrose Street office in the winter of 1878. One, starving and utterly exhausted, had walked from Govan with a note from the parish board explaining that she could not be admitted to the poorhouse there because she was not a pauper – despite having spent the previous few nights 'sleeping about stairs in Tradeston and Kingston.' Russell wired for the Belvidere Hospital van and sent out for milk and brandy to revive her for the journey, but she died of enteric fever a few days later. The other woman, in a state of collapse, was examined by Russell and found to be suffering from inflammation of the lungs. Her unemployed husband, who was waiting outside with their infant in his arms, was referred by Russell to the City Parish for medical help for the woman, but this was refused on the grounds that the man was in good health and able to work. Although she was not suffering from fever, Russell arranged for her admission to Belvidere, where she duly recovered. 'We are entering upon a winter which promises to be full of hardship for the poor,' he reported to the Health Committee. 'There will be a great deal of general sickness. Who is responsible for the care of it?' He was outraged that 'no dependant of an able-bodied man is, even under the circumstances of lying in a public office and being unable to walk away, entitled to medical relief.'

The position of the sick poor was totally unsatisfactory, he claimed – legislation on medical relief couldn't be delayed much longer. 'Meanwhile,' he added, 'I feel there is a risk of lives being lost unless the local authority is prepared to act as the Good Samaritan.'[85] He flatly disagreed with a bland Board of Supervision statement that private philanthropy could be trusted to meet the need. He felt it intolerable that whereas the family breadwinner was entitled to medical assistance when ill, his dependants were not, although in England statutory provision was made for such needs. These anomalies were his daily experience, for as Russell pointed out, Glasgow had a higher proportion of working-class inhabitants than any other city, and to these people 'much sickness means much destitution.' In a long and passionate letter to *The Glasgow Herald* he pleaded with his readers: 'We hear constantly of improvidence and intemperance, but do not let us forget vicious buildings, houses whose surroundings debase and brutalise the soul as well as impair the body, or our unnecessarily polluted atmosphere.' The community, he added, had contributed to this situation, and it was right that the community should pay for it – 'but the bulk of the community stands aloof.' The *Herald*'s own response was to attack Russell for trying to 'break down the self-dependence of the nation's character in order to save ourselves the pain of watching momentary suffering' and of working up the feelings of the public by appalling descriptions of human misery.[86]

To which Russell felt bound to reply: 'I am sorry that you dislike my mode of giving utterance to this opinion; but what can I do save "work upon the feelings of the public" by describing that which, in fact and reality, has worked upon my own feelings?'[87]

Chapter Twelve

A Family Tragedy

The harder ingredients seem to appear more prominently as we get older. Our lives become more valuable, our pleasures become deeper, more intellectual and moral, less emotional.

Russell's early years as MOH were ones of acute personal stress. A family tragedy which had been in the making for several years finally occurred in 1876. By then the Russells had three children. A son, David, had been born in the autumn of 1871, but the joy was not unalloyed. The boy had a cleft palate, at that time still an inoperable condition causing a permanent speech defect. Only two weeks after his birth Russell's father, after whom the child was named, died of pneumonia at the age of 63. Some years earlier he had returned from Australia to settle in Cambuslang, incurring the disapproval of Russell's clerical father-in-law who seems to have been unwilling to let him visit the young couple's Bath Street house.

A daughter, Mary, was born a few weeks after Russell had taken up his post as MOH, and her sister Helen two and a half years later. Helen was only a few months old when the crisis came. One Saturday in January, 1876, Russell's wife was certified insane and taken to the Glasgow Royal Asylum for Lunatics at Gartnavel. Over the previous few years Russell had noticed disturbing changes in her behaviour. Morbid suspicions of her husband and close relatives were accompanied by memory loss, delusions, occasional bouts of violence, and finally epileptic fits. Russell appears to have done his best to keep her at home as long as possible, but finally petitioned for a certificate of insanity. The petition was signed by two of the most eminent physicians in the city – his friend William Gairdner, who was a director of the Asylum, and William Leishman, Professor of Midwifery at Glasgow University. Gairdner testified to Helen Russell's 'generally demented condition' and her 'total incapacity for the most ordinary duties of her station and position', while Leishman stated that he had seen for himself her incoherence and 'various delusions chiefly in regard to imaginary sights and noises.' Before giving their testimony, the two doctors had interviewed Helen Russell's sister, Jessie Davidson, who was evidently staying in Bath Street at the time, and the resident nurse employed by Russell.[1]

On arrival at Gartnavel Helen Russell was taken to West House, the part of the Asylum reserved for paying patients. Behind its Tudor Gothic turrets and battlements this wing was furnished and decorated like a private mansion, but it is clear from the few surviving case notes[2] that the unfortunate woman was in no state to appreciate her surroundings. To present-day specialists her symptoms appear consistent with some form of organic disease. A degenerative brain disorder is a strong possibility, and it has been suggested that Pick's disease, a form of lobar atrophy which was not identified till later in the century, may be a possible contender.[3] The diagnosis of Helen Russell's own day was dementia, which was at that time regarded as a hereditary condition. Russell, who described his wife's family history as 'suspicious', must have feared for his children (his elder daughter was later warned that she should not have children). He would have received little comfort from Dr David Yellowlees, the Asylum superintendent, who uncompromisingly defended the heredity theory even when environmental explanations of mental disorders became more fashionable later in the century.[4] Gairdner, who had been his senior colleague in Edinburgh and had recommended him for the Gartnavel post, was of the same mind.

Helen Russell never left Gartnavel. At breakfast time one summer day in 1884 Russell announced: 'Children, your mother died yesterday'. The cause of death was intestinal cancer.[5] Aged 42, Helen Russell had been in the asylum for eight years. She was buried in the Russell family lair in Glasgow Necropolis.

The real break in family life had come with her departure for Gartnavel. Russell's sister Agnes had joined the household to look after the children, and the family moved west from Bath Street to Foremount Terrace (now part of Highburgh Road) on the southern slopes of the new Dowanhill Estate. The move may have been influenced by Russell's cousin, Robert Cassels, who had taken charge of the development of the estate when it ran into financial difficulties under its original proprietor.[6] The three-storey terrace house, with its elegant L-shaped drawing room, was conveniently situated for Russell, who could travel to and from his work on the Partick horse-tram.

He was 47 years old when his wife died. He had acquired a scholarly stoop and a flowing beard. His habits were ascetic: he still abstained from spirits, although possibly not from wine. At work he drove himself hard. At the time of his wife's death he was shouldering extra responsibilities because of the long illness of the Sanitary Inspector, Kenneth Macleod. He took little in the way of compassionate leave. He was not indestructible: in 1880, his health failing after a period of exceptional pressure during an epidemic of enteric fever, he had been granted two months' leave on medical grounds and spent the time holidaying in the United States. But even then he took the opportunity to meet sanitary leaders in the various cities through which he passed.[7]

There is no indication that he ever considered remarriage. Ill health, according to some of his friends, made him increasingly reclusive in later life. Yet in the earlier years of his widowhood he retained some at least of the love of good company that had marked his earlier years. He socialised with his medical colleagues at gatherings of the Western Medical Club, to which he was elected at a dinner 'enlivened from time to time by the singing of a professional glee party' helped by some of the members and guests.[8] As well as attending the WMC's champagne dinners and its summer excursions by train or steamer, and serving his turn as president, he was a frequent guest at the picnics of the Glasgow Southern Medical Society. On a fine June day in 1876, for example, he was among the company who consumed 'an excellent dinner' while reclining in a green meadow in an estate near Killearn, and the following year joined the same society in an excursion by saloon carriage to Tillietudlem in rural Lanarkshire.[9]

His closest friends included two future Glasgow University professors who had held public health appointments earlier in their careers, Joseph Coats and Samson Gemmell. Coats, who was to become the university's first Professor of Pathology, had been Russell's assistant at Parliamentary Road Fever Hospital, and later Gemmell had been its superintendent. 'He is infinitely worked up in 30 years of my life,' Russell once wrote of Coats. 'Many a time have I in trouble been comforted by his quiet, effective sympathy and helped by his wisdom, not hurled at me in set advice but dropped in seeming casual asides, bearing on the situation of the hour.'[10] When Coats, seriously ill, was despatched by his doctors to Guernsey's milder climate, he in turn was helped by Russell, who took the time to visit him there. The two men shared a love of the hills – Coats was a founder member of the Scottish Mountaineering Club. They also shared qualities of resoluteness and orderliness, had both been deeply influenced by William Gairdner's broad philosophical view of medicine, and had overlapping professional interests. In 1881 they travelled together by train to be present at the great international medical conference in London, attended by some 3000 doctors. Unfortunately they were seated so far back in the gallery of St James Hall that they missed most of James Paget's presidential address – 'but what we heard was really splendid stuff', Coats wrote home. Afterwards, en route to David Livingstone's grave in Westminster Abbey, they were surprised to see excited crowds outside the House of Commons. The atheist Charles Bradlaugh, barred from the Chamber because of his refusal to take the oath, had announced his intention of forcing his way in.[11]

Gemmell, too, had much in common with Russell. A former medical superintendent of Belvidere Fever Hospital, he had also worked as Gairdner's assistant and shared his philosophical approach. His interests ranged widely over history, poetry, and archaeology. One of his most distinguished former students, John Boyd Orr, thought him 'the man with the widest outlook on medical and world affairs generally that I have ever met' and described how in the middle of a lecture on infectious diseases he would launch into an exposition of Buckle's *History of Civilisation*. Gemmell, who was later to become Professor of the Practice of Medicine at Glasgow University, was also Russell's family doctor.

Another close friend was James Christie, medical officer of

the adjacent burgh of Hillhead, who had taken over Russell's duties during his sick leave. An ordained minister, he was unable to pursue this calling because of a weakness in his throat. After graduating in medicine at Glasgow University, where he was a near-contemporary of Russell's, he lived in Zanzibar while making a laborious study of trade routes to show how cholera spread between India, Africa, and Arabia. On his return to Glasgow he was in 'constant intercourse' with Russell, who liked his apologetic manner, his enthusiasm for sanitation, and his investigative skills.[12]

Not all Russell's associates were medical men. At meetings of the Philosophical Society of Glasgow, which he had joined in the early 1870s, he saw not only the familiar faces of Gairdner and other colleagues but also scientists and engineers, architects such as James Sellars, shipowners such as Charles Cayzer, and assorted manufacturers, brass founders, and yarn agents who gathered for 'the discussion of any and every problem that had direct or indirect bearing on the well being of the community at large'. Russell, who later became president of the society, delivered numerous papers and made the most of his opportunities to educate such an influential audience. 'A gutter child of the Bridgegate is a very complicated production,' he told them once. 'More forces have contributed to the pitiable result than those which have operated within the short span of his own life, or even passed into his body from the parents who begot him.'[13]

His church activities also brought him into contact with people outside his own profession. He became a deacon of Elgin Place Congregational Church in Bath Street, which was the latest home of the congregation in which his grandfather had played such a prominent part. The Rev. Albert Goodrich, a Londoner who was as expert in philosophy as in theology, attracted a congregation which 'was not confined to any class' and included many students.[14] Its pillars included Robert Henry, a well-known hatter who became one of Russell's close friends. Another prominent member was John Glaister, whose professional path crossed Russell's at many points, for although it was his work in forensic science that won him renown, he combined this subject with public health.[15] The surgeon H. E. Clark, a future president of the Faculty of Physicians and Surgeons who had been a house physician at Belvidere Fever Hospital and had worked closely with Russell on the *Glasgow Medical Journal*, was also among influential members of the congregation – and a force for tolerance and ecumenism.

Undoubtedly the church played an important part in Russell's life. 'While his creed was not a long one, it did not shorten as you measured it,' observed one of Elgin Place's pastors.[16] And Russell's diplomatic skills helped to resolve some awkward congregational wrangles. His local residents' association, too, had the benefit of his services. Hardly had he moved into Foremount Terrace than he wrote a letter on their behalf, urging the Dowanhill Estate Company to do something about the 'parties of lads playing cards and swearing foully' in the pleasure grounds nearby. Barbed wire fences, he went as far as to suggest, might prevent these invasions.[17]

What with these activities, and his numerous public speaking engagements, Russell can have had only very limited time to spend with his children. Nevertheless he took them on country walks, gave them picture books or the *Tales of Uncle Remus* on their birthdays, took them to Skelmorlie in the summer, and invented family jokes. Once, when his elder daughter had lost her spectacles during a family walk, he told her that a grouse would be wearing them – a small incident but one that she found touching enough to recall to her own daughter. All the same, what with their high-minded father and their stern aunt, Russell's children had an upbringing that in some ways resembled his own.

Chapter Thirteen

A Semi-asphyxiated City

*It is a curious optical fact that a sixpence may obscure
the sun.*

RUSSELL's work in the 1880s brought him into collision
with a great array of vested interests and professional
bodies – not just landlords and factors but industrialists
and businessmen, architects and teachers, and finally even the
medical profession. Enormous hostility was aroused by two great
enterprises in which he was engaged during this decade, the
push for more effective public health legislation and the attempt
to establish tighter environmental controls.

The prevalence of lung disease, described by Russell as the
scourge of Glasgow, made the city's smoky atmosphere a matter
of urgent concern. Russell advocated more radical measures to
purify the air not only of this 'semi-asphyxiated' city but of the
whole country.[1] 'We must purify,' he warned, 'that vast canopy
of smoke which envelops our towns and even invades the
country, not only directly injurious to the lungs but perhaps
even more injurious indirectly by cutting off the sun.'[2]

He believed that the city could be made as healthy as the
countryside. He wanted broad passages left for the entrance of
air from the open country. He wanted the slums replaced with
decent buildings and wide streets. He called for parks and
squares and green spaces so that the devitalised air could be
renewed and the children would no longer be pent up in backcourts and stairheads. Money would be better spent in this way,
he maintained, than on suburban parks, which were 'useful for
the cultivation of aesthetic sense rather than improvement of
health', because they were out of the reach of those who needed
them.[3] He wished that more working-class families would move
to the outskirts of the city. On his daily tram journeys it pained
him to see that while the middle-class breadwinners travelled
into town in the mornings and home to the suburbs in the

evenings, the working-class current moved in the opposite direction, from East End factories to city-centre slums. He found it 'quite sad to see these men leaving their wives and children daily to be stifled and confined in a restricted and contaminated atmosphere and returning at night with the their grimy faces to sleep amid the same unhealthy surroundings.'[4]

The combination of fog and frost was lethal. Russell correlated the weather records and the death rate, at first relying on readings supplied by schoolchildren (undependable because of the holidays) and from 1880 using the Sanitary Department's own meteorological station at Belvidere Hospital. Glasgow's mortality rates, he noted in 1881, had over the previous 20 years peaked during 'the foggy calm of continuous frost' rather than during epidemics. (Infant deaths, however, rose during summer when diarrhoea was rife.) In the bitter cold of January, 1881, the death rate soared in a way that made him feel helpless. He appealed to the comfortably off to remember the destitute. 'Sanitary inspectors can do nothing to keep down a death rate such as the present unless they carry about with them food, and especially bedding and fuel, on their daily rounds,' he reported.[5]

As well as dirty factories, smoky domestic chimneys poisoned the air breathed in by Glaswegian lungs.[6] 'We are a catharral, coughing, expectorating people, because we live in a huge industrial city, situated at the seaward end of the trough of a valley, which from one end to the other is covered with smoke, drifting in wreaths and clouds with the wind or in calm filling up the trough so that nothing is to be seen between the higher ground on either side but a sea of smoke,' he observed sadly.[7] He noted that Glasgow's drinking water was the purest, its air the most impure, in the whole kingdom.[8] This he was able to quantify with the help of a Mr Dixon, a college lecturer in physics who 'placed his personal services at our disposal without fee or reward' and who had devised an apparatus for measuring the impurities in the air.[9] Glasgow housewives needed no such device: they kept the windows permanently shut to exclude the smuts and smells.

The remedy, Russell believed, lay in improving the layout of streets and buildings, the 'more rational' use of coal, and the enforcement of the Smoke Act by alert local authorities.

Numerous companies were prosecuted for contravening the regulation permitting a maximum of five minutes' uninterrupted smoke emission per hour or 15 minutes' intermittent discharge, but the magistrates' fines were too small to be a serious deterrent. A delegate at the British Medical Association conference in Glasgow in 1888 was greeted with cries of 'Hear, hear!' when he remarked that Glasgow Corporation, though consisting of distinguished men of intellect, 'allowed the atmosphere to be polluted by various manufactories, the owners of those works being themselves in many cases members of the Council.' Or as Russell preferred to put it: 'It is a curious optical fact that sixpence may obscure the sun.' [10]

He was more than ready to make a nuisance of himself. The MOH's work had always had an industrial element. The 1867 Scottish Public Health Act had included controls against 'offensive trades.' This was partly in the domain of the Chief Sanitary Inspector but, as in the case of nuisance removal, medical assessment was necessary. Tallow melters, horse-slaughterers, bone-boilers, tripe-cleaners, gut-scrapers and the like, all needed Russell's consent when setting up in business. Industrial diseases were also within his province. After a case of lead poisoning he visited a firm of white lead manufacturers in Maryhill and saw women standing barefoot in the trough used for washing off the carbonate of lead, having laid aside their respirators so that they could chat. He told the firm to enforce the safety rules more strictly and improve its safeguards. [11]

Sometimes he recommended structural alterations – as in the case of a Cathcart paper mill which he inspected with remarkable thoroughness after some of its workers had been brought to Glasgow with smallpox. The willowing and riddling machines should be partitioned off, he confidently proposed, and all rag workers should be vaccinated or revaccinated because of the danger of breathing infected dust. [12] This was a minor investigation compared with his classic study of an outbreak of a ghastly and fatal disease at the Adelphi horsehair factory in Hutchesontown, which he identified as anthrax. In a paper which displayed a grasp of Continental medical literature as well as a close knowledge of the Adelphi factory's industrial processes he demonstrated that Russian horsehair, which was used in the factory, was invariably the source of such outbreaks. The paper, which influenced public health policy in England as well as Scotland, advocated safety measures and emphasised that 'every means ought to be adopted to inform the workers of the risks attendant upon their employment.' [13]

Where necessary Russell was happy to take on industrial giants. He fought a running battle with Charles Tennant, the most influential Glasgow business leader of his day, who usually received treatment worthy of royalty in that age of industrial mandarinism. Tennant is said to have symbolised Glasgow's transition from provincial status to second city of the Empire, but he was also a major contributor to industrial pollution. [14] Russell had been pursuing him for years about the sulphurous discharge from his St Rollox chemical factory, known locally as Stinking Ocean. The stink became even worse after the collapse of a waste pipe which had been routed to the Clyde via a convenient public sewer. Tennant replied to Russell's protests with polite promises, but nearly a year later a sanitary inspector who had been dispatched to the works found the noxious yellow liquid mingling with the city sewage. Russell himself explored the factory grounds before sending an acerbic reprimand to Tennant. 'I have to say that the existence of this by-way into the Public Sewers seems to demand an explanation on your part,' he wrote. 'It is no business of mine to be constantly on the watch and to warn you of preventable escapes, as I have repeatedly had to do, still less of deliberate abuse of the public sewers.' This reproof entered the public record via the Health Committee minutes. [15]

Other offenders received similar treatment. The Distillers Co. Ltd., another discharger of waste into public sewers, was given an ultimatum, and its protests that revenue would be seriously affected were swept aside. Steamship owners were prosecuted in the River Bailie's Court for smoke offences, although again the penalties were light. The tramway company, which had not yet been municipalised, was ordered to stop allowing old-clothes dealers to take their bundles on board and warned that dirty and badly ventilated trams would spread infections from the lower to the upper classes. Russell became particularly concerned about ventilation after boarding a foul-smelling tram in Queen Street and asking the conductor to open the ventilators, which proved to be stuck. Writing 'as a regular traveller by the Partick tram' as well as in his official capacity, he informed the company that better ventilation was needed and noted that the worst trams were on the routes on which fresh air was most required.[16]

The arm of the Medical Officer was long. It reached shipping agents in Leith who were criticised for their slack management of the thousands of unvaccinated European immigrants who in the 1880s streamed across Scotland on their way to North America; under pressure from Russell the companies agreed to notify the Sanitary Department about smallpox cases detected at the Tail of the Bank and decanted to Glasgow.[17] Public as well as private bodies were chivvied, schools as well as factories. Glasgow School Board was bullied into keeping playgrounds open after school hours for the use of all children of school age despite protests that they would be 'frequented by dirty, ill-mannered children' who would infect respectable children with their bad habits as well as their diseases.[18] Pressure was brought to bear for the closure of a Catholic industrial school in the East End after several boys had died in a mysterious outbreak of fever. After calling in Gairdner and others to help with investigations Russell rejected the suggestion of the school officials that tobacco-chewing was the cause, though he acknowledged that the habit could well have contributed to the lowered vitality of the victims. He pointed his finger instead at the school's polluted environment, its appalling structural defects, and its generally insanitary state, and reported that it was impossible to justify its retention in the city.[19]

The key to this aggressive strategy was the Health Committee. The partnership between Russell and its leadership developed into a powerful engine of reform. The pattern was set in the 1870s when the committee chairman was John Ure, the councillor who had pushed so hard for the appointment of an MOH. It continued in the 1880s under Ure's successors, W. R. W. Smith (sometimes known as 'Alphabet' Smith because of his predilection for initials) and Robert Crawford. These men were

A lanky Russell in his late teens (top) with his grandmother, Margaret Macdonald Russell, who helped to bring him up, and his young sister Agnes, who was his playmate in rural Rutherglen. Russell a few years later (bottom) as a student at Glasgow University and protégé of both Kelvin and Lister.

Helen Fenton Davidson, Russell's ill-fated wife (top), was the daughter of a well-known Edinburgh cleric. After their married life had come to an early and tragic end Russell's sister Agnes (bottom) became his housekeeper and looked after the three children.

Two of Russell's closest allies: Councillor John Ure (top), the grain merchant who became one of the pioneers of the public health movement in Glasgow, and Professor William Tennant Gairdner, his mentor, friend and father 'in the faith of sensation'. Ure's caricature is from the monthly magazine *The Bailie*.

Russell (top) at the peak of his career, when he had acquired an international reputation, and a more venerable Russell (bottom) in his sixties, when ill health and the burdens of his work had left their mark.

Councillor Robert Crawford (top) was a strong ally of Russell's and a passionate and persuasive advocate of municipal enterprise. Their opponents included Councillor Samuel Chisholm, a future Lord Provost (bottom), who was influenced by Russell's lectures but fell out with him over slum clearance plans. Both caricatures are from *The Bailie*.

Russell was a familiar presence where living conditions were most vile, as in these overcrowded tenements at No.80 High Street, photographed by Thomas Annan in the 1860s. But he believed that the city could be made as healthy as the countryside.

High Street tenements, such as these, Nos.97 and 103 Saltmarket, pho-
tographed by Annan, were among the most notorious slum properties in
Glasgow. Russell was exposed to the squalor of this area as a student at
Glasgow University in the decade before it moved to Gilmorehill.

Russell (above, third from the right on sludge boat) braves the 'pestilential odours' of the River Clyde, about which he complained in a report on river sewage and (below, second from right) takes a break during a conference, probably the huge and chaotic International Hygiene Congress in Budapest in 1894.

what Russell described as 'day-to-day committee men rather than fortnightly town councillors.'[20] All had a deep interest in public health independently of Russell, but all looked to him for guidance, professional expertise, and even inspiration; all became his close personal friends. And it was with these men, rather than the leaders of the full Town Council, that Russell conferred on politically sensitive issues.

Smith, a yarn merchant and the son of a former deputy governor of Sierra Leone, was an unconventional reformer, an advanced Liberal who pleaded in vain for a programme of municipal housebuilding and argued that the city must acquire more power over the surrounding land on the principle that 'the Earth is the Lord's and the fullness thereof.' He had an interest in sewage which some people thought bordered on obsession. He 'thought sewage, talked sewage, and wrote sewage,' critics claimed.[21] Councillor James Martin described him as the biggest blether on the Town Council. Although Smith was committee chairman for only a few years, and left the council soon afterwards when his business ran into trouble, he remained in touch with the committee leadership and, as Russell put it, was 'always invited to the little junketings with which municipal work is occasionally promoted.' He was the least powerful of the three men who shaped policy with Russell, but was possibly the one with whom he had the closest understanding. Smith, who was chairman when Russell lost his wife, had also been widowed at an early age and never remarried. Both men were shy and reserved, both were deeply religious, and Russell might have been referring to himself when he remarked that Smith 'enjoyed the wine of life, but at times would go from the feast out into the darkness and silence.' He seemed to dwell habitually, Russell remarked, on 'the borders of the unseen.'[22]

Crawford, who succeeded Smith as chairman in 1886, was a much younger man with a more modern approach. Though idealistic, he was a practical man with shrewd commercial sense – a partner in a successful fancy goods and stationery business which had connections with the Continent. He had a 'singularly acute intellect', was an eloquent and persuasive speaker, and gave public lectures on literary as well as political topics. Though it was only in the 1890s that he was to come fully into

his own as the publicist for Glasgow's great era of municipal
enterprise, he was already an influential figure in the 1880s. As
chairman of the art galleries committee as well as the health
committee he was a driving force behnd the establishment of
the People's Palace and was given much of the credit for the
success of Glasgow's first International Exhibition in 1888. A
great admirer of Russell, he worked particularly closely with
him in closing unhealthy properties and in extending the surveillance of the milk trade.[23]

These key allies would defend Russell's position at meetings
of the health committee, which was often deeply divided. They
would present Russell's fortnightly reports sympathetically at
meetings of the full Town Council, highlighting the points that
Russell wished to emphasise and which would then be reported
in the press. The same men worked closely with Russell on the
numerous small sub-committees where the important work was
done. They could count on influential support from councillors
like James Moir, the former Chartist. Outside the Town Council
they had powerful allies in William Gairdner (always ready with
a timely letter to the press), John Glaister, and Sheriff W. C.
Spens, a leading proponent of sanitary reform.

It was with the backing of such allies that Russell achieved
one of his most important aims – free hospital treatment for all
Glaswegians suffering from infectious diseases. This was a huge
achievement. The previous arrangement, whereby the parochial
authorities paid for paupers treated in Belvidere, had caused
endless disagreement and bureaucratic delay. Russell wanted to
remove the stigma of pauperisation and to see the treatment of
infectious diseases brought completely under municipal control
and out of inept parochial hands – thus completing the process
that had begun when the Royal Infirmary withdrew from the
treatment of infectious diseases. Ideology played no part in the
decision (Russell saw no inconsistency in later introducing pay
beds at Belvidere) but the move was nevertheless controversial
and passed the committee by only one vote.[24]

With the Health Committee often as divided as the full Town
Council, Russell relied on the political skills of its leadership to
steer through controversial measures. It was with their help,
too, that the committee was turned into an efficient legislative

machine. When John Ure became Lord Provost in 1880 he was determined to crown his municipal career with a last great contribution to public health, and began a drive for reforming legislation based on Russell's proposals.[25] Russell had long been drawing attention to the defects in the existing legislation, which lagged badly behind England's. The Scottish Public Health Act of 1867 was outdated, its procedures cumbersome. Even in Scottish terms Glasgow was falling behind. Edinburgh had made notification of infectious diseases compulsory in 1877, Greenock had established control over milk supplies, while Aberdeen and Dundee had also acquired new local legislation. Russell also looked enviously across the Atlantic, where city health boards enjoyed powers unknown in Glasgow. New York's board could close unhealthy buildings within 24 hours. Russell thought of this when attempting to help a woman who was afraid that her children would be bitten by the rats popping in and out of an open drain beneath the floor of their single end. He fumed because of the weeks that had to be spent in serving notices, inspecting, certifying, and again notifying, before the landlord took steps to put things right.[26]

Ure at first tried to rally all the Scottish burghs in a united push for new legislation, but when his overtures met with apathy he set about framing local legislation. Word then came that the Government was to initiate new legislation for Scotland, and for a while the energies of Ure and company were devoted to an attempt to influence the Bill. But its progress was so slow, and its contents so disappointing, that the decision was made to push ahead with a new Glasgow Police Bill after all. The Government's legislation was based on the lowest common denominator because, as Russell noted, it was impossible to apply the same stringent laws in Auchtermuchty as in Glasgow. The local Bill, based on Russell's ideas and drawn up by a special sub-committee, was more sweeping. It contained powers to compel the removal of patients with infectious diseases from their homes, even if the disease was not notifiable – an important power which found its way into Scottish legislation and is still of significance a century later. There were powers to enforce the cleaning of unhealthy houses, to ban wakes (on the grounds that they spread infection), to prevent children from attending school when there was infectious disease in their families, and to fine teachers who turned a blind eye to these children. Power was provided for the closure of uninhabitable houses – a Health Committee delegation having been most impressed by the way that similar powers were being exercised in Edinburgh [27] – and, not least, for the compulsory provision of internal sanitation. Regulations were laid down for the milk and meat trades.

These proposals were greeted with shouts of rage. The Bill was denounced as arbitrary and intrusive. Opposition came not only from the Factors and House Factors Association but even from the Faculty of Physicians and Surgeons of Glasgow. Insults were hurled across the long mahogany tables in the Council Chambers in Wilson Street. The Bill was denounced as tyrannical, particularly the clause giving the Health Committee authority to condemn unhealthy buildings on the MOH's recommendation. The milk regulations were described by one councillor as arbitrary and ridiculous. Dr Henry Wilson, an East End GP on the Health Committee, who was no friend of Russell's, objected to the proposal for the compulsory notification of infectious diseases, which he said had done nothing to lower Edinburgh's death rate.[28]

Lord Provost Ure made a powerful defence of the Bill, arguing that in this densely packed working-class city it was surely humane that the sanitary officials should come to the aid of the poor.[29] He said pointedly that he trusted that members of the Town Council would not be influenced by vested interests. But the battle was not won in Ure's day. It took almost a decade to put the legislation on the Statute Book, and concessions had to be made when the Bill ran into trouble in both Houses of Parliament – the right of appeal to the Sheriff Court was preserved for the proprietors of condemned buildings. Nevertheless the Health Committee had won the long battle. The Glasgow Police (Amendment) Act came into force in 1890, seven years before the new Scottish Public Health Act. Together with another of the Health Committee's efforts, the Building Regulations Bill, which became law two years later, it made Glasgow the pacemaker for sanitary reform.

The building regulations legislation, also denounced by interested parties as arbitrary and objectionable, was intended to put an end to what Russell described as 'notoriously defective' structures. He especially objected to the fashion for 'hollow square' tenements which were replacing the customary parallel rows. The squares in the centre were 'boxes of stagnant air' and quickly became filled up with more buildings, which shut the light out of the original tenements.[30] The situation had deteriorated because of a legal technicality which nullified the regulation against houses being built too close together. Russell also found it deplorable that the Glasgow builder digging his trenches for the walls of a tenement could not be compelled to make ventilating openings or install damp courses. As well as dealing with these anomalies the new legislation laid down that streets must be wide in proportion to the height of the tenements lining them – a step towards Russell's ideal of a city whose streets were corridors for country air. A minimum height of 9ft. 6in. was set for ceilings, bringing complaints from Councillor James Martin that poor people would have to pay a higher rent for the sake of empty space over their heads.[31]

The legislation also aroused the wrath of proprietors (and the Faculty of Procurators) by removing their right to subdivide houses without reference to the Dean of Guild Court. Most ticketed houses were 'made down' in this way. The practice was so lucrative that sometimes houses passed by the Dean of Guild Court as a single unit were almost immediately subdivided to bring in additional rent. This was done simply by throwing open the front door and letting each room to a separate tenant, thus creating dark and noisome lobbies which Russell described as conduits for 'aerial sewage.' As well as rectifying this situation the proposed regulations limited the number of dwellings entered from a common staircase to 16. This would have the incidental benefit of making life a little simpler for the sanitary inspectors. Russell sympathised with their difficulties when they found themselves in a close whose number was used for a front land and several backlands, 'with no end of turnpikes, stairs, flats, and lobbies.' The proper address, he pointed out, would be something like: 'Bridgegate, No. 29, back land, stair 1st left, 3 up, right lobby, door facing.'[32]

Many of Russell's most important objectives were secured by these new building regulations and the sanitary clauses of the new Police Act. Builders and landlords were being made more accountable. If the city streets were hardly being transformed into corridors for country air, at least a halt was being called to the worst excesses of overbuilding. More effective powers were being obtained for dealing with infectious diseases, and compulsory notification had meanwhile been achieved through national enabling legislation which Glasgow adopted on Russell's recommendation.[33]

But many enemies had been made in the process. There had been attempts to stop the legislation in its tracks. Opposition had come not only from vested interests but from a variety of other critics, some of whom had raised libertarian objections. Many people thought that the Health Committee was getting above itself. The *Glasgow Herald* noted that 'the itch of law-making had seized the committee' and that its building regulations would 'dent Glasgow's reputation for common sense.' In the paper's correspondence columns the committee was accused of seeking 'authority and by-laws which no Russian Emperor or Turkish Sultan would dare to enforce.'[34] There were more protests when, following Russell's report on an outbreak of bovine tuberculosis in a city dairy, it moved successfully to transfer responsibility for meat inspection from the City Slaughter House to the safer hands of the Sanitary Department. When details of the manoeuvre were leaked to the *Herald* the committee was accused of poaching power from the Markets Committee and the Chief Constable. The *Herald* on this occasion thought the committee had acted in the public interest, but one councillor saw it as 'just another of the Health Committee's actions' and claimed that this troublesome bunch were 'taking to do with far more things than they had anything to do with.'[35]

Russell was the target of much of this hostility. He was extremely closely associated with the committee – too closely, some thought. The new legislation was based on his ideas; he had worked out the details with the sub-committees concerned. He had gone to London to impress upon the Lord Advocate the committee's views on national legislation – lobbying, for example, for the milk trade to be brought under direct sanitary control in Scotland as well as England. All this made him unpopular not just with vested interests but with those who opposed sanitary reform on financial grounds or on principle, or who disapproved of the way Russell was doing his job.

This hostility surfaced when the Chief Sanitary Inspector, Kenneth Macleod, died in 1885 and Russell and his supporters moved to end the ambiguity in the MOH's status by establishing him as undisputed supremo of the Sanitary Department. Russell, who had taken over the Sanitary Inspector's responsibilities during Macleod's long periods of illness, wrote a memorandum in support of the change.

But the proposal, having narrowly passed the Health Committee, was rejected by the Town Council after a turbulent debate in which some unflattering things were said about Russell.[36] Although some councillors objected only to the principle of putting the MOH in direct command of the sanitary inspectorate, others were more personal. There were claims that the Council 'would always be in the Sheriff Court' and 'would soon get into hot water with buildings and factors.' His most outspoken opponents in this debate came from within the ranks of the Health Committee. The two river bailies on the committee seemed particularly unimpressed with Russell's practical qualifications for running the Sanitary Department. Dr Russell, said one of them, claimed to know more about the construction of a house than an architect, more about building than a mason, more about pipes than a plumber, more about bricks than a bricklayer, but nobody else believed it.

An even stronger attack was made by Dr Wilson, the GP on the Health Committee who had objected to the proposal for compulsory notification of infectious diseases. He alleged that Russell 'had not performed the duty of MO as it should be done in Glasgow' and that the Sanitary Department was a disgrace to the city. When chided by the Lord Provost for 'saying some very unhandsome things'. Wilson retorted: 'What I said is true, and I am prepared to prove it.' Wilson, who had claimed a few years earlier that there were a great many things that 'needed looking into,' had a strong dislike of sanitary officialdom, which he saw as irrelevant to the problems of poverty and disease. He complained about 'red-tapism' and cases of misdiagnosis by epidemic inspectors with no medical training. It was pointed

out to him during the debate that Russell had no say in the
appointment of these inspectors, which was one of the anomalies
that the proposal was designed to remove.

The critics, however, had their way. A few weeks later Peter
Fyfe, a mechanical engineer in the Cleansing Department, was
appointed to the post of Sanitary Inspector on the same terms
as his predecessor. All that Smith, Crawford, and company could
then do was initiate a revision of the departmental regulations
with a view to shoring up Russell's position.

This was the second time within a few months that he had
been at the centre of controversy in the Town Council. Some
councillors were unhappy about his choice of contractors for the
milk supplies to Belvidere Hospital. They wanted to know why
they were having to pay more than before despite the falling
price of milk. There were rumours of 'underhand dealing' – if
not by Russell, then by his subordinates – until a councillor
visited the farm of one of the unsuccessful bidders and confirmed
Russell's claim that the water supply was suspect.[37]

Even his ordinary fortnightly reports could sometimes arouse
strong feelings. When he reported that a group of workers were
careless about health regulations in their workplace, Councillor
Martin accused him of making 'an unblushing, barefaced attack'
and of using 'abominable, insulting, filthy language to the
citizens of Glasgow, and that too at a moment there were
thousands every day taking advantage of the public baths, which
I glory in being an instrument in procuring for them.'[38] On the
other hand, when Russell described a typhus-stricken family
living in grossly overcrowded conditions as 'cleanly and respectable Scotch folk', he was pounced upon by another councillor
and accused of traducing the Scottish character – until Robert
Crawford intervened with the sardonic observation that 'these
people, having paid their rates, had a right to have the fever if
they thought proper.'[39]

Controversy was an inescapable part of Russell's job. As a
letter-writer in the *Glasgow Herald* saw it, the MOH and his
staff 'incur the ill-will of many persons, more or less influential,
in the prosecution of their work, but they are animated, I believe,
by the sense of responsibility that is laid upon them, and
persevere in the face of obstacles that are placed in their way.'[40]

Russell seemed not to care whom he upset. As well as publicly admonishing Sir Charles Tennant for polluting the public sewers he denounced the Lord Advocate who 'had not the courage apparently' to admit that small burghs were incapable of undertaking the public health function they were being accorded in the Government's plans for local government reform. After objections by a number of councillors the criticisms were expunged from Russell's report.[41]

He spoke as plainly about his own profession. In 1889, when notification of infectious diseases became compulsory, he deeply upset many leading Glasgow practioners by claiming publicly that the error rate in diagnosis was unacceptably high. He had been particularly struck by the case of a 10-year-old boy in the East End who had been certified as having typhus. When the ambulance arrived there was no one at home – 'the patient and the whole family had gone, no one knew whither.' Several months later it transpired that they had moved to a Paisley lodging house and had later been taken to Paisley Royal Infirmary as cases of enteric fever. Russell, in a report to the Health Committee, described this as a striking example of the routine experience of the Sanitary Department. Too many mistakes, he said, were being made in the diagnosis of typhus, enteric fever, and diphtheria. Fully 44% of patients sent to Belvidere with a diagnosis of typhus turned out to be suffering from other diseases, from pneuomonia to alcoholism, and half should not have been sent to hospital at all.

Russell acknowledged that 'even the wisest physician sometimes makes mistakes,' and that he himself had made errors in a one-room house which he would not have done in a hospital. It is plain from his report that his intention was not to attack his local colleagues but to highlight a national problem – gaps in medical education and experience resulting from the decline in infectious diseases and from their treatment in local authority fever hospitals rather than general teaching hospitals. He pointed out that this had become 'a burning question' to the General Medical Council and quoted a provincial medical officer who was experiencing a year-by-year increase in misdiagnosis. The aim of the paper was evidently to advertise the fact that Belvidere was now offering free clinical instruction to medical students, and Russell may also have hoped to persuade the Town Council to provide additional funding.[42]

Some doctors nevertheless took the report as a slight on their professionalism, and even those who took a broader view were furious at Russell for bringing it before the Town Council, and thus the newspapers, instead of a medical society. Dr James Hamilton, leading a Glasgow Southern Medical Society discussion, described this as a glaring (if possibly unintentional) transgression of professional ethics. The society, with whose members Russell had picnicked so happily at Tillietudlem, was almost unanimous in its disapproval – only one speaker rose in his defence. Even John Glaister, Russell's fellow-Congregationalist and public health colleague, was critical of the way the report had been made public although he was sure that Russell had no other thought in his mind than of doing a public duty. Several speakers expressed the fear that general practioners would delay sending cases to hospital until the diagnosis was beyond doubt, thus frustrating the MOH's own wishes. Others cited mistakes made at Belvidere itself. Tensions between general practitioners and sanitary inspectors were also reflected in the debate. The highly regarded Dr James Tindal recalled that he had once written to tell Russell that the inspector had no right to interfere, and Russell had replied: 'I hope you will see that the patient is moved as I suggest, otherwise I shall have to take stronger measures.' Later, a doctor who had handled one of the cases cited by Russell suggested that 'the position he has taken up is much too autocratic for the commonweal of the profession.'[43] The controversy eventually reached the *Lancet*, which in a magisterial leader expressed respect for Russell but suggested that 'a cordial co-operation' could best be achieved if medical officers communicated directly with doctors about errors in diagnosis.[44] The fury then abated, although Russell picnicked no more with the Glasgow Southern Medical Society.

Yet these were also years of growing prestige and influence for Russell. By the time he celebrated his fiftieth birthday in May, 1887, his contribution to public health had been recognised. Glasgow University awarded him the honorary degree of LL. D in 1885, the year in which he was being publicly disparaged by his opponents on the Town Council. Soon afterwards he was elected president of the Philosophical Society of Glasgow, and arranged for one of their meetings to be held in Glasgow University's natural philosophy classroom so that his old mentor Sir William Thomson (soon to become Lord Kelvin) could give an experimental demonstration of his electrical measuring instruments. In 1889 the Royal College of Physicians of London gave him the first Bisset-Hawkins memorial medal for zeal in the promotion of public health, which was quickly followed by the British Medical Association's Stewart prize for his researches on epidemic disease. He was made a Fellow of the Faculty of Physicians and Surgeons of Glasgow and laboured on its library committee along with Gairdner, Joseph Coats, and H. E. Clark. He sat on the boards of the Western Infirmary, Anderson's College Medical School, the Glasgow Sick Poor and Private Nursing Association, and the new children's hospital in Garnethill. Seeing such institutions as almost an integral part of the public health movement, he was particularly enthusiastic about the children's hospital. Thoroughly disagreeing with the medical establishment's view that children should be treated in general hospitals, he had played an energetic role in the new hospital from the outset, travelling to England to interview the short leet of candidates for the post of matron, and constantly testing the milk supplies – finding, for example, the level of boracic acid to be 'perfectly intolerable.' He had also become chairman of the Glasgow Central Dispensary in George Street, the result of the movement he had generated for general dispensaries – medical outposts where the poor could receive advice and simple treatment.[45] And he was in at the birth of the Victoria Infirmary. With the City Architect, John Carrick, he helped to adjudicate the architectural competition organised by the promoters and thought that the winning entry, by James Sellars, bore 'the marks of true genius.'[46]

As one of Russell's supporters remarked during a stormy Town Council debate, the MOH had 'made a name for himself not only in Glasgow but throughout Scotland.' His advice was much in demand. Neighbouring burghs asked him to pronounce upon the sanitary condition of a burn or to be a witness for the prosecution in a nuisance case. The Board of Supervision made him a commissioner to report on sanitary affairs in Perth. Dairy farmers throughout the south of Scotland also had reason to be aware of his existence: in 1885, in the absence of an effective public health authority for Scotland, he issued a memorandum 'On the Sanitary Requirements of a Dairy Farm' for everyone engaged in supplying Glasgow with milk.[47] And he was becoming known abroad. In 1886, attending the American Public Health Association conference in Toronto, he was embarrassed to be asked to address the assembly. He declined, on the grounds that he had nothing to say, then felt remorse at his 'shabby' response, and delivered an address on Scottish public health legislation. Scotland as a whole, he told them, was 'one of the most benighted countries on the face of the earth' in sanitary matters: 'It is an unhappy fate which has cast a Scotchman upon your coasts rather than a representative of England proper.'[48]

More importantly, Russell had become much better known to ordinary Glasgow citizens. It was in the '80s that he blossomed as a public lecturer. The art of public speaking did not come naturally to him. He had difficulty in expressing his views even in committee meetings. Some of his earlier attempts to address audiences went badly. In 1877 William Gairdner wrote to congratulate him on 'an admirable paper ... so far as I could follow it.' Gairdner entreated him ('if you are to attempt lecturing') to speak more slowly and distinctly, emphasise the complete words, speak every word and even syllable as if he were thinking it out at the moment of speaking it, and keep his eye as much as possible on his audience – 'and rouse up any fellow who ventures to incline to fall asleep as I did.'[49] This must have been cruelly demoralising for a man who was already pathologically afraid of public speaking, but Russell evidently benefited from the advice. His wish to communicate was intense: he felt impelled to break through the public ignorance that had been demonstrated in Glasgow's reaction to the rectorial speech given by John Bright, the veteran Liberal politician, at Glasgow University in 1884. The students had shouted with incredulous laughter when Bright stated that 41 out of every 100 Glasgow families lived in one-room houses, and the shock waves reverberated in the press and pulpits. Yet the new rector was merely quoting from the official census.[50]

Though Russell was obviously not a born public speaker his literary skills served him well. He inserted apt quotations, caught the attention with striking images – the nomads of the city, he once said, were like Arabs, folding their tents and silently stealing away. He drew on his own experience to paint pictures of the city which were once described as 'almost Zola-esque' in their vividness.[51] Though often addressing small audiences, he reached a large cross-section of people and tailored his lectures according to his listeners. Addressing Park Church Literary Institute, he quoted Stendhal, Lamb, and Carlyle, as well as discussing the obligations of practical Christianity. In his presidential addresses to the Philosophical Society he made use of statistics, tables, and diagrams to drive home his message to his scientifically minded listeners. When speaking to professional groups he explained the role of local government, which he defined as the administrative expression of community interest. Invited to speak to an Airdrie audience, he described the shameful deficiencies of their town's public health record, then added: 'The only consolation I can give you is that Coatbridge is worse!'[52]

When delivering his public health lecture series he took the opportunity to give practical advice – open the windows, pull up the blinds, never neglect a smell, do not be satisfied with landlords who observe only the letter of the law. West End audiences, on the other hand, would be asked to imagine themselves living in single-ends: 'You mistresses of houses, with bedrooms and parlours, dining rooms and drawing rooms, kitchens and washing-houses, pantries and sculleries, how could you put one room to the uses of all? You mothers, with your cooks and housemaids, your nurses and general servants, how would you in your own persons act all those parts in one room, where, too, you must eat and sleep and find your lying-in room and make your sick bed?'[53]

In 'The Children of the City,' one of his most celebrated lectures, he made a similar appeal to people's imaginations. 'Have we not all been children?' he asked. 'Are our Members of Parliament and Town Councillors some strange order of beings

who sprang like Minerva, full-grown, into life, and had no
experience of nurseries, or playgrounds, or cricket fields?' His
idea of childhood was notably un-Victorian. He wanted children
to know that they were 'a recognised constituent of life.' Parks
should have playing fields for 'lads who cannot afford to lease
fields like the golden youth of the wealthy'; they should not be
'places for merely dawdling along looking at flowers or admiring
grass through iron railings. Cities should be made more like
places where children formed part of the population, less like
places laid out by some Board of Bachelors.' If women had the
vote, Russell suggested in this 1886 lecture, children would not
be forgotten (and he also wanted to see more women become
sanitary inspectors).[54]

These lectures made an enormous impact. Their success was
crucial to Russell's whole strategy. They prepared the ground
for change by arousing the public conscience and making people
aware of the price that would be paid for neglect. Their credi-
bility was boosted by the continuing fall in the death rate.
Russell's approach seemed to be getting results. Councillor
James Martin continued to mock the mortality tables, but it
was in the 1880s that Glasgow narrowed the gap with other
Scottish cities. In 1881 its crude death rate was 25.6 per thous-
and, well above Edinburgh's 20.8, Aberdeen's 20, and even
Dundee's 22.5. A decade later the Glasgow figure was down to
22.7 compared with Edinburgh's 20.8, Aberdeen's 20.9, and
Dundee's 22.[55]

But in some respects Glasgow still lagged badly. As Russell
noted in 'an apology for Glasgow' in 1885, it remained the
unhealthiest city in Scotland.[56] The air was heavily polluted –
sixpence still obscured the sun. The Clyde was still the city's
principal sewer. The problem was becoming more urgent as more
and more water closets decanted more and more untreated sewage into the river. This may have contributed to Russell's initial
opposition to the installation of WCs in small houses. But his
main reason was that sewer gases could blow back through badly
trapped WCs inadequately supplied with water. When mechanical improvements were made in the mid-80s he changed his
opinion and argued successfully for the compulsory introduction
of internal WCs – a major item in the new legislation.[57]

Housing was the worst of many unsolved public health problems as the 1880s drew to a close. With typhus nests still
featuring regularly in his fornightly reports, Russell recognised
that it would take more than building controls and sanitary
regulations to remedy the worst conditions. When he travelled
to Edinburgh in 1885 to give evidence to the Royal Commission
on the Housing of the Working Classes, he emphasised that
some property was utterly beyond repair.[58] He continued to
drive home the connection between bad housing and bad health.
In a classic analysis in 1888 he compared the healthiest district,
Kelvinhaugh and Sandyford, with the notorious 'District 14' –
Bridgegate and the Wynds, which had replaced the High Street
as the worst part of town. Russell described District 14 as the
headquarters of those who lived in open defiance of the law.
When he entered the houses he found not only the mothers at
home, as in other areas, but 'men and women sleeping by day
in preparation for the dismal work of the night.' District 14 had
the largest proportion of inmates per room in the city, and the
second largest proportion of single-ends. Its 7000 or more
inhabitants had 105 WCs among them. Its death rate was 32.45
per thousand compared with Kelvinhaugh's 13.89. Its infant
death rate was 239 compared with Kelvinhaugh's 88. A quarter
of its children died without reaching their first birthdays compared with 9% in Kelvinhaugh.[59]

The houses of these people, Russell said, were radically bad:
the only remedy was demolition and reconstruction. But the
City Improvement Trust, which was supposed to be tackling
this problem, had been dormant since the late 1870s. Its own
property had deteriorated disgracefully. Under pressure from
the Health Committee and other quarters it bestirred itself
towards the end of the decade, but the housing problem was
largely shelved till the 1890s. Like the sewage question, it would
be one of the recurrent themes of that decade. It would also
lead to the gravest crisis of Russell's career.

Chapter Fourteen

Breaking the Mould

*The sanitarian is like the lifeboat or the lifebelt to the
drowning man – 'a very present help.' The theorist is like
a lecturer on the art of swimming – any good he may do
is in the future.*

THE mid-1880s brought Russell to a crisis-point not only
in his personal and professional lives but also in his
politics. When he lifted his head from municipal affairs,
he found no comfort in the wider political scene. Discontents
and disagreements were growing among Liberals, not least in
the West of Scotland. Gladstone's espousal of Home Rule for
Ireland, in the spring of 1886, was for many of them the defining
moment. Thousands left the party, and prepared to fight the
forthcoming election on Unionist principles. Russell was among
them.

This was a wrenching decision. Russell had been a Liberal
since his debating days at Glasgow University 30 years earlier.
His political commitment was certainly no handicap when he
became MOH. Almost everyone else was a Liberal too. The
party had dominated the Scottish political scene since the
Reform Act of 1832. Russell's Health Committee allies – Ure,
Smith and Crawford – were fellow-Liberals. So for that matter
were most of his opponents, both inside and beyond the Town
Council. Sir Charles Tennant, who was attacked by Russell for
polluting the public sewers, was president of the Glasgow Liberal Association. Shared political allegiance was no reason for
pulling punches. Scottish Liberals, more factionalised than their
English counterparts, were a loose coalition which could accommodate old-fashioned whigs like William Gairdner and radicals
like W. R. W. Smith. They argued against one another in municipal debates, stood against one another at municipal elections.

Their disagreements had become more serious long before
the final split in 1886. There was widespread disapproval of the

leftwards drift of Gladstone's government and its handling of foreign policy: William Gairdner, for example, was 'profoundly shocked' by the death of Gordon at Khartoum.[1] Gladstone's Irish policy was the final blow. The impact on Glasgow and its hinterland was particularly heavy because of the strong commercial and sectarian ties with Ulster. The business community, at this time of growing imperial sentiment, were also afraid that Irish Home Rule would mark the beginning of the end of the Empire. Businessmen were prominent among those who left the party, made common cause with the Conservatives in the general election that followed, and soon afterwards established a Liberal Unionist Association.[2] Between 1886 and 1891 they made up about a quarter of Glasgow's 50 civic representatives, with the Liberals accounting for just under one-third.

Russell gave them his full support. He had become disenchanted with the Liberals. He regretted that Gladstonianism had become 'the measure of men's fitness to be a Liberal.'[3] He became active in the Unionist cause in his home patch in Partick, one of the key constituencies in the 1886 election. Sir William Thomson, who with his Ulster background was playing a leading part in the campaign against Home Rule, came to speak on behalf of the local MP,[4] who had defected from the Liberals and was duly returned to Parliament – one of nine victors among the 30 candidates put forward by the defectors in the West of Scotland. When the group formally turned itself into the Liberal Unionist Association, Russell became vice-president of the Partick branch[5] and consorted with the wider membership at the Imperial Union Club in St Vincent Street, the social wing of the movement.

This seems bold behaviour for a public official, who might have been expected in the circumstances simply to withdraw quietly from the Liberal Party. Yet all Russell's allies were becoming Liberal Unionists – Thomson, Gairdner, Smith, Crawford. His own views were strongly held. As a Congregationalist he may have hoped at one stage that Gladstone would disestablish the Church of Scotland, but such hopes were a thing of the past and many dissenters were now ready to desert the Liberals – within Russell's own circle Gairdner was a Unitarian, Smith an Episcopalian (and latterly a Swedenborgian), and

Crawford a United Presbyterian. For all of these men Ireland
was the overriding issue – Gladstone's Home Rule Speech
converted Gairdner to Unionism 'in a single day.'[6] Russell had
been interested in Ireland since his visits there during the
Atlantic Cable expedition, and his spell some years later at the
Rotundo Hospital in Dublin. His support for the Protestant
cause had long coloured his political opinions. As a medical
student he had applauded the anti-papal foreign policy of Lord
John Russell and deplored the 'baneful' influence of Britain's
alliance with France.[7] On his Atlantic cable expedition he had
equated the Catholic Church with 'the spirit of intolerance' that
was 'the ruin of Ireland.'

His religious beliefs were certainly involved in his pro-
Unionist stance. He was allying himself with a party whose
orators were not always above tapping the sectarian bitterness
of the time.[8] Some of them found subtle ways of playing on
entrenched prejudices against Irish immigrants, suggesting that
economic trouble in a devolved Ireland would have an impact
on the Scottish labour market. Yet two of William Thomson's
most recent biographers[9] argue that he, for one, was motivated
not by narrow bigotry but by a genuine belief that full membership of the United Kingdom offered the best guarantee of
liberty for all Irishmen; and such an attitude seems consistent
with Russell's own value system. It is true that Russell sometimes expressed harsh-sounding views about Glasgow's
underclass, with its large proportion of Irish Catholics. He spoke
of the 'social debris'; of reckless people who were 'spendthrift
of their own and the public money';[10] of a 'central mass of people
who cannot be trusted to live without supervision and guidance.'[11] He found Highlanders also prone to overcrowding but
identified the Irish as the 'most obstinate' overcrowders and
related this to drinking. According to Russell, 'that worst form
of overcrowding – the introduction of lodgers within the family
circle' – was mainly confined to the Irish, habitual overcrowders
who diverted money from rent to whisky.[12] Yet in practice he
co-operated with priests and had their backing for the banning
of wakes in order to limit the spread of infectious diseases. He
was also emphatic that the evils which he condemned were the
result not of national character but of living conditions. In an

effort to bring home this message to middle-class audiences he invited them to imagine what slum conditions were really like, morally as well as physically:

'Are they lovely though deadly, are they pleasant though poisonous? If they kill the body, do they ennoble the spirit and sanctify the soul? Is death in the wynds a euthanasia? Is disease made comely there by some drapery of dreams and hallucinations? If when we enter these precincts with dainty feet, stepping warily, with garments carefully drawn closer to our shrinking limbs, our every sense is outraged, and strange thoughts stir in our minds, and the world seems more unintelligible than ever; if, when we regain the open street, we feel as if we had escaped from Hades ... if all this be so, what of the people who live there? What of the children who are born and grew up there? What sort of citizens are they likely to turn out under the perpetual influence of conditions which have, in a few minutes, so disturbed the placid currents of our lives? What sort of a man is he likely to be who stumbles up and down through the twilight of those stairs night and morning; where sickness is never absent, where death is frequent, where the ambulance driver carrying the fever patient, or the undertaker's men piloting the coffin down the strait passage to the street, are familiar obstacles!' [13]

Was it not likely, he asked, that the hearts of such people would be filled with bitterness and hate, and harbour a sense of injustice? Although Russell was trying to warn middle-class Glaswegians that the price of neglect would be not only infectious disease but social unrest, his language was not that of the mere social engineer. He sympathised with the political struggles of the oppressed 'in the blindness of despair, burning mills, clamouring for the suffrage, rioting, ridden down by the cavalry at Peterloo, gradually gaining the protection of the factory acts and emancipation from the new slavery of the apprenticeship system ... finally, struggling through chartist riots towards political enfranchisement and the Ballot Act.' [14] He was not a Socialist, although he had read widely in socialist literature. He was opposed to State medicine and thought that charitable giving was better for the soul than paying taxes, because it cultivated the habit of giving. He was particularly scathing about the socialism of William Morris (who had marked down Glasgow as the outstanding indictment of the capitalist system) and dismissed his views as 'all very pretty and worthy of your aesthetic imagination.' [15] But he was even more scathing about the laissez-faire doctrine of Herbert Spencer, who claimed that sanitary intervention was contrary to individual liberty and evolutionary law. The best way to criticise Spencer, suggested Russell, was to quote him at length, which he proceeded to do before demolishing his arguments in detail and calling instead for 'the solidarity of human interest in the face of communicable disease.' Russell argued that 'there must be co-operation, with the unavoidable concomitant of sacrifice of some individual liberty.' [16] He believed that the evils of urbanisation could be redressed, that 'we may live together in society and not the sooner die.' As he once put it: 'The modern industrial revolution brought people together with disastrous results. To sanitation belongs the task of showing how men may live in cities and be healthy.' His faith was that sanitation could accomplish as much as socialism could, and offered a quicker route. Quoting Charles Lamb's essay on roast pig, he commented: 'We can get roast pig without burning the house down.' [17]

Conversion to Liberal Unionism signified no shift to the right in Russell's thinking. The new party was anxious to maintain a separate identity from the Conservatives. Its members linked imperial unity with social reform, equated the Empire with jobs, and were sympathetic to trade union rights.[18] Though derided by their opponents as 'self-sufficient, superior people who know everything better than anyone else,' [19] they included not just members of the whiggish tendency but radicals like W. R. W. Smith and Robert Crawford. These men believed, as Russell did, in strong local government, and in the 1890s some of them were to play a leading role in Glasgow's great age of municipal enterprise – which some of them were even content to refer to as municipal socialism. Joseph Chamberlain, the pioneer of civic power, had after all led the way by leaving the Liberals. His followers in Glasgow saw no contradiction between strong imperial rule and strong municipal government.

This meant that for a time Russell was able to continue his efficient working partnership with key town councillors. All the same, he was now operating from a narrower political base. He had thrown in his lot with a party which was dominated by business interests and branded by critics as 'either Lords or Whigs' whose aim was to 'keep the people down and dole out gifts of charity to them.' [20] Politics were becoming more polarised along class lines, and eventually this would make Russell's position harder to sustain. For better or worse he had taken a different path from his old friend James Bryce, by now a junior Minister, whose cogent advocacy of Irish Home Rule had raised him in Gladstone's esteem.

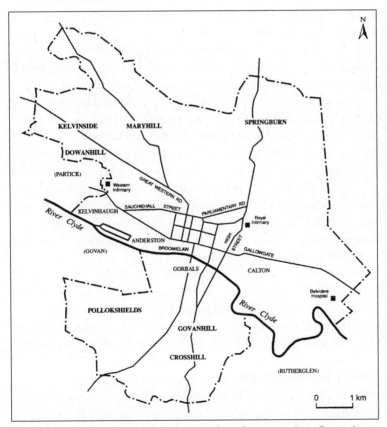

Map 2. Glasgow in 1892, after the great boundary extension of 1891 (see Chapter 15). Broken line shows boundary.

Chapter Fifteen

That Pale Multitude

We would preach the gospel of cleanliness, fresh air, and sunshine, from a new text.

THE 1890s were Glasgow's great era of municipal enterprise, when it throbbed with the kind of civic energy earlier associated with Joseph Chamberlain's Birmingham. The local economy was booming again. Public trust in the civic leadership, which had been torn to pieces by the City of Glasgow Bank failure and associated scandals, was on the mend. A mood of almost cosmopolitan confidence had been inspired by Glasgow's International Exhibition of 1888, with its electric lighting, switchback railway, and oriental pavilions full of whirring new machinery. The exhibition ground became known for the duration as Baghdad on the Kelvin, but civic pride found more durable expression soon afterwards with the opening of the imposing new City Chambers in George Square – a suitable command post for a local authority that was extending both its territorial boundaries and its sphere of activitiy. The Town Council, which had now matured into Glasgow Corporation, was reaching out and taking charge of everything from electricity supplies to telephone services – not out of ideological conviction but because it made good business sense.

The outside world was suitably impressed. American delegations arrived to inspect the model muncipality, to learn from the municipal trams, parks, libraries, baths and steamies, and to tour the municipal markets, the municipal farms, and the workshops where the Corporation built its own fire apparatus and tramcars.

The trams, municipalised in 1894, were the showpiece. American delegations were told of their significance for public health as a means of bringing the countryside nearer to the city.[1] American progressives also interested themselves in the milk regulations, and in the municipal provision for fever treatment.

A professor from Columbia University, New York, declared that he knew of nothing in the United States comparable to Belvidere Hospital.[2] A Midwestern mayor commented that Glasgow was 'immensely modern' like Chicago, but that unlike Chicago it had cleansed itself, and its slaughterhouses bore no relation to Upton Sinclair's muckraking novel *The Jungle*, with its shocking revelations of conditions in the stockyards.[3]

Russell helped to forge this special relationship. At the request of his old friend James Bryce he gave a briefing to Dr Albert Shaw, American journalist and reformer,[4] who became 'the best publicist the city of Glasgow ever had.' Shaw's chapter on Glasgow was the longest in his book on municipal government, and he remarked that 'these new municipal undertakings find their true center in the bureau of the medical officer of health' which produced the critical statistics.[5]

Shaw and other transatlantic visitors found in Russell an administrator who was familiar with the public health scene in their own country. Ever since his visit to the U.S. in 1880 he had kept in touch with developments, constantly comparing Glasgow's mortality statistics with those of the big American cities and citing the example of New York and Boston health boards in his quest for summary powers.[6] Russell's professionalism, together with the business background of Robert Crawford, the health committee convener, also reassured American visitors that reform was good for business rather than the first step towards socialism.

Both men displayed a blend of pragmatism and idealism which must have appealed to transatlantic progressives. It was this that helped to make Crawford, through his lecturing and writing, influential in the U.S. He became the chief exponent of Glasgow's brand of municipal government, its publicist and philosopher at home and abroad. Though never a Lord Provost himself, he was rumoured to be the *éminence grise* behind Lord Provost John Muir in the early 1890s.[7] Crawford himself was deeply influenced by Russell, whom he always referred to as his 'chief.' The two were in almost daily contact during Crawford's two decades on the Health Committee, which he once described as 'years of intense conviction, burning desires, and remarkable progress in the development of Glasgow towards a clean and healthy life for all its citizens.' This 'period of incandescence' had produced, Crawford said, 'a revolution in my whole outlook on the world and its affairs.'[8] Like Russell, he viewed public health within a broad context of civic well-being. Though cheerfully contradicting himself when in full rhetorical flight, Crawford seemed to share Russell's views of socialism – he applauded its 'divine instinct' but condemned its 'destructive fury.'[9] Like his 'chief' he was idealistic and on occasion visionary; he once said that he felt running within him 'the lifeblood of a great city.' He had dreamt of a city, he said, to which the sun would have constant access, through which its river ran clear as crystal, in which the streets were always clean and the people always happy and joyous, 'every man and woman thinking more of the whole community than himself.'[10] This sounds like a somewhat overblown version of Russell's ideal of a city that was as healthy as the countryside, with streets that were corridors for country air.

Russell's own power was at its peak. He and his allies had always argued for strong muncipal rule. They had established a municipal monopoly of hospital treatment for fever and through their enthusiasm for law-making had contributed to what Robert Crawford proudly described as 'a code of special laws bulky and intricate enough to serve for the government of a small kingdom.'[11] In the early 1890s, when these measures reached the Statute Book, Russell enjoyed greater authority than he had ever known – summary powers to close unhealthy houses, or to order improvements to be made. The new powers were rapidly utilised. By the end of 1895 the Health Committee, acting on Russell's recommendation, had closed 288 dwellings, mostly one-room and two-room houses, including such revealingly named properties as Piggie Close in Rottenrow.[12] Negligent proprietors were ordered to remedy bad drains and structural defects, or to deal with foul and uncovered cisterns which were being used 'for dietetic purposes.'[13] Under the new police legislation, which made internal sanitation compulsory, lists of properties without water closets or sinks were submitted fortnightly to the Health Committee with recommendations for legal action against the owners. Brick stacks housing communal closets on each half-landing were tacked onto the back of tenements, so that by the end of the decade WCs were in more common use in Glasgow than in any other Scottish city or large town.[14] Tenants, too, had their duties, such as cleaning houses judged by Russell to be in a filthy or unwholesome condition. A threatened cholera outbreak was met not just with the usual burst of limewashing but with new by-laws providing for the cleaning of common stairs and closes by rota.[15] The results of all this activity could be dramatic, though one councillor may have exaggerated when he suggested that 'Paradise Regained' would be a suitable name for a property previously known as 'Beelzebub's Castle.'[16]

Russell's empire was expanding. The boundary extension of 1891, embracing many of the adjacent burghs and districts, increased the city's population by more than 90,000 and nearly doubled its territory. The sanitary inspectors had to be issued with tram tickets because the distances were too great to be covered on foot.[17] For Russell – whose own house remained just outside the new boundary line, in the recalcitrant burgh of Partick – the annexation meant a hugely increased workload. He had been strongly in favour of the move, and often pointed out that the exclusion of salubrious suburbs like Pollokshields distorted the city's mortality statistics. But the new territory was not all as leafy and prosperous as Pollokshields. There were properties in Maryhill (sometimes known as 'Clartyhill') with earth-floored privies flooded with urine. Equally bad conditions existed south of the river. In Govanhill, Crossmyloof, and Strathbungo combined privies and ashpits were to be found close to the windows of old properties.[18] Polmadie, where 89% of the population lived in houses of one or two rooms, attracted Russell's 'anxious attention' because its room density (2.7 persons) was higher than in any of the city districts.[19] Glasgow's weekly cleansing system was quickly extended to these areas, and priority was given to the abolition of drop privies.[20] The Sanitary Department had to be reorganised and the statistics adjusted; a new, suburban category was added to the four territorial groups which Russell used for comparative analysis.

It was time to demand help. In a memorandum to the Health Committee Russell called 'after mature reflection' for an assistant. It had become, he said, a physical impossibility for one man to discharge his statutory duties throughout greater Glasgow. His idea was that the assistant would have the authority to perform these duties, while Russell himself would be at the operational centre, receiving all notifications of infectious diseases and issuing information and instructions to the districts. When some councillors objected on the grounds that the MOH had already been given a salary increase on account of his added responsibilities, Robert Crawford responded by claiming that Russell's work had increased so much that he was 'likely to break down.' The resolution was passed by 21 votes to six. Russell and Crawford dealt with the applications. In December, 1891, the appointment of Archibald K. Chalmers was announced.[21]

Chalmers, then 35, was surgeon to an iron and steel company, and a former superintendent of Knightswood Hospital. Among his assets was a knowledge of the law – he had served an apprenticeship with a solicitors' firm in his native Greenock before distinguishing himself as a medical student at Glasgow University.[22] A surgeon-major in the field artillery branch of the Volunteers, Chalmers had a military bearing and a neat moustache and cut a very different figure from Russell, with his beard and his scholarly stoop. His terse, matter-of-fact writing style lacked Russell's literary opulence, but the two were alike in their philosophical approach to public health and their analytical grasp. In due course Chalmers would carry forward the tradition of Gairdner and Russell into the twentieth century – not least in his demonstration of the continuing connection between room density and the death rate.

The boundary extension cleared the way for an attempt to make the Clyde a little less like an open sewer. Down the years a variety of proposals had come to nothing because of the number of local authorities involved, and arguments over costs. Russell had taken part in successive investigations into the problem. In the 1870s he had twice gone on deputations to various English cities, examining outfall stations, precipitation works, and sewage farms, and admiring the mangel wurzels cultivated with the help of Birmingham's best sludge. Once he had gone on an inspection tour with Dr William Wallace, Glasgow's city analyst, who proved to be a quietly congenial companion as well as a valued instructor in chemistry. Both had put their names to a report describing the condition of the Clyde as shameful and looking forward to a day when salmon would again leap in the river, the banks would be beautified by the innumerable villas of city merchants, and citizens could stroll by the riverside or take boat trips without having their senses 'shocked by pestilential odours.'[23]

Sanitary improvements had actually made the problem worse, in the short run. By the early 1890s well over 100,000 WCs were connected with drains discharging into the harbour – and the smell sometimes reached Russell's house in Partick.[24] Measures to prevent cholera were improvised after an outbreak in several English cities. The sewer pipes were lengthened to prevent the formation of stagnant pools, and a police constable was put on duty on the banks of the Clyde near Belvidere Hospital to prevent bathing.[25] But a more satisfactory solution was on the way. The Caledonian Railway Company undertook the realignment of the sewers when constructing their under-ground Glasgow Central line, which ran roughly parallel to the river. The sewage of about one-fifth of the city was conveyed by this system to new municipal treatment works at Dalmar-nock, which were soon judged to be a great success. Lord Provost James Bell noted that 'perhaps no better testimony to the generally innocuous character of the effluent can be cited than the fact that the works' manager had kept live goldfish in it apparently in perfect health for several months.'[26]

Meanwhile Russell and the Health Committee were using every available power to try to staunch the flow of industrial waste into the sewers. 'Dr Russell has been all over our works recently,' reported the management of the St Rollox chemical factory, now part of the world's biggest chemical empire but still up to its old tricks.[27] He had also visited Custom House Quay, where the St Rollox discharge 'was distinctly perceptible to my senses,' and had interviewed the captain of the S.S. *Penguin*, the master of a lighter, the driver of a steam crane, and a constable of the Marine Division, 'all of whom spoke very emphatically of the offensive, and at times intolerable, smells given off from the discharge of the pipe.' With masters of vessels complaining that they were unable to sleep on board because of the foul stink, the company was forced to take action and pipe the noxious liquid down to the river bed.[28]

Glasgow, with its thrusting municipal government and array of statutory powers, was ideally placed to play a leading role in the anti-tuberculosis crusade of the 1890s. No other city, in the early 1890s, had local powers for the control of milk as a medium for the spread of bovine tuberculosis. Glasgow's strong public health movement may also help to explain why its death rate from respiratory tuberculosis declined faster in the late nineteenth century than the rates for other Scottish cities and very much faster than those for English cities.[29]

By the late 1890s Russell had become an internationally recognised authority on the prevention of this dreaded disease, which struck down thousands of young adults and devastated their families – as had happened in Russell's own case. Yet he had not been prominent in the initial stages of the anti-tuberculosis campaign, which followed the discovery of the tubercle bacillus by the German bacteriologist Robert Koch in 1882. By demonstrating that the disease was infectious and not hereditary, as had been widely believed, Koch's discovery brought tuberculosis for the first time within the province of preventive medicine, but it was only gradually that the implications worked their way through to health management. Russell was not among the advance guard of MOHs – notably James Niven of Oldham – to launch campaigns against the disease; and when finally he took action it was at the prompting of the Medico-Chirurgical Society, which seized the initiative in 1891 by calling for preventive measures and public information. The signatories, headed by Russell's friends William Gairdner and Joseph Coats, made a point of referring to 'the splendid sanitary organisation which Glasgow possesses.'[30]

Russell, immersing himself in the medical literature, much of which he read in the original German, took almost four years to reply to their request. He was playing a waiting game until the numerous investigations prompted by Koch's discovery had been concluded. Better to delay, he maintained, than to react too quickly because 'in the enthusiasm naturally inspired by a new discovery, there is always an element of danger.'[31] Yet he was not dragging his feet. Like other progressive MOHs in London and elsewhere he had been conducting a covert campaign against pulmonary tuberculosis, or consumption, for many years.[32] As a former student of Lister's he was naturally among the many doctors who suspected that pulmonary tuberculosis was infectious long before Koch's discovery put the matter beyond doubt. He must have discussed the subject often with his friend Joseph Coats, who as pathologist to the Western Infirmary was investigating bovine tuberculosis.

Glasgow's unique small-area statistics, based on the 24 sanitary districts established by Gairdner, put Russell in a position to make his own investigations into consumption. By the early 1880s, before the discovery of the bacillus, he was noting the correlation between consumption and room density (and even air-space, to take account of the higher ceilings in newer working-class homes). If the word tuberculosis never featured in his regular reports of that time, this was because it was a taboo subject as long as the disease was popularly supposed to be hereditary. An awareness of the disease, however, was implicit in his repeated reminders of the virtues of fresh air and good ventilation, and in the way his campaign to close uninhabitable houses focused on dark and damp dwellings. In a public health lecture in 1881 he described sunlight as 'a universal disinfectant' which could destroy bacteria and warned his listeners to 'have no dark places inside your houses, which may be haunted not by imaginary ghosts, but by these microscopic impurities.'[33] Tuberculosis was not mentioned in this address, but the words anticipate his reply 15 years later to the Medico-Chirurgical Society petitioners which declared that 'sunlight is the only disinfectant which sustains the man while it kills the microbe.'[34] Russell's campaign for parks and playgrounds in the city centre predated his declaration that every park, every playground was a precaution against consumption. He also gave priority to ventilation and daylight in a report on overcrowding in workshops.[35]

He must also have had tuberculosis in mind when pushing for stronger legislation to bring the milk and meat trades under sanitary control. He was aware of the claims by Joseph Coats that food was the probable source of infection among the huge number of children under 10 who died of this disease.[36] Russell attempted to tackle this problem long before the Medico-Chirurgical petitioners drew up their demands. In 1889 the Town Council won a test case over its condemnation of the sale of tuberculous meat, and in the following year powers of seizure and prosecution were inserted at a late stage into the new Glasgow Police Act.[37] This put Glasgow in an exceptionally strong position to prevent the sale of infected meat and milk.

Russell's attempts to make the most of the new powers soon made him as unpopular with farmers, dairymen, and butchers as he was with builders and factors. 'They discover Glasgow everywhere mining and countermining, adding a deeper tinge of black to the cloud of agricultural depression, ruining the trade of the meat salesman, thwarting the speculations of the butcher, invading the prerequisites of the veterinary surgeon,' he complained.[38] He also parted company with other local authorities on the question of meat inspection. Glasgow was unrepresented at a conference of Scottish local authorities at which a clearing-house system was adopted. Russell thoroughly disapproved. He thought this 'most mischievous to the consumer' because the carcases were already carved up at the point of inspection, making detection difficult because the principal evidence was in the viscera. Much of the meat, Russell insisted, would be 'dubious rubbish' bought by the carrion butcher who took the risk of selling bad meat. Ideally Russell would have liked a system of public slaughter houses, but since this was not a practical proposition he adopted the detective system. Inspectors watched railways stations, wharves, and carriers' quarters, intercepted horse-lorries and suspicious-looking butchers' carts on the streets, searched the vehicles for clandestine consignments from unscrupulous suppliers, and travelled to the country to interview farmers and veterinary surgeons. Dubious mince and suspect sausages were seized from the shops of low-class butchers. The missing quarter of a cow confiscated in Glasgow was found buried in the dunghill of a suburban butcher. Even at the best of times Russell found meat traders frustrating people to deal with because of their artificial concept of meat. 'To the butchers,' he remarked, 'tongues and sirloins, rumps and quarters, chops and steaks are things which are knocking about the world as God made them.'[39]

Suppliers of milk (actually a much more significant source of bovine tuberculosis) received similar treatment. Russell's advice to farmers, 'The Sanitary Requirements of a Dairy Farm,' published in 1889,[40] was a sign that he meant business, and soon afterwards the new Police Act provided for the elimination of tuberculous cows from Glasgow, which still had 100 byres, and the surrounding countryside. The first inspection took place at a dairy farm at Carstairs, near Lanark, in 1891 when it was reported that 'one brown and white cow looks ill' and tuberculosis was diagnosed.[41] Armed with his new statutory powers, Russell continued his long-established policy of intervention in farms where infection was suspected. He pursued the owners of two Ayrshire farms even after they had stopped supplying milk to Glasgow – and was scathing when he discoverd that the factor of one of them was also member of the local council which was refusing to supply information to Glasgow.[42] Although seriously handicapped by Glasgow Corporation's slowness to appoint a veterinary inspector, Russell sometimes co-opted the principal of Glasgow Veterinary College in his investigations.

His response to the Medico-Chirurgical petitioners' call for preventive action was in effect a reaffirmation of existing practice. However, there was nothing perfunctory about the 12,000-word paper[43] which surveyed the main European and American reports, analysed the causes of the disease – unlike other authorities he thought that infected milk was at least as important as spitting – and examined possible lines of action. He took the opportunity to call (successfully this time) for the appointment of a city veterinary surgeon and to remind the various municipal committees of their responsibilities. The Parks Committee, he said, should see that the parks drew people from all classes of the community – 'flowers are wanted for some, music for others, but always space for the young.' The Dean of Guild Court should rigidly enforce the building regulations. The Magistrates Committee should not treat the anti-smoke laws and overcrowding rules as petty restrictions. The Tramways Committee should enforce the no-spitting rule.

His recommendations were comprehensive but conservative. Russell was opposed to the policies of the more enthusiastic disciples of Koch, whom he labelled 'the extremists.' He was against isolating consumptives in special hospitals, though in favour of hospices for advanced cases. He was against compulsory notification, as frequently recommended by the same experts, whose advice he regarded as a warning of the direction in which science, if applied indiscriminately, would move. Since 1890 local legislation had given him the power to remove any case of infectious disease to hospital, whether notifiable or not, and he had no desire to disturb the status quo. He wanted to avoid the middle-class hysteria then current in the West End of London, where consumptives were shunned because of the fear of infection. For Russell, this raised questions of personal liberty. The extremists, he claimed, were trying to 'out-Herod Herod' in their treatment of the consumptive: 'They would surround him with restrictions, and cover him with differential marks, which must make him almost as conspicuous in society as if he were clad in the grey gown and sounded the clapper of a medieval leper.'

Russell, with his passion for literature, was also mindful of the 'representatives of that pale multitude' who had enriched our culture – 'Keats, with all his golden store of verse; Chopin, tuneful throughout his long decline ... the frail, but fruitful, life of Stevenson.' He tried to imagine the consequences of such men being labelled as consumptives, forced to obey a code, confined to certain parts of the house, and made to abjure pocket handkerchiefs and keep their cutlery separate. His report emphasised instead the virtues of general hygiene and health education; and the 'natural disinfectants', sunlight and air. In his anxiety to persuade people that the only real danger lay in dust from sputum he seriously underplayed the risks of transmission by coughing.

This underemphasis was characteristic of the attempt by the British preventive movement to minimise social damage and avoid individual tragedies by presenting tuberculosis as a disease that could be kept at bay by domestic hygiene and sanitary measures. Such caution delayed the adoption of compulsory notification and new preventive techniques, but it enabled

Russell and others to reinforce their arguments for environmental improvements. The indications are that mortality from consumption, as a disease closely linked to poverty, was significantly reduced by general sanitary measures of the kind also directed against other infectious diseases. Russell, recognising that mortality was falling because of greater resistance to the disease rather than reduced exposure, was in no doubt that 'the higher the standard of public health, and especially the sounder the lungs of the population, the fewer will succumb.'[44] While this would not explain the mortality decline, which was general throughout the industrial world, it helps to explain its exceptional speed in Glasgow from an early stage in the sanitary movement. During the last three decades of the century mortality fell in Scotland by 40% and in Glasgow by 55%, from an even higher level.[45]

The specifics of his tuberculosis memorandum were probably less important than the boost that it gave to his drive for improved living conditions and better public education, with particular emphasis on sunlight and pure air. Soon regarded as a standard work, it attracted widespread interest, particularly in the United States, where it was issued as a State paper by Massachusetts, one of the most advanced states in public health provision.[46]

As Russell himself was aware, the decline of other infectious diseases may have helped to raise resistance to tuberculosis. Some had been almost defeated by the 1890s, in Glasgow as elsewhere. The two remaining typhus wards at Belvidere Hospital were often empty.[47] Cholera was a distant memory, although the limewashers were out in force during the scare of 1893;[48] and an outbreak in St Petersburg caused such concern about the number of Russians passing through Glasgow en route for the United States that a special sanitary inspector was appointed to keep a watch on the lodging houses where emigrants stayed. Common lodging houses were likewise the target during recurrent smallpox outbreaks in the 1890s,[49] when Russell also negotiated a controversial agreement with the prison authorities for the vaccination of all unvaccinated inmates – and for the others the offer of revaccination at municipal expense. He defended this policy on the grounds that the main source of infection was the criminal population, 'largely interfused with the tramp element.' [50] Against critics who wanted the tramps to be supervised and their movements restricted, he argued that vaccination was quicker, cheaper, and more practical.

As these old enemies were being beaten into retreat, a new menace appeared – influenza. 'This mysterious disease', as Russell called it, had been making its way across Europe and reached Glasgow in 1890. [51] It caused many deaths in the foggy winter of 1891, when the mortality rate from respiratory disease reached its highest level since 1877. Russell, who was accused by some councillors of being alarmist in his warnings, realised that hospital treatment was pointless as a community health measure. Nevertheless he sometimes sent lodging-house dwellers or the children of tramps to Belvidere on humanitarian grounds, just as he sometimes did with measles and chicken pox cases. 'Humanity makes one glad,' he remarked, 'when an excuse can be found in their diseases to send them to hospital.' [52]

The struggle against childhood diseases was still having mixed results. Scarlet fever was becoming less virulent. Diphtheria, despite a surge in 1893–4, rose less alarmingly in Glasgow than in London and elsewhere, which Russell thought might have something to do with the Sanitary Department's policy of co-operation with the School Board. Mortality declined after the introduction of anti-toxin treatment for diphtheria in 1894 although sanitary measures undoubtedly also played their part. But whooping cough and measles were another matter. Whooping cough remained in Russell's words 'the most formidable infectious disease known to Glasgow.' More than half the registered cases in the first half of the 1890s resulted in death, and while the rate dropped to a third in the second half of the decade, so many more children caught the disease that the deaths were more numerous. Measles, which was responsible for more than 6000 deaths during the decade, followed a similarly depressing pattern. Russell's main strategy was to persuade the infant departments of city schools to close their doors when pupils were infected, but many of the cases were under school age. As well as causing the highest short-term morality rates in the city, measles contributed indirectly to the statistics by leaving the survivors more susceptible to lung disease, which in the 1890s continued to account for an increasing proportion of deaths.[53] All the same, Russell's anti-measles campaign was at least responsible for damage-limitation. Mortality from the disease declined slightly during his years as MOH, in contrast with a rise in Scotland as a whole.

More surprising than the toll taken by these diseases, for which no effective drug treatment existed, was the alarming rise in mortality from diarrhoeal diseases, including dysentery, among children under five. Not all the cleansing and scavenging, limewashing and hosing, milk controls and modern conveniences could prevent the deaths of more than 2000 infants under the age of one from this 'filth' disease in the course of the decade, and almost 1000 deaths among children between one and five. In the second half of the decade the death rate among infants was as bad as it had been before the introduction of Loch Katrine water.[54]

Difficulties associated with the introduction of WCs provide part of the explanation. During what the Sanitary Department called the 'educational period' the WCs, which were shared by four or five families, were often choked with debris of all kinds. The water commissioners sometimes refused to provide a sufficient volume for the flushing of WCs on stair landings. Spillages were identified as the cause of a rise in enteric fever. It hardly helped, either, that the hosing of backcourts was replaced by sweeping when the WCs were installed, until the Health Committee realised the dangers. Another problem was that the doors of private WCs leading off courts and closes were often broken into by passing tradesmen and tram drivers who had been accustomed to making use of tenement privies. 'Round the Cross and along Argyle Street every privy was virtually a public privy,' Russell pointed out. The change, he added, had been much to the advantage of the householders, but greatly to the inconvenience of the public.[55]

His own explanation for the 'summer plague' was that sanitary reform 'does not so intimately reach the environment of the child as of the adult.' Domestic cleanliness and maternal control, he claimed, were what counted. Environmental improvements benefited older children, but for the infants 'the mother is after all the domestic sanitary inspector.'[56] During the hot late-summer weather overcrowded single-ends easily became breeding grounds for flies (not yet identified as a cause of contaminated food). Exceptionally hot weather in the late 1890s was associated with a general rise in infant diarrhoea throughout urban Scotland.[57] And, as always, it was in slum tenements that the disease was rife. In Port Dundas and Gorbals the death rate from the disease was double the city average.

The summer plague largely accounted for a rise in infant mortality in the late 1890s despite a continued fall in the mortality of adults and even of children aged one and over. Glasgow's rate – 149 deaths per 1000 births for the decade – was much worse than the Scottish one, although the gap had narrowed considerably and the rate was now much better than England's. Even more striking than the disparities among the infant death rates in various districts was the exceptionally high mortality among the babies of unmarried mothers[58] – a discrepancy which Russell had recorded in his early days as MOH and which was general throughout the country. Russell attributed it in part to the lack of legal protection for very young children from neglect by guardians, although obviously the anomaly must also have reflected the severe social and economic disadvantages of unmarried mothers. He also frowned upon the growing practice of bottle-feeding because of the inferior milk on sale in the worst areas of the city and poor supplementary diet (not only in the poorer districts). 'A woman who can suckle her child, and will not, increases a hundred-fold the risk that child runs of losing its life, and, should it die, to that extent causes its death,' Russell warned in his hints on child management.[59]

But the problem was largely beyond his resources: it awaited twentieth-century solutions in the form of antenatal care, child welfare, and medical advances.[60] In one respect, though, Russell helped to point the way forward to the new era of public health – through his backing for the emergent science of bacteriology. As well as helping Professor John Glaister to advise Glasgow University on the setting up of a public health laboratory,[61] he persuaded the Sanitary Department that it should have one of its own. Later, Russell would also be involved with some of the wider questions of health and welfare that opened up with the dawn of the new century – but not as Medical Officer of Health for Glasgow.

Chapter Sixteen

The Old Order Changes

*I fancy that as it is nowadays in war, so the armament of
sanitation will tend to greater scientific precision and
complication, and its methods to greater refinement.*

ARMED with an unprecedented array of statutory powers, Russell was at the height of his authority in the mid-1890s. Public health was now a recognised function of local government throughout the country, and Glasgow's pioneering role was acknowledged. As medical officer of the model municipality Russell had established an international reputation. It must have been widely assumed that he would stay at his post for the remainder of his career.

Approaching 60, he had begun to look venerable, with his grey beard and balding head. His way of life remained austere, except that he had uncharacteristically taken up cigarette-smoking (he was later to give it up). With his work, his public lectures, his court appearances as an expert witness, and medical conferences all over the country, he had only limited time to spend with his children, although at the evening meal he would insist on hearing about their daily activities. In 1894, however, he became much concerned about his middle child, Mary. A tall, thin girl, who was always losing her glasses and was acutely conscious of her large feet, Mary hardly conformed to the Victorian ideal. Less spirited than her younger sister, Helen, she was less able to stand up to her father, and family life left her with a lifelong sympathy for middle children. After attending the recently established Park School for girls, Mary enrolled in a domestic science course, but at the age of 19 suffered a nervous breakdown and was advised by her father's friend and physician, Dr Samson Gemmell, to go on a Continental tour.

Accompanied by her Aunt Jessie (her mother's sister) and a young cousin, she set off from Central Station for Holland, Belgium, Luxembourg, and France. Throughout the tour, in the

spring and early summer of 1894 she kept a diary [1] which was
almost as detailed, if not as dramatic, as the one her father had
kept at about the same age, on his Atlantic Cable voyage. In
the Ardennes she met a couple from the West of Scotland who
knew Russell's name well, but what struck her was simply how
small the world was (as it also proved to be in Paris, when she
and her Aunt saw Joseph Chamberlain walking round a picture
gallery). Russell wrote to his daughter during her tour, and
sent a postcard to Paris to ask why she had not written. But
she knitted socks for his 57th birthday and, following the advice
of the Paris postal authorities, sent them to Glasgow in two
parcels so that they could be classed as samples and cost her
less. She also bought a cigarette-rolling machine and was taught
by the shopkeeper how to use it so that she could save her
father the expense of buying cigarettes in boxes. Still emotion-
ally fragile, she was thrown into turmoil when advised to extend
the tour. After a 'dear, dear helpful letter' from her Aunt Agnes,
who still kept house for her father in Foremount Terrace, she
remarked: 'Oh, dear, how often I wish I were more obedient,
loving and helpful to those dear ones at home, for I never will
be able to repay them for all the thought, anxiety and trouble
I have caused them, not even in performing my filial duty
towards them.'

Russell was travelling too. When in need of respite from the
problems of overcrowded Glasgow, he felt instinctively drawn
to the wide open spaces of North America. He travelled on the
transcontinental railroads and once stayed with an Ontario
farmer, 'a stalwart old Scotchman' who years before had cleared
his space in the backwoods and built a log house. Russell was
fascinated by his stories of bears, Indians, and the privations of
pioneer life. He went into the forest to watch the old man 'hew
at a tree until it fell with a crash which shattered the stillness
of the forest' and mused about the romance as well as the
hardships of pioneer life.[2]

More hectic was his visit to Budapest in the autumn of 1894
to attend the International Hygiene Congress – a huge and
ill-organised jamboree whose widely scattered meeting places
signposted in Hungarian 'necessitated long walks and tiresome
ascents and descents of stairs.'[3] The hot weather 'made this

exertion irksome and fatiguing', and what made it worse was that most of the interest was concentrated on a few lectures given in overcrowded rooms, while others remained empty.

But among the 2500 conference-goers there was a buzz of excitement about the latest developments in bacteriology. There was much talk about how the definition of hygiene had to be widened to include preventive medicine. Speakers like Professor Edward Seaton, of St Thomas's Hospital, London, emphasised that the public had to be made to understand the need for systematic observation and research bearing on public health.[4] There was discussion of the possibility of artificially producing immunity from infectious diseases. Dr Emile Roux, who had recently discovered the diphtheria bacillus, 'astonished the Congress with the recital of the efforts of his work in vaccinating.' In view of the arguments then raging on the relationship between diphtheria and insanitary conditions Russell was interested to hear him conclude that the natural habitat of the bacillus was dirt and darkness. This meant, he reported to the Health Committee, that 'we were referred back to our old warfare against dirt and darkness.' The discussion also reinforced his conviction that 'a bacteriological and chemical laboratory is an indispensable adjunct of a municipal sanitary department.'

Russell gained the impression in Budapest that public health on the Continent lagged behind Britain 'so that we cannot say there is much in general to be learned by us.' He and the two Health Committee members who accompanied him did, however, find much to learn from Budapest's tramway system, which unlike Glasgow's was electrified. After making an inspection they noted the particulars for the benefit of the Corporation's Tramways Committee.

Along with other conference-goers Russell was invited to a reception at Count Esterhazy's castle outside the city. The event was described in the *Glasgow Herald* by a 'special correspondent' who is highly likely to have been Russell. Budapest at that time was rivalling Vienna as the leading city of the Austro-Hungarian Empire, and the article expressed unease at the military display all around. Even the ticket collector on the train to the castle came marching in with a sword. 'One hardly feels comfortable,' noted the correspondent, 'especially if one has lost his ticket among the multitude of papers which a Congressist carries.'

There were more uniforms at the castle – 'porters and footmen in magnificent military uniforms of blue; 50 gamekeepers in military uniforms of green, and the head game keeper dressed like a general.' The visitors inspected the stables, racecourse, deer park and vineyards, savoured 'the pleasure of being allowed to pluck the ripe blue grapes from the vine,' not to mention the estate's own wines. The Glasgow contingent, while listening to the 'seductive strains of Dvorak' as they sipped, amused themselves by watching the amount of wine being consumed by their Continental colleagues. The Count and his permanent company of actors gave a theatrical performance, after which 'actresses did their best to entice us all to eat and drink, and it was a most humorous sight to witness grey and grey-headed sires clicking glasses and cracking jokes with the gaudily dressed performers.' The British visitors expressed their appreciation by singing 'For He's a Jolly Good Fellow' and 'with many "hip-hip hurrahs", all of us somewhat elated, we were driven back to the station.'[5]

Russell also attended less exotic conferences, and was prominent in their public health sections. He was president of this section at the British Medical Association's conference in Bournemouth in 1891 – an occasion which stirred sombre thoughts, to judge by the lines pencilled on the back of his conference agenda:

> *Looks he also wistfully on to the long burial aisle of the Past, where only winds and their low, harsh moan give inarticulate answer!*

and

> *Obedience is our universal duty and destiny.*

In Budapest Russell had witnessed the excitment and ferment of a new era in public health. In Glasgow the dawn of the new age was symbolised by the elaborate ceremony accompanying the laying of the foundation stone of the new Sanitary Chambers in Montrose Street in the summer of 1895. The Sanitary Department had not moved to the new City Chambers in George

Square lest some of its widely assorted visitors spread infectious diseases, but its importance was reflected in the design for the new building – 'in the style of a modified Italian renaissance,' and with a bacteriological laboratory and heating by steam pipes. On the morning of the ceremony the windows of nearby ware-houses were crowded with onlookers. In Montrose Street, lines of flags and streamers fluttered in the June sunshine. After the ceremony, which was performed on a crimson-lined platform in the middle of the site, speakers recalled the old days over the official lunch in the City Chambers. The first Sanitary Office in Montrose Street, it was recalled, had been purchased for £180 compared with the £17,000 being spent on the new premises. In those days the sanitary inspectors had numbered 43; now they had increased fourfold to 172. Robert Crawford, speaking as Health Committee convener, was applauded when he spoke of the 'great victory over stubborn and ignorant public opinion, which persisted in ascribing to Providence diseases and death which were the result of dirt and neglect.' The people, he said, had been led to an understanding that 'the doctrine of soap and water' was a good doctrine and worth paying for, and now they were living 'in an atmosphere with every throb of it progressive and not retrograde.' Russell, too, came in for praise: infectious diseases, said one councillor, were 'treated in a manner which made Dr Russell's name second to none in this country.'[6]

But Russell was not there to hear it. His health was apparently buckling under the strain of work. He was confined to bed for much of the summer – and took advantage of the enforced solitude to write a sanitary history of Glasgow, hailed by one reviewer as 'a romance of sanitation.'[7] A few weeks after com-pleting it, in the autumn of 1895, he took official leave on doctors' orders, just as he had done in 1880. A certificate signed by his friends Samson Gemmell and Hector Cameron, and by William Snodgrass, a Glasgow University physiologist who specialised in 'nerve cells', was read to the Health Committee by Robert Crawford. The nature of the illness was not recorded in the committee minutes but the doctors expressed the opinion that a rest period of at least six months, especially if spent in a less rigorous climate, would 'result in his complete restora-tion.'[8] Perhaps the smoking was intended to soothe his nerves.

Nine months later, though back at work, Russell was 'still in rather unstable equilibrium.' One morning Samson Gemmell, correctly guessing his friend's intentions, dropped in to the Sanitary Office to forbid him to attend the jubilee banquet for Lord Kelvin, who had completed half a century in the Chair of Natural Philosophy.[9] 'I have to walk circumspectly, both literally and metaphorically,' he explained in a warm letter of congratulation to Kelvin. He declined an invitation to preside over the congress of the British Institute of Public Health at Glasgow University later that summer, but agreed to be president of its preventive medicine section provided that no one expected him to give an address. When the time came, however, he asked to be excused if he 'violently took possession of a portion of the time of the section to read a paper on the subject of contagion.' In this controversial paper he contended that disease-producing microbes could not survive in sewers, a conclusion which was instantly challenged by Sir Charles Cameron, who was a Glasgow MP as well as a doctor, and later questioned in the medical press.[10]

This was nothing to the controversy Russell was experiencing in his role as MOH. He had returned from his illness to face the biggest crisis of his career. At the Public Health Institute congress Glasgow was congratulated for having 'for many years taken a foremost place in all matters connected with public health', and Russell was lauded as 'a gentleman whose name is known the length and breadth of the land', but in Glasgow his position was becoming increasingly difficult. For a start, the Health Committee was not having things its own way. It was becoming more difficult to obtain local legislation. Crawford complained that post-prandial pledges of visiting politicians were writ on water – 'MPs have lauded us to the skies – especially at civic lunches.'[11] Often, too, the committee met with rebuffs in its attempts to influence national legislation. It had been so determined to influence the Food and Drugs Act, because of Russell's difficulties in obtaining convictions for contraventions, that it dispatched a shorthand writer to record a speech given to the London Chamber of Commerce by the only Scottish MP on the select committee on this subject. But the committee refused to hear Glasgow's witnesses on the grounds that they had read all their papers.[12] It was the same story when the city attempted to influence the new Scottish Public Health Bill. This landmark legislation, enacted in 1897, provided for the compulsory notification of infectious diseases – a practice already followed in Glasgow – but provoked much controversy by giving sanitary inspectors the same power as medical officers to decide what constituted a health nuisance. The Government dropped the first version of the legislation after Russell had described it as 'seriously prejudicial to the interests of public health' but was less yielding when the Health Committee used the same phrase about the second version and set about drawing up amendments. The Scottish Secretary, Lord Balfour of Burleigh, refused to meet the Glasgow delegation who had come to London to state their criticisms.[13]

Municipal politics, too, were becoming more difficult. Even as the admiring delegations were arriving from Boston and Chicago, the consensus underpinning municipal socialism was giving way. The Corporation was becoming more politicised. With the emergence of pro-labour political groups Conservatives and their sympathisers began to look askance at anything labelled municipal socialism and to question the costs of sanitary reform.[14] The middle of the decade brought a backlash against rising capital expenditure by the Sanitary Department – caused among other things by the decision to build a new hospital at Ruchill to absorb the pressure caused by compulsory notification of infectious diseases. One leading councillor wanted to delay river purification plans and objected to the practice of sending people who had been bitten by rabid dogs to Paris at the Corporation's expense for treatment at the Pasteur Institute.[15]

Sanitary expenditure was also questioned from the left, by a new breed of working-class Liberals. Some of these 'Lib-Labs' were on the Health Committee – men like John Battersby, compositor and leading member of Glasgow Trades Council, which had backed Keir Hardie in the Mid-Lanark by-election of 1888. Battersby once maintained that it would be a waste of public money for the Corporation to send representatives to a forthcoming sanitary conference in Newcastle for he had never heard a report worth listening to as the result of such events.[16] He and his allies, whose mission was to win better pay

and conditions for municipal employees, managed to block a
salary increase for Russell on the grounds that the Sanitary
Department's cleaners and street sweepers should have pay rises
first. Although not automatically opposed to Russell's policies,
the Lib-Labs were often at odds with his Liberal Unionist allies,
who were marked down as representatives of the moneyed
classes. The Liberal Unionists were in a somewhat vulnerable
position. The boundary extension had caused an influx of Liberal
councillors into Glasgow Corporation. The Liberal Unionists
remained a powerful force, thanks to such influential politicians
as Robert Crawford and David Richmond, but their share of
seats had declined.[17]

This weakened Russell's position in the final and most furious
controversy of his career as MOH. The issue was housing – a
subject close to Russell's heart. For years he and his allies had
been trying to stir the City Improvement Trust into action. In
the mid-1880s a small group of councillors, including Robert
Crawford, was elected to help Russell investigate the Trust's
slum properties – a survey which was later broadened to include
all the insanitary housing of the city. They were appalled by
what they saw – a rat-infested property in the Saltmarket with
stinking drains and a wet earthen floor; Trongate houses in
which every sink was used as a WC while the backcourts and
outhouse roofs were covered with excrement flung from the
windows.[18]

Their descriptions caused shock waves in the Town Council.[19]
One councillor said that a report of Russell's had revealed 'a
state of things most disgraceful in a city of boasted civilisation.'[20]
The sub-committee described some of the houses as being utterly beyond repair, a verdict underlined by Russell in his
evidence to the Royal Commission on the Housing of the Working Classes.[21] Though guarded in his responses to the searching
questions of the chairman of the commission, the radical politician Sir Charles Dilke, he did testify that the Trust owned 'some
of the worst property in town.' The Commission's report put
added pressure on the Trust to fulfil its social obligations by
building on its own account rather than merely making sites
available to private constructors, whose inadequacies Dilke skil-
fully exposed.[22] The idea had been mooted on the Town Council

from time to time by Russell's allies, but always with a negative response. 'There it is again – the usual "no, no!" complained Councillor W. R. W. Smith, who was a strong advocate of municipal building.[23] Robert Crawford accused the Trust of being more interested in the financial side of its affairs than in public health. He mocked those who claimed that strong drink rather than bad housing was the core problem. Referring to a tenement in Bridgegate, he said that even if they were to 'bombard the place with missionaries', they could not make it fit for human beings to live in.[24]

Finally the Trust relented and, as one local politician put it, dipped their hands in the mortar tub. Their early efforts were on a small scale and consisted of tenements for artisans rather than for the impoverished denizens of District 14, but the operation gained a new impetus when Councillor Samuel Chisholm became chairman of the Trust. Chisholm, a wholesale grocer from Dalkeith, was a man of strong personality who was seen by his opponents as autocratic and inflexible. He was a strong prohibitionist, with a loyal following among left-wing temperance supporters, and a sense of mission not only about temperance as the key to moral redemption but about housing. He had been influenced by Russell's lecture, 'Life in One Room', and when he became chairman of the City Improvement Trust set his mind to slum clearance and redevelopment.[25] The City Engineer was asked to draw up plans and Russell was consulted by the Trust about 'providing cheap, wholesome houses for the well doing poor,' which he was known to regard as a prerequisite of further slum clearance.[26] In June, 1896, the Corporation resolved to seek statutory power to acquire land for building.

So far, so good. Finally the Trust was being brought to life – and by a man who had been influenced by Russell. But soon things began to go very wrong. The lines of communication were weak. Russell, only recently returned to work after his illness, was not kept in touch with developments because the legislation was being drawn up by a sub-committee of the whole Corporation rather than of the Health Committee. Moreover John Carrick, the City Architect, with whom he had collaborated closely, had died in 1890 and had been replaced by A. B. McDonald, with the new title of City Engineer. When Russell

was finally shown McDonald's maps, in which 50 areas were
scheduled for development, he protested that they 'went far
beyond the scope of my consultation' and also 'beyond the
apparent sanitary necessities of the case.' He felt unable to give
the scheme his support until it had been submitted to the Health
Committee, but this was not to happen. Instead Russell received
'an urgent telegram' summoning him immediately to London
where Chisholm, the Town Clerk and the City Engineer were
putting the finishing touches to the draft legislation. The consent of the Medical Officer was required for the areas scheduled.
Immediately on receiving this summons Russell consulted Crawford, as Health Committee chairman. Crawford advised him to
stay at home. Russell stayed.[27]

He was now in a perilously exposed position. He and the
Health Committee had often opposed national legislation. Never
before had they attempted to block one of the Corporation's
own bills. It must have seemed almost perverse for them to
oppose a measure apparently designed to bring about a development for which they had been arguing for years. Yet Russell
and Crawford had their reasons. Although they had supported
the original idea, the final plan went far beyond what they had
been led to expect. It was a block plan for comprehensive
redevelopment which, they complained, cut across the work of
the Sanitary Department. Properties which they had painstak-
ingly sought to improve, dwellings in which water closets had
been installed at their insistence, were included in the red areas
on the city engineer's map. In a letter to the Town Clerk – the
formidable James Marwick – Russell pointed out that in several
of the properties workmen were at that moment 'carrying out
improvements at our instance.' He compared the proposal to a
surgical operation in which the physician who had looked after
the patient during long years of ameliorative treatment was to
have no say. 'I can scarcely say,' he added, 'how much I regret
to find myself an obstructive in the way of the Improvement
Trust, for the past work of which I entertain the deepest
gratitude.'[28]

Crawford was just as angry. Improvement Trust plans, he
insisted at a Corporation meeting, ought to be determined
primarily by the Health Committee: no other department should

be allowed to introduce confusion into their operations 'and paralyse the policy which had been going on for a good many years.' Their policies were being 'invaded' by the Chisholm plan, which he had originally thought was designed to give the Health Committee added powers to deal with some particularly difficult insanitary areas.

This attitude met with fury in some quarters of the Corporation. The Health Committee was accused of having acted in a most 'unconstitutional' and 'irregular' way in intervening through an official of the Corporation. Russell, one councillor insisted, owed as much loyalty to a sub-committee of the full Corporation as to the Health Committee, and to ignore that committee and report to another was 'quite irregular and unprecedented.' Samuel Chisholm provoked laughter in the City Chambers when he declared that the Health Committee had gone on a hunt for a mare's nest; they had gone tilting, he said, not against windmills, but against a phantom fortress of their own disordered imagination. Chisholm also argued that it was because Russell was unable (presumably because of illness) to help undertake a joint report that the City Engineer had had to draw up the plans on his own.[29]

The issue became politically polarised. The Lib-Labs moved onto the attack. John Battersby claimed that the Health Committee were simply afraid that their powers were being usurped. *The Glasgow Herald* agreed: 'The question with Dr Russell and the Health Committee seems to be not whether drastic treatment is called for but who should take charge of it.'[30] The Liberal Unionists and Conservatives backed Russell and mounted what was later described as 'perhaps the most violent opposition to which any legislative proposal of the Corporation has ever been subjected.'[31] Representatives of the wealthier suburbs, fearing a rates increase, joined them. For the first time Russell and his allies found themselves on what was apparently the unprogressive side of the argument. Yet this was not simply a power struggle. Russell and Crawford genuinely believed that public health was being given too low a priority in the Chisholm plan. They were not alone in this view. *The Glasgow Herald*, though unsympathetic to their cause, saw a 'conflict between the sanitary and aesthetic aspects.' Russell was also opposed to

Chisholm's idea of building the new houses in the city centre
rather than the suburbs, where land was cheaper and rents
would be lower (the idea of subsidised rents did not yet figure
in the argument).

The argument raged during the campaign for the watershed
municipal poll of 1896 – a 'general election' in which all seats
were contested after a ward redistribution resulting from the
boundary extension.[32] The Liberal Unionists fared badly. Having
once commanded almost a quarter of municipal seats, they were
left with a meagre 13%. They continued to exercise dispropor-
tionate influence through Russell's ally David Richmond, who
became Lord Provost – the last in a line of Liberal Unionists
to preside over municipal socialism because of dissent and wave-
ring in the Liberal ranks. But this time the waverers were fewer,
and the anti-Unionist cause was bolstered by the election of a
handful of pro-labour 'Stalwarts.' [33] Russell had also lost a powerful ally in Robert Crawford, who ended his municipal career at
that time. The heyday of the Health Committee was over. Lord
Provost Richmond manoeuvred to modify the Chisholm plan,
which passed into law in diluted form in the summer of 1897.
Half a dozen 'congested and insanitary areas' out of the original
50 were scheduled for clearing and rebuilding and the Corporation was empowered to spend up to £100,000 on land for
building. It was the signal for a phase of energetic house building
by the city. Before long there would be a ratepayers' backlash,
but meanwhile Samuel Chisholm had emerged as the coming
man for Lord Provost. He took over from Richmond in 1899.

But Russell had by that time left Glasgow. In 1898 he accepted
the invitation of the Local Government Board of Scotland, the
body which had replaced the Board of Supervision, to become
its Medical Member. This was not the first time of asking.
When the board was set up in 1894 the Liberal Secretary of
State for Scotland, Sir George Trevelyan, had tried to headhunt
him,[34] but according to one of Russell's contemporaries he 'feared
that so great a departure might be too much for his strength.' [35]
This version has always been accepted, but in fact Russell did
signal his willingness to accept the position. The trouble was
that by the time he did so it was too late. The Scottish Secretary
had already offered the job to someone else. In the autumn of

1894 Russell returned from Budapest to find a letter of apology from a highly embarrassed John Skelton, the chairman of the board, who expressed coded fury at Trevelyan and described the bungle as 'a public calamity.' Russell had either dithered too long, or changed his mind too late.[36]

When the post became vacant again in 1898 Russell's appointment was widely expected. As the *Bailie* commented: 'What with the regular duties pertaining to Dr Russell's present office, and the always-increasing worries entailed on its holder by Father Chisholm's new City Improvement Act – the end whereof no man can foresee – no surprise need be felt should he resolve on migrating to the capital.'[37]

The public health world held its breath. Every MOH in the country wanted Russell to be appointed, but there were fears that the Conservative Scottish Secretary, Lord Balfour, might make a political choice.[38] Already that year Russell's backers had met with a disappointment: Glasgow University could not afford to create a chair of public health as urged by William Gairdner, who undoubtedly had Russell in mind for the post.[39] Balfour, however, rose to the occasion. He chose his man on merit. The official announcement was made on October 4, 1898. Two days later Russell sat down to write his resignation letter to the Lord Provost.

'I can honestly say that I have served the Corporation with all my heart,' he wrote.[40]

Less than a week later he started his new duties in Edinburgh, leaving a typical trail of controversy behind him in Glasgow. The announcement of his appointment had been much delayed because of a disagreement over his terms. His age precluded him from entitlement to a Government pension, and Balfour thought that it was up to Glasgow to meet the need. He offered to 'feel the way' with Lord Provost Richmond, who responded positively, and on that basis Russell accepted the job.[41] But Richmond's proposal for an annual payment of £250 was savaged when it came before the Corporation. A substitute proposal for a £1000 honorarium was also attacked – some said it would be a subsidy to other employers, an inducement to poach Glasgow officials 'of most mature judgement and ripe experience.' Councillor Battersby questioned the legality of spending the ratepayers' money in this way. Dr James Erskine, an eye surgeon and radical Liberal, suggested that subscriptions should be raised to provide a proper testimonial, but added that some councillors were singing Russell's praises a bit too loudly. He pointed out that Loch Katrine water had done much to reduce the death rate in Russell's day. He 'certainly had not been a sort of sanitary saviour of the city.' But another doctor on the Health Committee, John Carswell, spoke in a very different vein. Thanks, he said, to Russell's philosophical insight and scientific acquirements, not only Glasgow but the whole human race had been put in possession of the first principles of public health. Russell, he added, had not merely done his public duty: he had devoted his days and nights to ascertaining the scientific principles underlying the mysterious process of contagion, and more than any man alive in this country or anywhere else, he had contributed to the sum of human knowledge on the subject. The honorarium proposal passed by two votes: Russell received his £1000.[42]

Leavetaking had its more agreeable side. The management and staff of the Western Infirmary gave a dinner to thank Russell for his efforts as a director and for his advice at times of crisis. Lord Kelvin was among the guests, and William Gairdner, in London on medical business, sent a telegram to say that Russell had made Glasgow's sanitary administration an object lesson to the whole world. In replying to the toast Russell said that he thought it right that hospitals for non-infectious diseases should be supported from charity rather than taxes or rates. 'Unless the alabaster box is broken by the hand of love,' he said, 'the very precious ointment will have no sweet odour.' He also recalled the testimonial he had received from his medical colleagues when applying for the post of MOH, and signed by some of those who were at the dinner. 'I preserve the original with pride,' he told them.[43]

An occasion that possibly touched him more deeply was his presentation from the Sanitary Department and fever hospital staffs, who gave him a tea service and an armchair ('for my *re*-clining years'). It was a time for reminiscing. Recalling the old farmer he had met in the Canadian backwoods, Russell reflected on the romance of pioneer life. 'As I, an old man, look now upon this assemblage, in its numbers and in the diversity of functions which it represents, and think of the material resources which it commands, the stringent and detailed statutes which it administers, and the genial and fostering atmosphere which surrounds its appreciated labours, I cannot but revert to the beginning of things,' he said.

He referred to 'the greybeards among you' as he recalled the old times. 'I am sure,' he said, 'that if those veterans were sitting together with me, our feet to the fender, smoking a friendly pipe, recalling all the incidents of the past, you younger men would soon learn that after all there is a romance about making bricks with straw.' He contrasted the old days with the humdrum present. 'What a glorious thing it is,' he declared, 'to have lived before the days of hospitals and hospital committees, when the enemy came in like a flood, and from sheer necessity all forms and punctilios of representative government were thrown aside ... No official will ever have such a time of unbridled liberty in Glasgow again. The days of romance are over.' Turning to 'men like Nicol and MacDiarmid and Macdougall, who have grown grey in the service as epidemic inspectors', he asked them to remember the days before compulsory notification, with the ceaseless search for information about infectious diseases which now came to them every morning by post with the regularity of rolls for breakfast. 'No more spying from afar the movements of doctors,' he said. He invited Nicol to remember the time when he had sent him up a ladder to remove a smallpox case through a Gallowgate window – 'and how near he was to being annihilated by a navvy, a brother of the patient.' Addressing another inspector, he recalled their adventures on the trail of milk infections: 'Mr Armstrong here could tell you of our drives in all sorts of weather, of our descents by train and gig upon remote farms.' He asked Mr Warnock, a meat inspector, to recall 'those picturesque excursions into remote regions ...; those nights in wayside inns; those exhumations from dunghills and discoveries in pigstyes ...'

Russell concluded, however, with a warning about the precariousness of what had been achieved since those days. Lack of vigilance, he said, could open the way for the return of infectious diseases. 'Apart from your efforts,' he told them, 'there is no inherent stability in the sanitary position which Glasgow has gained by strenuous and purposive effort.' [44]

For Russell, there was an unreality even about the current operations of the Sanitary Department. Finding himself back in the City Chambers after several weeks at his Edinburgh post, he felt like a spectator. 'All that has hitherto been familiar to my eyes and thoughts has been fading away, and giving place to new scenes, to new interests,' he confessed. 'The scene shifters have been busy on the stage of my life. Now, finding myself once more inside the Municipal Buildings, which have already begun to wear a look of mystery and strangeness, and face to face with the officials of the sanitary organisation in all of its departments, I am like one who closes his eyes upon the act which is in progress, or who in dreams wanders through the corridors of the past.'

The words echoed his sentiments of 40 years earlier, when he returned to his grandparents' home in Auburn Cottage after his adventures on the high seas: 'Now it is all over, and it seems like a dream, for memory dwells close to the shadowy boundaries of dreamland.'

Chapter Seventeen

Edinburgh

*Not only as to pauperism, but in all its relations, health is
cheaper than disease.*

Russell's Edinburgh home, a large corner villa in Braid
Road, Morningside, was on a grander scale than his
Glasgow terrace house. He named it Auburn, after the
cottage in Rutherglen where he had been brought up. The name
must have pleased his sister Agnes, who moved to Edinburgh
with him along with Russell's two daughters – his son, set on
a career in farming, had left home some years before. Since the
entry date for the new house was not until the spring of 1899,
Russell established temporary headquarters at Edinburgh
Hydropathic in Craiglockhart (destined for fame as a military
hospital in the First World War), travelling daily to the Scottish
Local Government Board's offices in George Street.

The Board had been in existence for four years when Russell
became its Medical Member. In a shake-up intended to make
Scottish welfare more democratic and accountable, less legalistic
and bureaucratic, it had replaced the Board of Supervision as
the central body responsible for administering the Poor Law
and public health, and at the same time the old parochial boards
were replaced by elected parish councils. These reforms followed
logically from the creation of the Scottish Office in 1885 (partly
in order to ward off Scottish nationalism at a time when Irish
Home Rule was on the agenda). The new Scottish Secretary
found himself answerable to Parliament for Scottish welfare but
without control over its administration. The anomaly was
removed when the new Board was set up in 1894 with the
Scottish Secretary as its president. The other members were
the Solicitor General, a chairman, a legal member, and a medical
member.[1]

This was the first time that the welfare policy makers had
included a medical man, and one with a powerful role to play.

Sir George Trevelyan, the Scottish Secretary and architect of
the reform – and the man who had tried to recruit Russell in
1894 – envisaged the chairman and the medical and legal members as his inner circle of administrative officers. Looking to the
Irish Local Government Board as a model, Trevelyan said that
what was wanted was 'men who are paid to give their whole
time and to be always on the spot, always able to carry out the
necessities of administration.'[2] There was violent opposition on
the grounds that the administration would be 'doctor-ridden' or
dominated by 'faddists,' but Trevelyan prevailed, with the backing of a sanitary lobby eager to follow the Continental model
of a public health administration under professional control.[3]
This was a complete change from the workings of the old Board
of Supervision, which was run by Edinburgh lawyers and Poor
Law officials who gave a higher priority to economy than to
public health.

Russell was 61 when he began his new work. His health was
deteriorating. The new post offered greater anonymity than his
Glasgow one which had exposed him to continual public controversy. But the move to Edinburgh was not a mere escape
route. It was not in his nature to seek an easy life. There was
logic to the transition. Russell had always looked beyond Glasgow's boundaries and sought to influence health legislation for
the whole of Scotland. He had constantly related the municipal
health statistics to trends in other parts of Scotland. Back in
the 1870s, tracing milk infections to their source in insanitary
farms, he had warned that the 'neglected nastiness' in the
countryside was a threat to the cities. He had tried to spur the
Board of Supervision to action and when this failed had taken
steps of his own to persuade rural authorities to appoint medical
and sanitary officers. With his allies on the Health Committee
he had campaigned to have the Board of Supervision replaced
by a more effective public health body. He considered the Board
an 'absurd executive' because its paramount concern was the
stringent administration of the Poor Law. 'The virtues of the
Poor Law become the rankest of vices when applied to the
administration of the Public Health Act,' he pointed out in 1881.[4]

Faced once with an audience of Poor Law administrators, he
seized the opportunity to point out their shortcomings. At the

Poor Law conference in Glasgow in 1884 he blamed his listeners for allowing England to outstrip Scotland 'in the business of health-seeking.' Whereas England's death rate was lower than 20 years previously, he told them, Scotland's was higher – and it was only the large towns, which vigorously enforced national legislation and supplemented it with local acts, that were keeping themselves abreast of progress in England. His listeners must have winced when he added: 'I think it is particularly pertinent to the business of a meeting such as this, of parochial authorities and officials, that I should specially direct their attention to the fact that it is in their hands that the stagnation, I would say retrogression, of one third of the population of Scotland has taken place.' After berating parochial officials for their failures in the rural areas he added: 'I wish I could take leave of you with more gracious words; but I cannot concuss these facts into any other conclusion.'[5]

The new Local Government Board was not the ideal solution to these problems. Many reformers had wanted a separate public health board which had nothing to do with Poor Law administration. Moreover the new Board turned out to be less radical than Trevelyan had intended. The old thinking still prevailed. Trevelyan's successor, the Conservative Lord Balfour of Burleigh, was much less keen on social experiment. He appointed a former Poor Law superintendent, Malcolm McNeill, as the Board's chairman and may well have had misgivings about recruiting Russell. The scene was set for a continued struggle between traditional exponents of the Poor Law and the advocates of a more modern approach to social welfare.[6] Russell's position prevented him from publicly taking part in the debate but he was well placed to influence events. Applying the principles that had guided him as Glasgow's MOH, he shifted public health administration away from the passive and bureaucratic policy associated with the Poor Law.

Russell had a 'keen and troubled' look as he threw himself into this work,[7] giving the lie to fears that his energies might be ebbing. His predecessor, Dr James McLintock, a former MOH for Lanarkshire, had been perfectly able but lacked Russell's experience and authority. The difference showed immediately. Public health loomed larger in the Board's annual report;

statistics blossomed. Medical officers of health as well as sanitary inspectors all over the country were bludgeoned into submitting annual reports. The reports came rolling in and Russell read them all – thousands of pages each year, which he carefully annotated. Soon he introduced forms so that standardised information could be gathered on births, deaths, and disease in the various districts. He demanded much more detail than his predecessor had done – not just general birth and death rates but the rates for individual diseases and for different age groups, and the percentage of cases treated in hospital. Just as he had done years before as a young MOH in Glasgow, he tabulated the information and arranged it in categories, comparing the statistics for principal towns, large towns, smaller burghs, and counties.[8] The tables highlighted the diversity in infantile death rates – from 151 per thousand in the big towns to 105 in the counties. During a smallpox outbreak in 1900 he adopted the same approach, demanding regular and standardised information from medical officers in an effort 'to establish through the Board a centre for the spread of information and advice.' Up and down the country the medical officers responded well; soon many of them were undertaking to wire information to one another.[9]

This was a little like the communications network that Russell had established after Glasgow's boundary extension, with himself at the centre. This time he had to concern himself with matters that had been beyond his ken as Glasgow's MOH – the housing of potato diggers and berry pickers, by-laws for pigsties, the sanitary condition of St Kilda. Scouring these reports in his office in George Street, he received remarkable insights into social as well as sanitary conditions all over Scotland. From Matthew Hay, Aberdeen's distinguished MOH, he learned how up to 70 men could be seen entering a certain grocer's shop in the east end of the city every morning to buy methylated spirits. 'Each,' Hay explained, 'carries the necessary bottle, and after leaving the shop proceeds to a neighbouring water-tap to dilute the spirits and then drink it.'[10] From the MOH for Barra came an equally vivid account of life in a croft with no chimney apart from a bottomless cask stuck in the roof above the kitchen fireplace. 'In this room the wife and girls knit and sew, and the fathers and sons mend their fishing nets,' he recorded. 'During the long winter nights the neighbours come in and talk and discuss the latest accounts of the war in South Africa. The peat fire in due time is replenished, the house fills with peat smoke, and for a time all is fog. Those who mend the nets one by one throw off their jackets, all are perspiring ... and the kitchen is now a mild Turkish bath ...' [11]

Wherever possible Russell acted on the information. He rendered the board more interventionist. One of its main functions had always been to advise local authorities on questions arising from public health legislation, but Russell went further and tried to ensure that the law was enforced. No longer could local authorities fob off the Board with their favourite reply: 'The matters referred to are receiving our earnest consideration.' They found themselves under pressure to appoint public analysts as required by the Sale of Food and Drugs Act, 1899, though some of the appointments were then vetoed – on the grounds, for example, that it would be inappropriate for a medical officer or a GP to fill the post. [12] Russell also urged local authorities to see that meat inspection regulations were rigidly enforced, but criticised some of the regulations that they made under a new statutory milk order. [13] After serious illness had been caused in England by arsenic in beer he reminded Scottish local authorities of their statutory powers of detection of arsenic in sugar substitutes. [14]

Local authorities were also instructed to supply information to the Royal Commission on Sewage, of which Russell himself was a member; but after surveying the evidence he concluded that 'Scotland had but little information for the Commission' because its main industrial centres were either on the coast or on tidal waters. [15]

Russell was rigorous in investigating complaints about the failure of local authorities to deal with nuisances. The burgh of Kirkcudbright was taken to court over a midden which the Board had told it to remove. The Board claimed that the burgh had failed to discharge its functions as guardian of public health, and the Sheriff-substitute agreed – he ordered the burgh to fence off the midden and granted an interdict to prevent more deposits before this had been done. [16]

'There is not today in Scotland a parish that does not feel

the good influence of his energies,' noted the *Sanitary Journal* in 1901, praising Russell for giving Scotland a more integrated public health administration.[17]

He also concerned himself with the duties of medical officers and sanitary inspectors, whose relations remained strife-ridden and in Glasgow had reached the stage of 'acute friction.' Scrapping the draft regulations drawn up by the old Board of Supervision, he substituted a more elaborate code. When asked for guidance by an MOH who was experiencing problems, Russell must have recalled the 'jarring' between himself and Kenneth Macleod, Glasgow's Chief Sanitary Inspector. It may have given him some satisfaction to reply that, under the new model regulations, 'the Medical Officer was responsible for the Sanitary Inspector's actions relative to infectious diseases, and that the discretion as to their nature lay with the MOH and not the SI.'[18]

Russell's reports were anonymous, his circulars signed by the Board's secretary. Yet he put his stamp on what he wrote. The tone of his reports was often characteristically emphatic, not least in matters relating to the flurry of hospital building which took place in his years at the Board. Here he drew confidently on his vast experience, dating from the days when he was in sole charge of Parliamentary Road Fever Hospital. 'A hospital for infectious diseases ought to come up to the highest standard of structure prescribed for a wholesome dwelling-house directed to the prevention of damp and the exclusion of ground air; while the heating, ventilation, and isolation must meet a higher standard still,' declared the guidelines for local authorities drawn up in Russell's first year as the Board's medical member. As in his Parliamentary Road days, he emphasised the importance of 'the services of a good class of nurses' and added the warning: 'Good nurses cannot be retained unless they are made comfortable, as they ought to be in view of the risks of their occupation.'[19]

The sites and plans for new hospitals had to be approved by the Board, and Russell was a hard man to please. Some applications were turned down, or approved only on certain conditions; and sometimes more important projects were referred to an architectural commissioner. Russell took exception to a plan which included covered gangways between the wards and the administration block. The proposed site was exceptionally windswept, but Russell objected that covered passages were inconsistent with the pavilion system, which allowed the free movement of air between buildings. All the important hospitals in Scotland, he pointed out, were constructed on that principle and 'waterproofs and galoshes ... are found by the nurses to afford sufficient protection, and they enjoy better health.' [20]

He was equally insistent that smallpox patients should be treated in different hospitals – not merely different pavilions – from sufferers from other infectious diseases. He encouraged local authorities to co-operate in providing these hospitals and was gratified when Dumfries County Council took the advice and reached agreement with other authorities within the county for the opening of a combined hospital. [21] Local authorities were also left in no doubt about the need to provide the right kind of reception-houses for the accommodation of people whose houses were being disinfected although they themselves were not suffering from diseases. These places, he insisted, had to be seen not as prisons but as 'places substituted for ordinary residences.' He criticised the plans submitted by some local authorities as being 'too much of the nature of a barracks' with no suggestion of home about them, no provision for families, and no division of inmates apart from the segregation of men and women. [22] The best reception-houses, he told local authorities, were conversions of large self-contained houses, and that was the ideal to be kept in mind.

He also had ample opportunity to continue his long campaign against infected or impure food. In 1900 the Fishery Board of Scotland reported that they had received complaints from the Continent about the unsatisfactory condition of Scottish-cured herring. When the barrels were opened the fish were sometimes found to be 'perfectly rotten.' The Scottish Secretary, Lord Balfour, referred the matter to the Local Government Board, and a circular was sent to the local authorities in the areas concerned 'reminding them of their ample powers for dealing with unsound food and urging them to lose no time in applying these powers by the systematic inspection of the premises of curers and of herrings in transit on fishing vessels or being unloaded.' Later the Board's inspectors visited the ports and found that the local authorities appeared to be 'alive to the need for frequent inspection and supervision.' The Fishery Board wrote to say that this action had 'most beneficially affected' the quality of herring exported to the Continent.[23]

Russell also made the local authorities dance to his tune when some of them wanted to make consumption a notifiable disease. It was not among the infectious diseases specified in the Scottish Public Health Act of 1897, which required local authorities to adopt compulsory notification rather than, as before, merely empowering them to do so if they wished. Russell was not at all keen to add consumption to the list. He argued, as he had done in his Glasgow days, that compulsory notification would restrict the liberty of consumptives and encourage public hysteria. By this time there was added cause for fear because the 1897 Act had made it an offence for sufferers from notifiable diseases to use a hotel or lodging house, travel on public transport, or send their children to school – restrictions which clearly would have been intolerable if applied to consumptives. Russell therefore told the local authorities that it 'would not at present be expedient' to adopt their proposal. It would be better, he argued, to test the effects of notification through voluntary schemes, and although local authorities already had the discretionary right to apply to the Board to make consumption notifiable in their areas, he made it clear that they would have to satisfy extremely stringent conditions – such as having adequate resources and bacteriological facilities for dealing with the disease. He continued to put all the emphasis on general preventive measures such as improved living conditions and public education.[24]

This policy could not be sustained for much longer. By 1903 it had become clear to many authorities, Glasgow's included, that they lacked adequate information about the distribution of the disease. The Board changed tack, although not until after Russell's time, and decreed that local authorities should be empowered to make consumption notifiable under the Public Health Act. But at the same time some of the more oppressive clauses were removed from the legislation – thus to some extent meeting the libertarian objections that had been raised by Russell and others.[25]

In moving to Edinburgh, Russell did not become entirely desk-bound, confined to issuing circulars and scrutinising planning applications. In the early years at least investigative work took him out of George Street and in 1900 he found himself again among old friends in Glasgow, although for a reason that he could hardly have welcomed. In August an outbreak of bubonic plague occurred in the city – the first in the United Kingdom for more than 200 years. The long-forgotten scourge had made its appearance in Hong Kong in 1898 and quickly worked its way along the international shipping routes. In the summer of 1899 it erupted in Portugal, and the Local Government Board was soon sending confidential circulars to medical officers of health and dispatching its inspectors to report on preparations in the ports. Ships arriving from Spain and Portugal were inspected and dead rats found on board were examined bacteriologically. Despite these precautions an outbreak occurred in Glasgow in August, 1900, in an area to the south of the Clyde largely inhabited by dock workers 'with a sprinkling of persons of irregular life.' The initial cases were traced to a wake, but what was particularly worrying was that the disease had not been detected until it was well established.

Russell immediately took the train to Glasgow, examined the cases, arranged for the port of Glasgow to be officially declared to be infected with plague, and wired the Foreign Office and the local government boards of England and Ireland, while Scottish local authorities, particularly seaports, were warned to keep a watch on slum areas. Throughout the epidemic he made repeated visits to Glasgow, and in between times received daily bulletins from Chalmers, who had ordered the limewashers and scavengers into action and was presiding over a huge rat-hunt in cellars and basements, on ships, and around the harbour, where more than 6000 of the creatures were trapped and examined. When Glasgow was officially declared free of the disease in November, after 29 identified cases and nine deaths, Russell was full of praise for the 'skill and energy' with which Chalmers and company had checked the outbreak. 'It is not more than the bare truth to say,' he said, 'that Great Britain lies under a heavy obligation to Glasgow for the promptitude and efficiency of the sanitary measures taken in the presence of a national emergency.'[26]

The outbreak had attracted enormous attention. Medical officers from all parts of the country flocked to Glasgow to witness the phenomenon. The English Local Government Board sent one of its inspectors. Experts from Bergen, Budapest, Copenhagen, South Africa, New Zealand, and Australia arrived to study the outbreak. The Russian Government was represented by Professor Zabolotny, of the Imperial Institute of Experimental Medicine in St Petersburg. For Glasgow, which was accustomed to being viewed as a model municipality and a pacesetter in public health rather than an object of curiosity and concern, this attention must have been highly unwelcome. Embarrassment was compounded by the reappearance of the plague in August, 1901, when it coincided with Glasgow's great International Exhibition and with the numerous important conferences that were its by-products. This hardly helped the image of the city at a time when it was already struggling to bring a smallpox epidemic under control. To make things worse, the first crop of the 1901 plague cases was unexpectedly followed by a second, this time not in a crowded slum but in the superior ambience of the Central Hotel, three of whose servants succumbed. The danger was that the rats dislodged by nearby railway work would also find their way into neighbouring tenements, and Chalmers was at pains to allay fears and prevent panic – though also at risk of appearing complacent.[27]

The outbreak was soon over, but this time there were no plaudits from Russell. In such a sensitive situation (and with Chalmers at loggerheads with the Chief Sanitary Inspector, Peter Fyfe) tensions may well have developed between the city and the Board; at any rate there is an impression that communications between the two were not as smooth as on the earlier occasion.[28] One reason was possibly that Russell, who was repeatedly in Glasgow during the 1900 outbreak, remained in Edinburgh in 1901. The men on the spot were Sir Henry Littlejohn – Edinburgh's renowned MOH, who also acted as part-time medical officer for the Local Government Board – and Dr Leslie Mackenzie, recently recruited to the new post of Medical Inspector of the Board.

Mackenzie, then in his 40s, was the up-and-coming man on the Board and had taken over much of Russell's investigative work. Formerly MOH for Leith, he greatly admired Russell's passion for reform [29] and believed that public health policy should be guided by social insight. Like Russell, he was at odds with the laissez-faire approach to public health associated with Herbert Spencer; but as a socialist and a friend of Sidney and Beatrice Webb he went much further than Russell in advocating state intervention. His ideas must have been anathema to the Board's chairman, Sir Malcolm McNeill, and Russell's conciliatory skills may well have been called into play. Mackenzie created wider shock waves with a survey for the Royal Commission on Physical Training which drew attention to widespread malnutrition among school children and argued the case for school meals and school medical inspection.

Later, as Russell's successor, Mackenzie was to see these proposals implemented in the legislative programme that followed the Liberal landslide of 1906. Yet it was Russell who had prepared the ground for a more modern approach to public health. No one had done more to stir the public conscience, to challenge Poor Law thinking, or to shake the complacency of the old regime. He might not have agreed with all of Mackenzie's ideas but he remained progressive and forward-looking in his Edinburgh years. 'In these his latter days, as in his earlier, Dr Russell acts the pioneer,' noted the *Sanitary Journal of Scotland* in 1901. 'He is always in touch, always in sympathy, with the young minds of his time. He has behind him a well-filled past, but, at an age when others would think of ease and rest, he thinks only of fresh tasks for tomorrow. Long may it be so; for in Scotland today the service of man has no better or more faithful servant.[30]

But it was not to be so for long.

Chapter Eighteen

Shadowy Boundaries

The thought grows into a sense of boundaries, so far as
this world is concerned.

His Edinburgh post removed Russell from the glare of public controversy, no doubt to his considerable relief. The rough and tumble of his municipal career had failed to dent his natural reserve and shyness. The social round was not to his taste, and when a knighthood was offered he turned it down, apparently on the grounds that he had no wife to take care of the consequent entertaining. Yet he never became a complete recluse. He cultivated his friendships, both old and new, with a care that may have had something to do with his acute awareness of the transience of human life. His most regular correspondent was an old High School friend who had become a university administrator in New Zealand, but he also won the affection of his new colleagues on the Local Government Board. The board's chairman, Sir Malcolm McNeill, though a Conservative and the personification of old-fashioned Poor Law thinking, particularly enjoyed what he described as a 'crack' with the Medical Member.[1]

His old mentor William Gairdner had returned to his native Edinburgh on retirement and was still keeping a paternal eye on his 'son in the faith' of sanitation, as he liked to address Russell. Gairdner (who, for his part, had accepted a knighthood after what he described as a 'mental struggle') was trying unsuccessfully to persuade Russell to produce a collected edition of his papers. 'Pray do not lose sight of this little project,' he pleaded. 'It seems to me to be one of the best things I can do for humanity in the time that remains to me, to stir you up in the production of such a volume.'[2]

But some other old friends had vanished from Russell's life. On a chill and foggy day in January, 1899, he had shivered in Glasgow Necropolis at the funeral of Joseph Coats, whose early

death came only a few years after he had become the first
Professor of Pathology at Glasgow University. 'Poor Joe!' Russell wrote to Coats's wife, recalling their work together at
Parliamentary Road Hospital. 'I feel his removal very much.'
He also told Mrs Coats of a strange premonition of Coats's
death that he had had in a dream the night before her telegram
had arrived with the news.[3]

Russell had lost touch with his old friend James Bryce, then
on the Opposition benches, although he read and admired his
latest writings. On impulse he wrote to him in 1903 after
spotting the notice of Bryce's mother's death in *The Glasgow
Herald*, which he continued to read in his Edinburgh years. His
memory of Bryce's parents was still so vivid that he could, he
wrote, have drawn their faces if only he had had the necessary
artistic skill. He went on to muse about the records of human
lives contained in the memories of people's contemporaries,
adding: 'The thought grows into a sense of boundaries, so far
as this world is concerned.'[4] Bryce replied warmly, with sentiments about the value of old friends – 'I have hardly any left
who go back so far into boyhood as you do.'[5]

Russell's 'sense of boundaries' may by that time have owed
something to an awareness that his own days were numbered.
Under his contract he was to work till he was 70 but his hopes
of reaching retirement age were blighted when bladder cancer
was diagnosed while he was still in his mid-60s. Close friends
and colleagues were shocked when, during one of his absences
from work in the summer of 1904, they learned how grave his
illness was. 'I am afraid that we two must be content to feel
that in our very different ways we are both on the downgrade,
and must wait with such patience as we may the inevitable call,'
wrote Gairdner, who was suffering from a heart arrythmia. After
describing how he himself seemed to be losing ground without
any serious pain, he wrote: 'But in your case dear friend I feel
it is not in me to say anything about what you have written. I
only trust that it may be less than I fear, and in any case, that
you may escape suffering as much as I do.'[6]

The news also caused distress in the Local Government
Board's office. Sir Malcolm McNeill, who had missed his regular
chats with Russell during his absence, wrote to say that he was

about to 'hop along in the tram and invade your room.' He also bowed to Russell's demands by promising to 'send you along anything that puzzles us but always on the understanding that you send it back untouched if you feel ... "indisposed for shop." ' [7]

The remaining months of Russell's life were full of pain and suffering, but he tried not to let his illness interrupt his work and when unable to leave the house managed 'from his bedside to discharge such official duties as were possible in the circumstances.' [8] There was a possible motive for this in that Russell's contract made him liable to dismissal by the Scottish Secretary if he became incapacitated by illness.[9] Yet his addiction to work was enough to explain the paper-strewn state of his bedroom in Braid Road. Some years previously he had corresponded with Gairdner about possible English equivalents of a Latin motto to the effect that 'work is the essence of life' – a motto which Russell might well have adopted as his own.[10]

For his family it was obviously a trying time. None of his three children had yet married. David Russell, now in his 30s, had acquired a farm at Dalton, near Lockerbie, with financial help from his father and no doubt with words of advice about hygiene in the cowsheds. The two daughters remained in Braid Road with their father and aunt, but Mary, the elder, had become engaged to a young Congregational minister, William Collier. An Aberdonian and the son of a well-known photographer, Collier had been a distingished philosophy student at Aberdeen University and was briefly assistant pastor at Elgin Place Church in Glasgow while the Russells were still attending it.

The wedding was planned for December, 1904, in Morningside Congregational Church, but Russell did not live to see it. Some seven weeks earlier he underwent surgery that, it was hoped, would give some temporary relief to his pain. Two days later, on October 22, 1904, he died from a haemorrhage, at the age of 67. His death was sudden and painless.

One of his friends remarked that he died fighting in the line of battle. He had finished his last official deliverance on the day before his operation. The Legal Member of the Local Government Board, James Patten MacDougall, treasured his last memory of Russell 'resting very complacently in bed surrounded on all sides by our Local Government Board files – a perfect picture of devotion to duty.'[11]

Meanwhile in Glasgow 'much grief' was expressed at a Corporation meeting and the Lord Provost, John Ure Primrose – nephew of Russell's old ally John Ure – declared that in their hearts the memory of Russell's genial presence and great power would remain a heritage for years to come.

After a service at Morningside Congregational Church on October 26, Russell's body was taken by train to Glasgow. The funeral cortège went from Queen Street Station to Glasgow Necropolis, where a huge crowd had gathered. Russell's old friend Hector Cameron looked around him and noticed faces marked with an expression of universal grief. The sanitary staff, numbering nearly 200, lined the walks to the grave. Headed by Archibald Chalmers, Russell's successor and former colleague, they had marched in procession from the Sanitary Chambers. The Chief Sanitary Inspector, Peter Fyfe, and the Chairman of the Health Committee, Bailie James Dick, walked alongside Chalmers. The two oldest members of the sanitary staff bore a wreath on high and placed it on the family tomb, which already bore the inscriptions of Russell's grandparents and father.[12]

One mourner brooded over the scene and reflected on the massed ranks of sanitary inspectors. 'Here were the men now an army,' he wrote later. 'In his early days he fought single with the enemy. He now lies there in the heart of the Glasgow that he loved – the old Glasgow of the poor that have no helper; of the slum-owners that have no bowels of compassion; of the infirmary, which made death easier to the worn-out pilgrim or brought back life to the weary; of the Cathedral, which rises out of the Middle Ages in majesty to symbolise the undying pity, the enthusiasm of humanity, the undying service of man.'[13]

Chapter Nineteen

Russell in Retrospect

The whole weight of water is pressing against the embankment.

'NONE will, I think, venture to deny that no such services had ever before been given to the advancement of the health of the people,' wrote Matthew Hay. 'One of the greatest and gentlest of human souls has gone from among us.'[1] Russell's public health colleagues were in no doubt about his stature. He was assured, they thought, of lasting international fame. William Gairdner described him as one of the ablest sanitarians in Europe and 'a true living genius full of poetic imagination and fire.'[2] Dr John Brownlee, physician superintendent of Belvidere Fever Hospital, thought his supreme achievement was in arousing a sense of social responsibility towards the poor. The *Lancet* declared that 'he belonged to the modern public health movement and was of no time and no place.'[3]

A century on, how is his performance to be measured? One obvious benchmark is the death rate. During his years as MOH it fell from 29 per 1000 to 21 per 1000. Fewer people died in his final year as MOH than in his first, although the population had increased by some 200,000, almost 50%, with many of the newcomers arriving destitute from the Highlands and Ireland. A little of the improvement can be explained by the falling birthrate, which because of persistently high infant mortality had a favourable effect on the general death rate. A little can be explained by the infusion of healthy and wealthy suburbanites from Pollokshields and Hillhead which resulted from boundary extension. Some people at the time claimed that this alone accounted for the continued downward trend of mortality in the 1890s. But most of what was gained on the swings was lost on some extremely filthy roundabouts: average mortality for the annexed areas was only fractionally below the rate for the original city.[4] Lord Provost Richmond was therefore quite justified in claiming that there were 'thousands' walking the streets who would have been dead if things had remained as they were.

The crucial question is how many of these lives would have been saved even without Russell. As his critics pointed out, there were other forces at work – Loch Katrine water, which was introduced before his time, and the slum clearance programme begun in Gairdner's day. The first had had its main impact on the mortality statistics before Russell took up his post, but the second undoubtedly contributed enormously to the huge reduction in mortality in his early years as MOH. Wider influences were also at work. Mortality rates declined throughout Britain in the same period. Since infectious diseases, which accounted for much of the decline, were waning before the sanitary offensive started, it is sometimes argued that falling mortality was primarily due to an improved standard of living and particularly to better nutrition.[5] In Glasgow as elsewhere diet improved in quantity and purity, though Russell was among those who regretted that oatmeal was being ousted by white bread and tea.[6] The view that nutrition was paramount has, however, been challenged by scholars who draw on epidemiological research and local studies to argue that social conditions were more important in determining the pattern of infectious diseases.[7] The Russell story provides added evidence that social intervention was the critical factor in controlling the ill effects of unregulated urban growth. His own statistics and observations demonstrate the link between social dislocation and disease.

Although infectious diseases were retreating everywhere, it is significant that the retreat was so ragged. Disease was beaten back more rapidly where there was civic energy and sanitary initiative. From the 1870s there were fewer typhus deaths in the Scottish cities than in the larger Scottish towns, which had no sanitary movement to speak of, while enteric fever was more deeply entrenched in the rural muck than in the city slums. These were the classic 'filth diseases,' the ones most amenable to sanitary action. Typhus mortality, though generally worse during economic downturns, continued to fall even in the lean years of the late 1870s and early 1880s. These were years when Russell was throwing everything at the problem – disinfection,

isolation in hospital, an evangelical insistence on domestic cleanliness and fresh air.

Russell was convinced that this all-out war against the filth
diseases also inflicted damage on other lethal infections. For
many years he fought pulmonary tuberculosis under cover of
his attack on typhus, since both were associated with overcrowding and insanitary conditions. Tuberculosis was waning
throughout the industrial world and would have continued to
decline in Glasgow even without Russell's attentions – but
probably not at the same rate. During the Russell years and for
some time afterwards it fell more rapidly in Glasgow than in
the other Scottish cities and very much more rapidly than in
the Scottish countryside. One study of tuberculosis in Glasgow
concludes that while diet was important, so was the Scottish
public health tradition, permeated as it was with the scientific
and rational ethos of the Enlightenment.[8] Russell, through his
system of small-area statistics, was in a better position than
most medical officers to exploit that tradition. He could track
tuberculosis mortality through the city and demonstrate its link
with bad housing. With the backing of a powerful municipality
he could tackle it not only through general sanitary measures
but also through better building standards, more strictly regulated workshops, and close monitoring of milk supplies.
Environmental improvements were also of significance for the
drop in deaths from other respiratory diseases, which like tuberculosis declined more steeply in Glasgow than in the rest of
Scotland in these years – accounting, along with infectious
diseases and tuberculosis, for much of the mortality decline.[9]
The same measures, along with Russell's educational campaigns,
may also help to explain the considerable fall in child deaths in
these years. Recent studies of ninteenth-century mortality in
the city, while acknowledging the importance of rising living
standards, have tended to give the greatest weight to sanitary
and housing improvements.[10] Although housing conditions were
still appalling at the end of Russell's period, it has been suggested that the death rate may have been sensitive to the worst
level of housing – that is, a slight improvement made a big
difference. Russell certainly made his contribution to that
improvement.

Rather than by any single measure, Russell made his impact through the determination and thoroughness with which he pursued a wide variety of objectives – persecuting industrial mandarins and jobbing butchers, tracking down smallpox defectors, fighting pitched battles over uninhabitable houses, hammering out legislation, and pursuing miscreants through the courts with a regard for detail that made him almost invincible. He showed how much more there was to sanitary reform than buckets of limewash. Lighting and ventilation, parks and playgrounds, even food standards all fell within his sphere of interest. Operating on a broad front, he turned Glasgow's sanitary administration into a modern public health department. His contribution to the fall in the death rate could never be precisely established without disentangling the many strands of deprivation in the single-ends of late-Victorian Glasgow, but in any case it would be an unsatisfactory measure of his achievement. Russell himself warned that obsession with death rates could detract attention from disease, which unlike a deerstalker's bullet wounded many whom it did not kill. He improved living conditions in ways that are ultimately unquantifiable. 'Etiology may be left to others,' he said. 'Sewer gas does no good whether it causes diphtheria or not. The business of the Medical Officer is to get rid of it first, and afterward to find out if he can what part it plays in the depreciation of health.'[11]

Russell could not have achieved all this single-handed. The story has other heroes – not only Gairdner but John Ure, the prime mover in Glasgow's public health revolution, and his successors in the Health Committee leadership. Russell, unlike Gairdner, was able to establish a working partnership with these men. Together they grappled with the problems of this huge working-class city with its crammed single-ends and sunless wynds and vennels. Alhough Glasgow had the highest proportion of small houses of any city in the UK, they kept its death rate well below that of Manchester or Liverpool and narrowed the gap with the other Scottish cities. Under their own dedicated medical officers, men educated in the same broad tradition as Russell, the other Scottish cities also made great strides. They had the civic strength to keep abreast of public health progress in England by making their own laws and regulations. But it was Glasgow that led the way. Under Russell, who was for most of his career the only full-time MOH in Scotland, it took over the leadership of the Scottish public health movement and exploited the tradition that Gairdner had brought with him from Edinburgh to Glasgow. Glasgow's breakneck industrial expansion had caused its dire health problem, but its industrial power also gave it extra reserves of political strength. The public health movement had behind it the full weight of municipal socialism, powered by civic energy and pride. The spirit of confidence was so strong that Russell's ally Robert Crawford could advocate new public health legislation for Scotland in the interests, he explained, not of the cities but of the rest of the country. The cities had already gone to Parliament 'to bring their own powers up to date, and to assimilate them as much as possible to the Public Health Act for England.' From the beginning Russell was a most influential and energetic campaigner for that wider reform. 'We must agitate, agitate, agitate until the sanitary system of the rural districts of Scotland is reformed,' he insisted.[12] Eventually, in the 1890s, this determination was rewarded.

The remarkable power wielded by Russell and his allies made them less than popular in some quarters. Were they really, as their critics alleged, civic sultans and czars? Was the Health Committee too pushy for its own good? The ticketing of houses provided them with powers of surveillance which had no parallel in England, while the Improvement Trust operations could be seen as large-scale social engineering, with the dispersal of difficult tenants from the central areas (or their containment in strictly run model lodging houses) and their replacement with less disruptive elements. Russell himself certainly believed that the sanitary authorities had a supervisory role to play. 'Physical and moral chaos,' he warned, 'will gradually invade the original order if an eye, either the eye of the landlord or the sanitary inspector, is not kept upon the householders to prevent over-crowding.'[13] Of the 75,000 people who made up what he described as the social debris of the city,[14] only about 10% were in his view struggling bravely with poverty while the rest were 'bankrupt in character and fortune' and if neglected would form 'a fermenting mass of moral and physical putrefaction.' He once described the dispersal of 'the lowest elements' from the centre of Glasgow as 'obviously a change to the advantage of social order and good government'[15] and would have preferred them to be right outside the city. His allegiance to Liberal Unionism, which became increasingly identified with class interest, raises the question of whether his objective was social control. Both the Irish and the 'Scotch Celts' who formed the bulk of the underclass were guilty in his view of 'a propensity to overcrowding.' His strongest sympathies were with 'the well-doing poor.'

Yet it is impossible to read his writings and lectures, especially his appeals to middle-class consciences, without becoming aware that he was driven by compassion and a sense of outrage. Despite his association with the business-dominated Liberal Unionists he detested unrestrained commercialism. He repeatedly intervened to defend tenants from exploitation, for example by preventing the cutting-off of their water supplies. His support for ticketing is best seen as part of his unending battle against rapacious proprietors and landlords, who were subject to remarkably few legal constraints when Russell became MOH. Russell himself had grave misgivings about ticketing. He disliked the midnight raids by men with lanterns. He would have preferred to tackle overcrowding through slum clearance and rebuilding (through co-ordinated municipal and private action), which he strongly advocated during the years when the City Improvement Trust was too concerned about its profits to take this step.

Proof of Russell's concern for civil liberties can be found in his refusal to make tuberculosis a notifiable disease for fear that consumptives would be treated like lepers. Admittedly his concern for the literary and artistic representatives of 'that pale multitude' possibly helped to shape his opinion – for Russell could certainly sound elitist on occasion. Sometimes he spoke of the lowest layer of society as though it were beyond hope. Early in his career, at least, he sometimes endorsed the argument that the poor would be able to afford better accommodation if they were to spend less money on whisky. This is the most ambivalent area in his record. Yet again and again he expressed moral outrage at living conditions in the slums, and reiterated his conviction that these conditions created crime and poverty, not the reverse. Wherever insanitary conditions existed, he told his respectable middle-class audiences, there predictably would be found 'a people unhealthy, reckless, spendthrift ... tinged more or less by immorality and crime.' [16] Sometimes he seemed to despair of conveying the full horror of slum life to those who had never seen it for themselves. 'Where can I find language in which to clothe the facts of these poor people's lives, and yet be tolerable?' [17] he once asked. He was driven to fury by the inadequacy of poor relief for the ill-fed, ill-clothed miserable masses who endured the pinching cold of winter in scantily furnished single-ends. 'Are they so differently made and con-stituted from ourselves that we can possible imagine that "the voluntary benevolence of the public" has discharged itself of the trust of their "safety" while this is all that is done for them?' he demanded. 'We hear constantly of improvidence and intem-perance, but do not let us forget vicious buildings, houses whose surroundings debase and brutalise the soul as well as impair the body, or our unnecessarily polluted atmosphere.' [18]

Russell could not have tackled problems on the scale of Glasgow's without drawing on the relatively authoritarian Scot-tish urban tradition, linked in particular with the wider Scottish concept of policing. It seems significant that the Health Com-mittee was strictly speaking an operation of the Police Board – which by then was the Town Council under another hat, but John Ure, for one, liked to emphasise its distinct identity. An interventionist approach was needed not just because of the overwhelming nature of the problem but because Glasgow was a tenement city. With their common stairs and closes, their shared sinks and WCs, tenements were public in a sense that English working-class houses were not. Russell regarded it as axiomatic that any part of a structure in communal use necessi-tated the intervention of the public authority. [19] The sanitary inspectors spent endless hours enforcing by-laws for the clean-ing of closes and stairs and fixing the blame for choked WCs and sinks. 'When you have a whole stairful before a magistrate, the women each one objecting and objurgating, the practical result is very slight,' Russell told the Royal Commission on the Housing of the Working Classes in 1885. He believed that though tenement flats were not naturally conducive to health, their weaknesses could be overcome, and that this would be better than emulating the experiment with seven-storey model flats which he had viewed with disapproval in London. (He would not have approved of Glasgow's later experiment with multi-storey flats.[20])

Russell suffered some bad defeats. Clean air was a lost cause, and despite Dalmarnock treatment works the Clyde was hardly crystalline at the close of the century. The early experiment in treating measles patients in hospital met with failure. There were some serious reversals in court – not least when his interpretation of the Food and Drugs Act was overruled. His biggest disappointment must have been the persistently high infant mortality, which contrasted with the fall in deaths from childhood diseases. Though it remained throughout Russell's years well below the rate for Manchester and Liverpool, and in the 1890s even dipped below the English average, the death rate of infants under one year fell by only about a tenth as much as the general death rate and in Cowcaddens was as high as 194 per 1000. The problem awaited twentieth-century solutions in the form of maternity and child welfare services which were beyond the power of the Victorian municipal authorities to deliver even if they had recognised the necessity for them.

Even after the introduction of these services relatively high infant mortality continued to be associated with overcrowding until after the Second World War,[21] proving the accuracy of Russell's 'law of occupancy' – small houses mean higher room density and higher mortality. In Russell's day this was demon-strated dramatically by the sharp decline in mortality in districts whose population had been reduced by slum clearance and other measures to minimise overcrowding. The death rate in the High Street area, where as a student Russell had witnessed some of the worst slums in Europe, dropped from over 45 per 1000 to under 30 during his MOH years. Indeed the death rate in the unhealthiest of the four groups into which Russell arranged the sanitary districts of the city fell by 10 per 1000 over the period compared with five in the healthiest group – a more important index of progress than the general death rate. On the other hand one or two of the newer working-class districts, which had become more crowded with the dispersal of population from the centre, showed only a tiny improvement. At the end of the century the Cowcaddens death rate was still above what the average for the city had been three decades earlier. It was worse in Russell's final year than it had been in the early '90s.[22]

This reflected Russell's limiting factor, and municipal socialism's most serious failure: the lack of a proper housing programme. Of necessity his work consisted largely of an attempt, as he put it, to neutralise or lessen the evil effects of overcrowding. Only in the closing years of Russell's Glasgow career did the city decide to go in for house-building on any scale, and then only in a form which cut across his own environmental improvements; and even then the building was on expensive land and in the absence of subsidised rents could do little to solve the problems of the very poor. The prevailing attitude was that the poor could easily have afforded better accommodation had they chosen to spend less money on drink. It is true that a smaller proportion of working-class income was spent on housing in Glasgow than in any other major British city, but this partly reflected unstable wage levels and high food prices.[23] Municipal government could not supply all the answers to the problems of the poor and it was with typically apt timing that Russell moved on to a wider stage just as central authority was beginning to play a more active role – a process which he himself encouraged during his Edinburgh years.

Yet nothing could match his devotion to the city that he left behind when he joined the Scottish Local Government Board. He knew Glasgow as few others did, its wynds and closes, its factories and sweatshops as well as its law courts and learned societies. All the same it is easy to see what the *Lancet* meant when it described this Victorian Glaswegian as being of no place and no time. His writings are disturbingly relevant to our own day. There is, for example, something eerily prophetic about his description of the destructive side of the Industrial Revolution:

'The earth seems to grow chimney stalks; the highways become streets; the burns become loathsome and are buried out of sight in sewers; the rivers lose their sparkle and are expressionless as the eye of the dead; they stink like the rivers of Egypt; the fish die in them; the wells become poisonous; the air thickens; the sun is blotted out; the trees die; what we, with pleasing melancholy, call grass is mostly weeds.'[24]

At a time when infectious disease is again on the march, it might also be wise to remember James Burn Russell's farewell message to the sanitary inspectors:[25]

'There is in the achievements of man, whether they be physical or metaphysical, no inherent stability. What he gains by struggle he can retain only by effort. Withdraw the inhabitants from the structure known as Glasgow – which means, take away their daily care to protect and restore – and on the instant the disintegrating forces will prevail. The wind and the rain and the lever of the frost will overthrow it. The drifting dust and the burrowing earthworm will cover it over. The air will sow broadcast, and the birds deposit upon it seed of moss and grass, wild flower and the tree, the growth of which will hasten the triumph of nature over the artifices of man. Withdraw your Public Health Acts, your Police Acts, your Building Acts, and all the administrative and executive machinery through which they operate; abolish your hospitals, your reception houses, your refuse destructors, and all the elaborate apparatus by which you restrain the inroads of pathogenic organisms, and protect the commonweal from the operations of ignorance and selfishness. Their potential energy is as great as ever. The whole weight of the water is pressing against the embankment. Withdraw the restraint, and it becomes a devastating flood.'

Family Footnote

THE task of tracking down Russell's descendants was daunting. His only son, David, emigrated to Canada before the First World War, but the trail had gone cold. From Brenda White, who did research on Russell when she was a member of Glasgow University Economic History Department, I learned the name of the small community where he had settled in British Columbia. A letter to the editor of the local newspaper elicited two replies which established, among other interesting bits of information about Russell's son, that although he had married, there were no children.

Edinburgh street directories showed that Russell's younger daughter, Helen, had remained in Morningside, unmarried, until her death in the 1950s. The only hope was the elder daughter, Mary Collier, whose Congregational husband was pastor of a church in Bolton at the time of their marriage. On sabbatical from my work on the *Herald* in 1993, I went to Bolton to trace her footsteps. Church news in local newspaper files in the public library provided the next clue, and soon I was boarding a train for Stockport, where the couple had moved before the First World War. Street directories and voters' rolls yielded more information: the Colliers had had a daughter, who had evidently left home early in the 1930s when her name disappeared from the voters' roll. The registry office across the road from the library provided evidence of her marriage to a Scottish Flying Officer, Alexander Rodgers. Back in the Mitchell Library in Glasgow, the Air Force List showed that he had later become an Air Commodore. *Who Was Who* told me that there were two children. Since Alexander Rodgers had been a graduate of St Andrews University, it seemed worth checking its General Council Register for other members of the family. There I found not only an entry for the son but also one for his mother, whose Leicestershire address the university was able to supply by return of post. A couple of weeks later, on a sunny June day, I met Agnes Rodgers – Russell's granddaughter – at her son's house in East Lothian and spent the day leafing through family records arrayed on the dining-room table. Later Agnes Rodgers toured the places where her grandfather had lived and worked in Glasgow, and inspected Auburn Cottage in Rutherglen, where he grew up, which has miraculously survived amid a modern housing estate. At her home in Melton Mowbray she served me tea from the silver teapot presented to Russell by the sanitary staff when he left Glasgow.

Agnes Rodgers, who has continued to be actively involved in the research for this book, has added a vital dimension to Russell's story because of all that she was able to tell me not only about the man himself but about the whole family history, and not least about Russell's remarkable grandfather, who was such a powerful influence on his life. Another part of the story was pieced together with the help of Mrs Alice Carey, whose husband was a descendant of Russell's barrister uncle, John Archibald Russell. Mrs Pat Bayliss, an Englishwoman now living in Vernon, British Columbia, supplied much information about David Russell's life in Canada, which she uncovered in the course of her own historical researches.

David Russell's story was a colourful one. At the time of his father's death he was still farming in Dumfriesshire. In 1908, when he was in his mid-thirties, he married a cousin, Ethel Annie Russell, one of the youngest of the 12 children of John Archibald Russell, who had died in 1899. A few years later their lives took an unexpected course. After suffering severe internal injuries when he was kicked by a horse, David Russell decided that he would be better suited to fruit-farming in British Columbia than to the heavy work of his Scottish farm. He and his wife settled in a small Anglo-Scottish enclave near Vernon, where he named his orchard Fostermeadow after his Dumfries-shire farm. David Russell became a prominent member of the local community. As a councillor he served on the waterworks committee and rated a mention in a recent history of Vernon [1] for his part in a controversy over the proposed municipalisation of an irrigation scheme. On the centenary of Waterloo he arranged an exhibition of his great-grandfather's memorabilia in the window of the Vernon Hardware Company – including the dictionary that James Russell had carried with him through the battle, the letter he had written home to his wife, and a canister still smelling of coffee, all of which attracted much interest among soldiers from the nearby training camps. Russell also wrote to his father's old friend James Bryce, congratulating him on being made a viscount and enclosing a newspaper article that he had written about the Waterloo anniversary.

Soon, however, the fruit-growers were struggling to overcome the effects of the wartime labour shortage and other difficulties. Russell sold his ranch and moved to Departure Bay, on the east coast of Vancouver Island, where he farmed until, in poor health, he decided to return to the UK. To help finance the move he sold his grandfather's Waterloo souvenirs.

Edinburgh, where James Burn Russell had spent only six years of his life, remained a family focal point long after his death. His sister Agnes remained in Morningside until her death in 1911. His daughter Helen, engaging in charitable work and church activities, provided a longer thread of continuity, and the connection was kept up with the Davidsons, the rapidly proliferating family of Russell's unfortunate wife. One of them, Sarah Davidson, became one of Scotland's first women medical graduates – the only member of the family to follow in Russell's footsteps, although others have inherited something of his writing abilities: it was not for nothing that his grandfather carried a dictionary with him through the Battle of Waterloo.

The wedding of Mary Russell and William Collier went ahead as planned just after her father's death – Russell had urged that there should be no postponement if he were to die before the date. The bride resisted family pressure to wear black, but compromised by wearing grey. The wedding took place in Morningside Congregational Church on a rainy December day, and the Colliers' daughter Agnes still relishes the story of how her mother's elegantly attired bridesmaid forgot to remove her galoshes in church.

Agnes was the Colliers' only child – Russell's only grandchild. Although brought up in England, she spent long periods in Edinburgh during her childhood and remembers hiding under the bedclothes in her Davidson cousins' house during the Zeppelin raid in the First World War. She remembers her Aunt

Helen's flat in Greenbank Terrace, where the outer door was opened and closed by means of an iron lever on the first floor; and she vividly recalls Dr Sarah Davidson riding about in a pony and trap – and smoking.

Like her mother, Agnes was married in Morningside Congregational Church. At St Andrews University she had met a young RAF Flying Officer, Alexander Rodgers, later to become an Air Commodore. They had a son, Ian, and a daughter, Jenny, both of whom married and have children. Agnes Rodgers, whose husband died in 1973, now lives in Leicestershire. She has seven grandchildren – Julia, Tessa, Kate, Emma, James, Clare, and Adam: the great-great grandchildren of James Burn Russell.

'Life in One Room' [1]

I SHALL not readily forget an incident in the delivery of the Right Hon. John Bright's Rectorial Address to the students of Glasgow University in 1884. He had discussed certain questions of the future, arising from the relations of this country to our colonies and dependencies and to foreign nations. Turning to home legislation, he thought to make his remarks more impressive by a reference to the condition of the inhabitants of the city in which his youthful audience was assembled, and in which a considerable proportion had been born. Mr. Bright said: 'I was reading the other day a book which many of you have seen, called "Past and Present." In it there are some statements made from the Census of the Kingdom of Scotland. The writer states that in the City of Glasgow alone 41 families out of every 100 live in houses having only one room.' The right hon. gentleman was immediately interrupted with cries of 'oh! oh!' and shouts of incredulous laughter; whereupon he interjected the reminder—'That is the official statement of the Census'; and went on to give further information about the homes of the people of Glasgow, which I shall not quote, as Mr. Bright took his figures from the census of 1871 instead of 1881, to which I shall subsequently refer. I said to myself—was there ever a better illustration of the proverb that one half of the world does not know how the other half lives? Here were facts which had been lying for 13 years in the Census Report, and which were not only unknown to the 200 educated youths of the University, but which were so startling in their nature that when made known they were barely believed. Nay more. No passage in that long and eloquent address attracted more attention from the general public. The one and two roomed houses of Glasgow have almost passed into a proverb. They immediately became the subject of

[1] A Lecture delivered to the Park Parish Literary Institute, Glasgow, 27th February, 1888.

leaders in the newspapers, of speeches from statesmen, and the text of sermons. All thoughtful men were startled with the grave significance of those plain figures as to the physical and moral conditions under which our population lives. In short this passage set alight that flame of interest in the social circumstances of the poor which has spread over the land, and which, if the truth must be told, has been fed by facts which were perfectly well known to all men who in an official capacity or from special philanthropic impulses have been keeping touch with the poorer classes. Now, what does this prove? It proves that if the cup of cold water has not been borne to the parched lips, it is not because of want of sympathy, but because of the want of knowledge. It is the old story—the mendicant who holds up his feigned distress to the public eye is sated with undeserved alms, while the poor man who hides his real sufferings at home is unnoticed and unrelieved. Carry him out to the wayside, or better still, go and search for him; and there is that divine impulse in the heart of humanity which will make men rush to his relief; even as, when we see a child stumble, our arms are around it before we are conscious of a throb of sympathy. This being so, I hold that it is our duty as Christian men and women to acquire that knowledge of our fellow-citizens which will give us a reasonable ground for determining the measure of our duty towards them. It is one of the blessed prerogatives of childhood to remain in happy ignorance of the anxieties and cares, the schemes and forethought, which fill the minds of those who maintain about them the comforts of their homes. For all they know to the contrary those comforts come to them with as little effort or design on the part of anybody, and are as far beyond the possibility of miscarriage, as the sun which cheers them at play. They will sleep in full assurance of awaking to their customary bountiful repast, while their parents are sleepless with the anticipation of reverse of fortune. But that which is natural in the child is thoughtless and even sinful in the man and woman. We ought to know something of the social machinery which is kept moving around us. We ought not because *our* bread and water are made sure lazily to take for granted that the bread and water of others give them as little concern. We ought not to preen and expand *our* virtues to the sun in our self-contained houses, putting them in proud contrast with the vices of those who live in the one-roomed house, without asking ourselves how far both the virtue and the vice are native to the physical circumstances in which we find them.

When my friend,your President, asked me to give you an address, it was by thoughts such as these that I was led to choose to speak to you of the City in which we live. You go about the streets of this great city day by day, and I wish you to have an intelligent sympathy with the life of it. A heathen poet said—'I am a man, and nothing that concerns man is without interest to me'; and surely if this was truly felt by a heathen nearly two hundred years before the birth of Christ, we who live nearly two thousand years after that divine expression of sympathy for man, must adopt the words with a fuller, richer meaning. You have experienced the change which passes over our relations to a man as we come to know something about him. We see him day by day taking his place opposite us at the desk, or his seat beside us in the pew, or we meet him from time to time in the tramcar, or pass him as we walk to business at a certain corner of a street. Bit by bit we come to know where he lives, what he does, what his social circumstances are. The man ceases to be a pale abstraction, and in short becomes to us really a man. I cannot in the same sense make you to know the men and women of Glasgow. I can only build up in your minds by the aid of a few figures and general facts, some notion of the physical circumstances of an impersonal average inhabitant. When we think of a citizen of Rome or of Athens, we have before us the outlines of a being whose home-life and occupation and amusements and general surroundings we could describe. Let us see whether we cannot so distinguish in our thoughts the citizen of Glasgow from the citizens of other cities in the country.

The point of time to which my statements refer is the 4th of April, 1881, when the census was taken, and nothing capable of expression in figures as to the condition of the population was left to surmise. The inhabitants of Glasgow numbered 511,520 souls. The area of the earth's surface on which they lived extends from E. to W. 5 miles, and from N. to S. fully 3 miles, and contains 6111 acres or fully 9½ square miles. These data enable us to work out the most important physical fact in the condition of men in the aggregate, viz. the proportion of their number to the extent of the earth's surface on which they live. A man may learn to exist without air for several minutes if he wishes so to distinguish himself; a man may live for several days without food; and clothing is not at all essential to life, but *space* to live on and in is an absolute necessity. I do not wish to be led into a discussion of 'the rights of man' as a citizen, but it is well now-a-days to remember this at any rate, that if man has any rights at all, one of them certainly is—the right to enough of the area of the earth's surface to afford him standing room, and enough of the cubic space of air thereon at least to crouch in. You may call it a luxury to give him a room to lie down in, and space to stretch himself in, but to deny him standing and crouching room is to say in the laconic language of Aytoun's ballad, 'You shall not exist for another day more!' In the phraseology of vital statistics and proportion of population to the earth's surface is called the 'density' of that population. In Glasgow the density is 84 persons per acre. The exact meaning of this statement is, that if the whole population were distributed equally over 6111 acres, there would be on each acre 84 persons; or if each person were assigned his own share of this acre it would of course be the 84th part of an acre, or about 58 square yards. The significance of this fact can be brought home to your minds only by comparison with other cities. There is only one city in Great Britain which exceeds Glasgow in density, and that is Liverpool where there are 106 persons to the acre. The only city which approached Glasgow in density is Manchester, where are about 80 persons to the acre. The density of London is only 51, and of Edinburgh only 55. Excepting Greenock and Edinburgh no other town in Scotland exceeds half the density of Glasgow; most are far below that figure.

Let us endeavour to unfold to you somewhat the meaning of this first fact concerning the average citizen of Glasgow—that he has less of the earth's surface on which to live than the citizen of any city save one in the kingdom. This area gives us the proportion of the universal bounties of nature which he enjoys. The vertical space of the general atmosphere rests upon the 84th part of an acre on which he stands. We measure the sunshine and the rainfall by this area. Nor do we fully represent the state of the case if we infer that the inhabitant of the city gets a smaller share of the full quantity of these bounties of nature. The denser the city is, the more befouled is the earth with organic impurities; the thicker becomes the canopy of smoke which cuts off the sunshine; the fouler are the rain and the streams and springs which traverse the earth. The self-purifying functions of soil and air and water are over-powered by the amount of the work thrown upon them and the unnatural circumstances under which it has to be attempted. From these disadvantages of density therefore Glasgow suffers beyond all other cities, and as I have elsewhere said: 'Altogether we are as far shut out from the ministry of nature as the necessities of the case, combined with the aggravations of human ignorance, perversity, and wilful self-aggrandisement can place us.'

I have said that this element of density is calculated upon the assumption that all persons are equally distributed over the area of the city, each standing in the centre of his or her own plot. On this supposition another fact may be worked out, which is—the average 'proximity' of each person to his neighbour. This is simply the length of a straight line drawn from the centre of one plot to the next. In Glasgow this is slightly over 8 yards. You will understand at once that the proximity must vary exactly as the density, and therefore in Glasgow we are on the average nearer to each other than in any city save Liverpool. This means that in the various relations of our lives we are more apt to jostle against and interfere with one another, either for good or for evil. As I confine myself at present to physical relations, it is obvious that we are more apt to interfere with one another to our mutual disadvantage. This is absolutely and universally true as regards physical evil. Take infectious disease as a typical illustration. Throughout the community as a whole, infection, which means the passage of a material something from person to person, must take place in proportion to their average proximity. If that is in Glasgow 8 yards and in Edinburgh 10, then the chances favourable to infection in Glasgow must be in that proportion greater in Edinburgh, unless indeed by greater care in the treatment of cases of infectious disease we diminish those chances.

Now let us turn to the class of facts upon which Mr. Bright touched. As a matter of fact, the population is not equally distributed over the area of any city. The space in which people really live—that space the extent of which most influences their health and comfort, and even conditions the moral relations of their lives—is the space which is their own, viz. their house-room. The extent of this space or the size of the house determines the local density. While the average density of all Glasgow is 84 persons per acre, the local density varies from 26 to 348, in the 24 sanitary districts into which the city is divided. You can apply for yourselves to these facts all that I have said as to the evils of density. If we classify all the houses in Glasgow, we find that in every 100 there are 30 of only one apartment, 44 of only two apartments, 15 of three, and only 5 of five apartments and upwards. This enormous proportion of small houses will sufficiently explain the low average rental of a Glasgow house. The hovels of the East completely swamp the palaces of the West, and produce an average of only £11 6s. 9d. The size of this average house is only 2.3 rooms, each occupied by 2 persons fully (2.042). The highest average of rooms per house in any district is a little over 4; the lowest considerably under 2. The highest average of inmates per room is about 3; the lowest 1¼. I am unable to give you parallel statements regarding any other city, because the data have not been worked out. Indeed, the materials do not exist excepting for Glasgow, so that I may ask you to note this fact, that the authorities of Glasgow have a minute knowledge of the physical condition of their people which no other authorities possess, and therefore ignorance cannot be pled in extenuation of any back-wardness in improving this condition. I can, however, give you the exact comparative position of your city among the eight chief towns of Scotland as regards the proportion of their populations living in the various sizes of house. Mr. Bridge gave the proportion of families, but it is of more importance in estimating the extent to which the advantages and disadvant-ages of house-room are imposed upon the population to ascertain the proportion of individuals. Of the inhabitants of Glasgow, 25 per cent. live in houses of one apartment; 45 per cent. in houses of two apartments; 16 per cent. in houses of three apartments;

6 per cent. in houses of four apartments; and only 8 per cent. in houses of five apartments and upwards. There is no town in Scotland which has so large a proportion of its population living in one-room houses. There is no town in Scotland which has so small a proportion of its population living in houses of five rooms and upwards. In Edinburgh, above 27 per cent. of the people live in houses of five apartments and upwards, and only 17 per cent. in houses of one apartment. The dreadful struggle for life in Glasgow as compared with Edinburgh is shown by the fact that in Glasgow one-room houses contain more inmates on the average than in Edinburgh, and the large houses fewer. But even in Glasgow there are only 7.8 persons in the large houses as compared with fully 3 in the one-room houses—a difference in the physical circumstances of these two classes of citizens which alone places them far as the poles asunder in respect of the preservation of health and the opportunity for purity of life. I am anxious to emphasize this difference by the accumulation of facts which can be expressed in cold figures. Figures are beyond the reach of sentiment, and, if they are sensational, it is only because of their terrible, undisguised truthfulness. You must not think of the inmates of those small houses as families in the ordinary sense of the term. No less than 14 per cent. of the one-roomed houses and 27 per cent. of the two-roomed houses contain lodgers—strange men and women mixed up with husbands and wives and children, within the four walls of small rooms. Nor must I permit you in noting down the tame average of fully 3 inmates in each of these one-apartment houses to remain ignorant of the fact that there are thousands of these homes which contain 5, 6, and 7 inmates, and hundreds which are inhabited by from 8 up even to 13!

Percentages, though an accurate, are but a feeble mode of expression for such facts regarding men and women like ourselves. I have told you that in 1881 the population of Glasgow was 511,520 persons, and that of those 25 per cent. lived in one-room and 45 per cent. in two-roomed houses; but what does that mean? It means that 126,000 persons *live* in those one-roomed, and 228,000 in those two-roomed houses. But is that all I can say? I might throw down the statement before you, and ask you imagine yourselves, with all your appetites and passions, your bodily necessities and functions, your feelings of modesty, your sense of propriety, your births, your sicknesses, your deaths, your children,—in short, your *lives* in the whole round of their relationship with the seen and the unseen, suddenly shrivelled and shrunk into such conditions of space. I *might* ask you, I *do* ask you, to consider and honestly confess what would be the result to you. But I would fain do more. Generalities are so feeble. Yet how can I speak to you decently of details? Where can I find language in which to clothe the facts of these poor people's lives, and yet be tolerable? The words of Herr Teufelsdröckh [Thomas Carlyle, *Sartor Resartus*], when at midnight, from his attic lodging, he looked down upon the town of Weissnichtwo, will help me a little. He said to his friend—'Oh, under that hideous coverlet of vapours, and putrefactions, and unimaginable gases, what a Fermenting-vat lies simmering and hid! The joyful and the sorrowful are there; men are dying there, men are being born; men are praying,—on the other side of a brick partition men are cursing; and around them all is the vast, void Night . . . Wretchedness cowers into truckle beds, or shivers hunger-stricken into its lair of straw; in obscure cellars *Rouge-et-Noir* languidly emits its voice-of-destiny to haggard, hungry villains . . . Riot cries aloud, and staggers and swaggers in his rank dens of shame; and the mother, with streaming hair, kneels over her pallid, dying infant, whose cracked lips only her tears now moisten.—All these heaped and huddled together, with nothing but a little carpentry and masonry between them; crammed in like salted fish in their barrel; or weltering, shall I say, like an Egyptian pitcher of tamed vipers, each struggling to get its *head above* the others: *such* work goes on under that smoke-counterpane!'

It is those small houses which produce the high death-rate of Glasgow. It is those small houses which give to that death-rate the striking characteristics of an enormous proportion of death in childhood, and deaths from diseases of the lungs at all ages. Their exhausted air and poor and perverse feeding fill our streets with bandy-legged children. There you will find year after a death-rate of 38 per 1000, while in the districts with larger houses it is only 16 or 17. Of all the children who die in Glasgow before they complete their fifth year, 32 per cent. die in houses of one apartment; and not 2 per cent. in houses of five apartments and upwards. There they die, and their little bodies are laid on a table or on the dresser, so as to be somewhat out of the way of their brothers and sisters, who play and sleep and eat in their ghastly company. From beginning to rapid-ending the lives of these children are short parts in a continuous tragedy. A large proportion enter life by the side-door of illegitimacy. One in every five of all who are born there never see the end of their first year. Of those who so prematurely die, a third have never been seen in their sickness by any doctor. 'The tongue of the sucking child cleaveth to the roof of his mouth for thirst; the young children ask bread and no man breaketh it unto them.' Every year in Glasgow the deaths of from 60 to 70 children under five years of age are classified by the Registrar-General as due to accident or negligence; and it is wholly in these small houses that such deaths occur. Half of that number are overlain by drunken mothers, others fall over windows and down stairs, are drowned in tubs of and pails of water, scalded, or burned, or poisoned with whisky. I can only venture to lift a corner of the curtain which veils the life which is lived in these houses. It is impossible to show you more.

These are some of the worst fruits of life in the one and two roomed house, the ultimate products of that degeneration, moral and physical, which proves that the whole bias and tendency of life there is downwards. But let us ask ourselves what life in one room can be, taken at its best. Return to those 126,000 men, women, and children, whose house is one apartment, and consider whether, since the world began, man or angel ever had such a task set before them as this—the creation of the elements of a home, or the conduct of family life within four bare walls. You mistresses of houses, with bed-rooms and parlours, dining-rooms and drawing-rooms, kitchens and washing-houses, pantries and sculleries, how could you put one room to the uses of all? You mothers, with your cooks and housemaids, your nurses and general servants, how would you in your own persons act all those parts in one room, where, too, you must eat and sleep and find your lying-in-room and make your sick-bed? You fathers, with your billiard-room, your libraries and parlours, your dinner parties, your evening hours undisturbed by washing-days, your children brought to you when they can amuse you, and far removed when they become troublesome, how long would you continue to be that pattern husband which you are—in one room? You children, with your nurseries and nurses, your toys and your picture books, your space to play in without being trodden upon, your children's parties and your daily airings, your prattle which does not disturb your sick mamma, your special table spread with a special meal, your seclusion from contact with the dead, and the still worse familiarity with the living, where would you find your innocence, and how would you preserve the dew and freshness of your infancy—in one room? You grown-up sons, with all the resources of your fathers for indoor amusement, with your cricket field and football club and skating pond, with your own bedroom, with space which makes self-restraint easy and decency natural, how could you wash and dress, and sleep and eat and spend your leisure hours in a house of—one room? You grown-up daughters, with your bed-rooms and your bath-rooms, your piano and your drawing-room, your little brothers and sisters to toy with when you have a mind to, and send out of the way when you cannot be troubled, your every want supplied, without sharing in menial household work, your society regulated, and no rude rabble of lodgers to sully the purity of your surroundings, how could you live and preserve 'the white flower of a blameless life'—in one room? You sick ones, in your hushed seclusion, listen to Charles Lamb's description of you:—'Household rumours touch him not. Some faint murmur, indicative of life going on within the house, soothes him, while he knows not distinctly what it is. He is not to know anything, not to think of anything. Servants gliding up or down the distant staircase, treading as upon velvet, gently keep his ear awake, so long as he troubles not himself further then with some feeble guess at their errands . . . He opens his eye faintly at the dull stroke of the muffled knocker, and closes it again without asking—"Who was it?" He is flattered by a general notion that inquiries are making after him, but he cares not to know the name of the inquirer. In the general stillness and awful hush of the house, he lies in state and feels his sovereignty.' How would *you* deport yourself in the racket and thoughtless noise of your nursery, in the heat and smells of your kitchen, in the steam and disturbance of your washing-house, for you would find all these combined in a house of—one room? Last of all when *you* die, *you* still have one room to yourself, where in decency you may be washed and dressed and laid out for burial. If that one room were your house, what a ghastly intrusion you would be! The bed on which you lie is wanted for the accommodation of the living. The table at which your children ought to sit must bear your coffin, and they must keep your unwelcome company. Day and night you lie there until with difficulty those who carry you out thread their tortuous way along the dark lobby and down the narrow stair through a crowd of women and children. You are driven along the busy and unsympathetic streets, lumbering beneath the vehicle which conveys your scanty company to the distant and cheerless cemetery, where the acrid and deadly air of the city in which you lived will still blow over you and prevent even a blade of grass from growing upon your grave.

I think you will agree with me in this inference, that in the city in which we live there is great room for the development of practical Christianity. There is probably no better field in the three kingdoms for those who would imitate Christ in ministering to the bodies as well as to the souls of men: and there is no hope for the people who live in one and two roomed houses unless the Church, which is the healing hand of Christ still present in our midst, becomes the motive power in society, directing our rulers to wise public measures, and stirring the hearts of individuals to private beneficence. The question for us is, what can we do? The solution of the social problems of the age is for us the doing of something here and now. Our lives are fleeting: the lives of those who furnish the problem are fleeting, and if we act not now, we shall be 'unprofitable servants,' and those we might have profited will rise up in the judgement against us.

It is obvious that no manner of occupancy will make a one-room house a home in the proper sense of the word. Not that many an isolated man or woman or aged couple may not find in it a wholesome and suitable dwelling-place, and enjoy therein the privilege of independence. Even the young couple who have 'married for love' while yet in the stage of 'working for sillar' may light their first fire on the hearth of the one-room house. These are the anomalies of life, and under certain conditions I take no exception to the one-room house in itself, because it undoubtedly meets them; but, I repeat, a home in the proper sense of the word, a place for the nurture of a family it can never be. Therefore there is among us a large population which is, from whatever ultimate cause, absolutely debarred from the requisite physical conditions even of the lowest standard of home comfort, and which is always on the inclined plane of moral deterioration. We may discuss, if we please, the question whether there ought to be such houses, whether it is necessary that there should be such houses, whether their existence depends upon inadequate wages, or the mis-spending of adequate wages. Indeed these questions ought to be discussed; but let us not meanwhile forget that there they *are*, and that human beings are living in them under the physical and moral disadvantages described, and we are bound to endeavour to make their lives happier and better. I venture to believe this very endeavour is the most natural and most likely way bit by bit to do away with one-room houses, by recognizing that their inmates are our brothers and sisters, and so elevate their aspirations and restore them to self-respect. If we deny them this recognition I see no prospect for them but degeneracy into 'Dead Sea apes,' or something worse! It is encouraging to know that Glasgow is improving. In 1861 there were in a much smaller population 145,000 persons living in one apartment. There are now, as I have said, 126,000; and there is a corresponding increase in the inhabitants of houses of two and three apartments. We are therefore moving in the right direction, and that not by any revolutionary force from without, but by a higher standard of life growing in the minds of the people. Still the inhabitants of those small houses require our active Christian sympathy and assistance, and in a city which is the greatest aggregation of working people with the smallest admixture of the wealthy class to be found in this country there will always be this necessity.

Here let me interject a word on areas of local government in relation to social helpfulness and sympathy. Local government is the expression in administration of community of interest. Men are not driven together by fortuitous gusts like heaps of dead leaves. The locality of the city is determined by the satisfaction of some motive purpose—the shelter of the castle or the monastery, the stream favourable for traffic, for manufactures, the port for trade, the many various incidents of place which tempt the migrant to become the settler. So by harmony of motive aggregation goes on until in time comes the sense of the need of local government. A boundary must be defined, and it is drawn around the whole community; but frequently the community increases and overflows this boundary. Clearly there ought to be some automatic method of from time to time including these overflows, and so preserving unity of government in that which is essentially an organic whole. Unfortunately, boundaries have political as well as social importance, and are the subjects of gerrymandering; and so our lawgivers regard questions of boundaries with an eye to political issues. Within the family, which is the unit of society, there is mutual helpfulness and interdependence. Between one family and another in a community there is mutual helpfulness and interdependence. If it were not so communities never would have existed. Where, in the aggregation of families and householders on one soil, under the expanse of one sky, in the soft embrace of one atmosphere, shadowed by the same passing cloud, or made bright by one sun, smitten by the same disease or adversity, rejoiced by the same health or prosperity, where can we safely permit the erection of an administrative barrier, and say, here the necessity for this practical sympathy and co-operated ceases? "What God hath joined together, let not man put asunder." Social philosophy and social morality alike demand unity in the civic life, formal, corporate unity. If the employers have hived off the west and built themselves suburban villas; if the skilled artizans and mechanics have gathered in colonies, north, east, and south; if the old parent city has gradually become little more than a workplace, the centre of commercial life and the seat of the power which drives the complicated machinery of the communal activities, where she sits surrounded by the hewers of wood and the drawers of water, by the prodigals of her family, the bankrupt in fortune and the criminals, how distraught is the community! Does the political economist ask information as to the amount and the incidence of municipal taxation, as to the prevalence of poverty or crime and the expenditure in poor-rates and police, as to the state of labour, the number of unemployed and the method of providing for them. He can get no information which is not misleading. Does the statistician wish to follow the movement of the marriage-rate, the birth-rate, and the death-rate? The figures we supply are not those of the community at all. If the sociologist attempts to reason upon them he is sure to stumble into fallacies. Water-supply, gas-supply, hospitals, tramways, all those developments of municipal co-operation for the more efficient and economical satisfaction of common needs are essentially crippled in their application. Police, cleansing, sanitation, sewerage, and all the ordinary objects of local government are made more difficult to attainment. Taxation of every kind being sectional is unfair. The strong do not share the burdens of the weak. In one body, traversed by the same system of arteries and veins and nerves, there can be no such thing as a local benefit or a local injury. In such a distraught community as I am describing the local benefit so-called becomes a local injustice. Parks, museums, picture galleries, everything provided by local money for public use is unavoidably enjoyed by those who do not contribute to the cost or maintenance. There is a constant antagonism in the minds of several authorities between the broad dictates of state craft and the narrow impulses of parochialism. Some sense of the good of all moves blindly towards the former, but jealousies, rivalries, and the necessity of maintaining a show of local patriotism determine the supremacy of the latter. Glasgow has done much to supply by taxation those physical accessories of small houses which dwellers in large houses provide for themselves, which from mere want of space the poor cannot have, but which, if they are indeed brothers and sisters, they require as much as the rich. Taxation for such purposes is eminently Christian in motive and effect. It may be called Christian Socialism. All contribute, but the well-to-do are not taxed directly for their own benefit, although it is to be hoped we recognize the truth of one of those sayings of the late Prince Leopold which make us regret his untimely death—'Along the ways of wisdom and virtue we shall all advance further, if we all advance together.'

Our public baths and wash-houses are the best and most ample in the country. Every inmate of a small house may find there those conveniences for private ablutions which cannot be got at home, and the women may, at a trifling cost, avoid turning their homes into washing-houses. Our model lodging houses help to lessen the horrid evil of lodgers in small houses. The sick, in so far as their sickness arises from infectious disease, have access without special charge to what is the finest Fever Hospital in the country, and infected clothing, &c., is removed, washed and returned clean as punctually and carefully as by any commercial laundry company. We still require public mortuaries to lessen the necessity for the ghastly presence of the dead in the one-room house. Our parks, galleries and museums furnish means of recreation, culture and instruction, but we have no system of Free Libraries bringing books and quiet room for study to every district of the city. There is also a sad want of play spaces for the little children in Glasgow. I shall have something more to say on behalf of the children when I come to speak of various forms of private beneficiaries, but I wish our authorities would think a little more of the toddling 'things' who cannot walk to our parks, and whose mothers have not time to carry them thither. One often stumbles over them creeping about dark lobbies, and many a time one has to pick his steps carefully, so as not to interfere with their attempts to play at houses on the stairs. If they venture further they will find only the dead air and nauseous environments of the back courts, or the dangerous street. Probably the Glasgow boy is the wildest, most destructive specimen of a boy in existence, and why? It is a law of child-nature to be constantly moving, constantly doing something, and what can a poor boy do in Glasgow but pull bricks out of the walls of the ashpits, or climb on to the roof and tear off the slates. The landlords complain that the police do not protect their property. If they would not be so greedy of the soil, but provide more space for innocent games, the evil would be cured. I need scarcely say that I sympathize with the poor boys more than with the landlords. I also think that a few open spaces here and there, made clean and smooth with asphalt or granolithic, where boys could spin tops and little children could sprawl about in safety, would serve the necessities of the rising generation better than the parks. There also, some area, clear of shrubs and flower-beds ought to be preserved for young men. Where can working lads go to get a game at football or play at cricket? The young men of the West-end expend large sums of money to obtain space for these recreations; and even they are every year driven further away and put to greater expense. It is sad to see the poorer lads lounging at the close-mouths, when they ought to be developing their muscles, and acquiring that love of out-door sport which is the best antidote to the temptations of the music hall, the dancing saloon, and the dram shop. Yet, what can they do? Their poor pence will not suffice for the rent of a field, and they ought to be supplied out of the public funds. Let us have public gymnasia; and, if we are to be breeders of men and not of vicious loafers, do not let us confine our efforts to the growing of grass in our parks and the luxury of looking at it over an iron railing.

Now, let us turn to the development of practical Christianity by private effort. Hospitals for the sick are the special product of Christianity . . . Glasgow is well supplied with general hospitals; but not too well. Their resources are drawn upon to meet the wants, not of Glasgow merely, but of the enormous working population of Lanarkshire. Another [the Victoria Infirmary] is about to be built on the south-side. I do not think these hospitals are supported as they ought to be by the public of Glasgow. If the miseries of sickness in small houses were more vividly before the public mind, I am sure the benevolent gentlemen who give so much of their time to the management of those institutions would not be worried as they constantly are about their finances. They require more of the shillings and half-crowns of the middle classes. There is no way in which money can be charitably bestowed with less risk of being mis-applied.

But when thinking of the physical disadvantages of small houses as a subject of benevolent help and alleviations, what comes to my thoughts with ever recurring persistence is the dull, dead, unrelieved monotony of the conditions of life within them and around them. Mr. Buckle wrote a history of civiliza-tion, the philosophy of which was that in form and character civilization was determined by the influence of physical agents—climate, soil, food, and the general aspects of nature—on the races of mankind. Under general aspects of nature he contended for 'the influence exercised by the external world in pre-disposing men to certain habits of thought, and thus giving a particular tone to religion, arts, literature, and, in a word, to all the principal manifestations of the human mind.' Buckle went too far in his desire to make the moral and spiritual nature of man entirely the product of external and material agencies; so that, soul and body, he must change with the flora and fauna of his district. But it is certainly true that the physical surroundings even of the individual man will leave their mark on his soul as well as on his body; and the one result may be as regards his individual responsibility, as inevitable as the other. Place 126,000 human beings in one-room houses, and 43,000 in houses of five rooms and upwards, and, no matter who or what they are, you have at once determined for them much both of their moral and physical future. If their course is downwards, the one class has further to fall than the other before both reach the same depth. If their course is to be upwards, the one class has not so far to rise as the other before both reach the same height. All through life man divides his time between work and sleep and play,—play including all ways of spending those hours which are not absorbed in work and sleep. The education of the child and the toil of the adult are *regulated for him*, and imposed upon him. The *play* of both is in its character *a matter of choice*, and nothing shows more clearly the inner nature than the nature of the play. But the nature of the play is very much a matter of education and of opportunity; and the opportunity of the child is the education of the adult. If the child has only the dark lobby and the stair to play in, then the man and woman will find amusement only in the dram shop, the music hall, and the dancing saloon. The gutter child grows up into the loafer. The hard-working man when he gets a holiday does not know how to spend it. Even when he finds himself in the country, he has frequently no eye for the scenery, or for the beauties of the grass and the flowers. He carries too often a bottle of whisky in his pocket, and he makes himself an object of alarm and disgust. The hard-working woman either joins in the debauch or thinks no shame to be seen in the company of intoxicated men. There is no way of forming a just opinion as to these habits of the inhabitants of our small houses, but by calmly and conscientiously analysing what I might call the physics of our own morality. If Buckle has successfully proved regarding mankind in the mass, inhabiting different regions of the earth, that there is an 'influence exercised by the external world in predisposing men to certain habits of thought, and thus giving a particular tone to religion, arts, literature, and, in a word, to all the principal manifestations of the human mind,' and I believe he has, then is it possible that the one and two roomed house piled up in tenements, and these tenements again ranked in streets and packed into back courts, can produce the same manner of men as the large houses with all the luxurious space and opportunity of the softening ministration of nature *without,* and the tender wooing of light and warmth and comfortable domesticity *within?* I confess for myself that the physical circumstances of the poor in Glasgow are so contrary in their nature to those which have surrounded me throughout my life and I recognize such a close relationship between my physical circumstances and the general character of my life, that I can come only to one or other of two conclusions: Either the poor belong to a different species of the genus man, or the same relationship must exist between *their* different physical circumstances and the different general character of *their* lives.

I feel that I am occupying your time too much with general philosophizing. I have striven to lead you into an intelligent view of your relations as Christians to the city in which we live. I plead for general helpfulness to enable the inhabitants of the one-roomed houses to bear the burdens of their lives. I must leave you to find out for yourselves the various methods, which may lie to your hands and be adapted to your individual circumstances and capacities, of working in the general direction which I have indicated. I commend to your kindly interest and Christian liberality the Association for Nursing the Sick Poor at Home, the Kyrle Society, the Day Nurseries, the Day Feeding Schools. Poor Children's Dinner Tables, Flower Missions, Fresh-air Funds, Foundry Boys' Association, and the like. I put in a special word for the children because of their essential helplessness, and because they are the men and women of the future. It is so easy to make a child happy. If you only take a few poor children to the country for a day, or admit them to a garden or a plot or grass for an hour or two; or gather a few together on a winter's night and show them a magic lantern, or play to them and teach them a lively game, or sing a nursery rhyme, or tell them a nursery story, their happiness is secured. I read lately the life of Paul Merritt, a man who was born in the most miserable circumstances, but who grew up to be a well-known art critic; and the first awakening of his faculty was a peep through a keyhole into a garden. He writes—'I was in my eleventh year, meanly clothed, poorly fed, and penniless—an errand-boy in receipt of 1s. 6d. a week.' He discovered a garden, peeping with a boy's curiosity through the keyhole in the tall wooden gate. 'I looked through the keyhole every time I passed and that was four times daily, and always with increased interest, for my flowering aconite. But oh! trouble upon trouble, one day I found the keyhole stopped, and there was an end of my daily joy and of the interest which had awakened in me a new craving for the wonders of nature.' A few days after, grubbing among the rubbish thrown out from this garden he found a budding something which seemed to him to have 'the promise and potency of life,' though of what sort he know not. He nurtured it in an old teapot, and it shortly burst out—the first crocus he had ever seen. Years after, when surrounded with beauty in his studio in London, he described how—'one sunny, silent, Sunday morning, this crocus opened its golden glowing sacramental cup, gleaming like light from heaven, dropped in a dark place, living light and fire.' Let this experience teach you by what simple means—a flower, a song, one bright day in the country— child-nature may in its growth be turned upwards towards the light.

I have now in a way very fragmentary and not at all satisfactory to myself, but the only way possible to a busy man, brought before you the physical circumstances of the inhabitants of the city in which you live as a field for practical Christianity. I have said the only hope for Glasgow lies in the Church, which alone has the hand endowed with virtue to convey healing to those social sores. The same may be said of all our towns according to their special necessities. The constantly increasing proportion of the population of this country which is concentrating round our towns constitutes one of the most anxious features of the times. Be assured if the Church neglects this field, the devil and his ministers will not. Those one and two roomed houses are filled with restless, uncomfortable souls, wakening up to the contrast between their misery and the luxury of their neighbours, and ready to grasp at any theory or project however wild, which promises material relief. Nihilism, Communism, Socialism, Mr. George Bradlaugh—any sort 'of Morrison's Pill' will be eagerly swallowed. That is the future before us if the Church does not carry soothing and sanity to the physical discomforts of the people. I cannot find words in which to take leave of you and of my subject, better than those of Carlyle:—

'It is to you, ye Workers, who do already work, and are as grown men, noble and honourable in a sort, that the whole world calls for new work and nobleness. Subdue mutiny, discord, wide-spread despair, by manfulness, justice, mercy, and wisdom. Chaos is dark, deep as Hell; let light be, and there is instead a green flowery World. Oh, it is great, and there is no other greatness. To make some nook of God's creation a little fruitfuller, better, more worthy of God; to make some human hearts a little wiser, manfuller, happier—more blessed, less accursed! It is work for a God. Sooty Hell of mutiny and savagery and despair can, by man's energy, be made a kind of Heaven; cleared of its soot, of its mutiny, of its *need* to mutiny; the everlasting arch of heaven's azure overspanning *it* too, and its cunning mechanisms and tall chimney-steeples; God and all men looking on it well pleased.

Notes

Abbreviations

Preface

1. These encounters were described by Russell in a lecture in 1894 and reprinted in *Public Health Administration in Glasgow* (Glasgow, 1905), pp. 228–243. The book is a memorial volume of his writings edited by his successor, A. K. Chalmers.
2. JBR, *Public Health*, p. 564.
3. JBR, *Public Health*, pp. 231–2.
4. JBR, *Public Health*, p. 196. (His famous lecture, 'Life in One Room'.)
5. The ticketed housing system is described as 'totalitarian' by T. C. Smout in his contribution to *The Cambridge Social History of Britain, 1750–1950, Volume I: Regions and Communities*, edited by F. M. L. Thompson (Cambridge, 1990). S. G. Checkland in *The Upas Tree* (Glasgow, 1976) points out that there is little evidence that Russell and his contemporaries 'feared the people of the slums in any sense other than that of increasing social

and sanitary blight' and that 'there is a good deal to suggest deep human concern.'

6. The phrase was used by one of Russell's successors, Sir Alexander Macgregor, in *Public Health in Glasgow, 1905–1946* (Edinburgh, 1967). A later occupant of the post, Dr T. Scott Wilson, said that Russell 'was a bonnie fighter in his day and was well thought of by his successors and all who sat about Montrose Street.' (Interview with Dr T. Scott Wilson, 1993)

7. Brenda White has described his achievements in 'James Burn Russell, MOH, Glasgow 1872–1898', *Proceedings of the Scottish Society of the History of Medicine*, 1985–6, pp. 1–9 and 'James Burn Russell', *Glasgow Medicine*, July–August 1986, pp. 20–22. Olive Checkland describes him as 'a man of flair and vision' in Olive Checkland and Margaret Lamb (eds.), *Health Care as Social History: The Glasgow Case* (Aberdeen, 1982), p. 16. T. C Smout in *A Century of the Scottish People, 1830–195* (London, 1986), p. 44 claims that he 'did more than any other man of his age to bring home to the ignorant and complacent the horrible realities of slum disease.'

Chapter One

1. Sources of information on Russell's birth and family background include the family archives in the possession of Mrs Agnes Rodgers and records of Barony Parish.

2. Andrew Aird, *Printers and Printing in Glasgow, 1830–1890* (privately printed in Glasgow, 1891), pp. 58–59. The author was the brother of John Aird, David Russell's partner.

3. John Cassels's sederunt book; Marriage Trust of John Houston Cassels; Marriage Trust of John Robert Cassels, GCA T-MS/42–44

4. Steamboat Harbourmaster's Memorandum Book, Clyde Navigation Trust records, GCA T-CN/18–1.

5. Quoted in Dorothy and Alan Shelston, *The Industrial City, 1820–1870* (London, 1990), pp. 78–79.

6. Both Symons and Miller are quoted in JBR, *Public Health*, pp. 7–9. Other sources of information on Glasgow at that time include Edwin Chadwick, *Report on the Sanitary Condition of the Labouring Population of Great Britain, 1842*, ed. M. W. Flinn (Edinburgh, 1965); W. Hamish Fraser and Irene Maver (eds.), *Glasgow, Vol. 2, 1830–1912* (Manchester, 1996); R. A. Cage, 'Health in Glasgow', in *The Working Class in Glasgow, 1750–1914*, ed. R. A. Cage (London 1987); W. Hamish Fraser and R. J. Morris, *People and Society in Scotland, Vol. 2, 1830–1914* (Edinburgh, 1990); Olive and Sydney Checkland, *Industry and Ethos in Scotland, 1832–1914*; Michael Pacione, *Glasgow: The Socio-Spatial Development of the City* (Chichester, 1995); Andrew Gibb, *Glasgow: the Making of a City*; Stephanie M. Blackden, 'The Development of Public Health Administration in Glasgow, 1842–1872' (Edinburgh University thesis, 1976); C. I. Pennington, 'Mortality, Public Health, and Medical Improvements in Glasgow, 1855–1911' (Stirling

University thesis, 1977); J. M. Reid, *Glasgow* (London, 1956); and Maurice
Lindsay, *An Illustrated Guide to Glasgow, 1837* (London, 1989).

7. T. M. Devine, and Gordon Jackson (eds.), *Glasgow, Vol. 1: Beginnings to
1830* (Manchester, 1995), p. 410.

8. Devine and Jackson, *Glasgow*, p. 410.

Chapter Two

1. *The New Statistical Account of Scotland, Vol. VI: Lanarkshire* (Edinburgh,
1845).

2. Hugh Macdonald, *Rambles Round Glasgow*, 2nd edition (Glasgow, 1910),
pp. 106–107.

3. John Brownlee, 'Biographical Sketch of the Late James B. Russell, M. D.,
LL. D.', *Transactions of the Royal Philosophical Society of Glasgow*, February,
1905.

4. W. Ross Shearer, *Rutherglen Lore* (Paisley, 1922), pp. 229–230.

5. Macdonald, *Rambles*, p. 106.

6. JBR, 'Miscellaneous Papers', a scrapbook started in 1861, National Library
of Scotland, ABS 3.80.20.

7. Obituary of James Burn Russell, *Lancet*, November 12, 1904. The writer
was apparently confusing the generations when he attributed these
qualities to Russell's mother and father respectively, rather than to his
grandparents.

8. Rev. Ambrose Shepherd, *In Memorium James Burn Russell* (Glasgow, 1904).
Shepherd was the pastor of Elgin Place Congregational Church in Bath
Street, which was the successor to the West George Street chapel. *In
Memorium* is the sermon that he delivered at a memorial service.

9. 'The Late Mr Russell of the Clyde Police': obituary of James Russell, *GH*,
November 4, 1864.

10. The incident was described by Russell's son David in a letter to Lord
Bryce in 1915. 'The Papers of James Bryce, Viscount Bryce of Dechmont,
1838–1922,' Bodleian Library Mss 1–528, folio 122.

11. Letter from JBR to James Bryce, June 13, 1865, 'Bryce Papers,' folio 153.

12. 'Obituary of James Russell', *GH*.

13. David Russell, 'Soldiers' Wives and Children: or, forty years ago,' *Sydney
Morning Herald*, June, 1854.

14. Percy Groves, *History of the 2nd Dragoons—the Royal Scots Greys, 1678–1893*:
Illustrated History of the Scottish Regiments, Book 2 (Edinburgh, 1893), p. 15.

15. The letter is quoted in an article written by Russell's son David and
published in the *Vernon News*, Vernon, British Columbia on June 15, 1911.
It differs considerably from the version given in the *Sydney Morning Herald*
by JBR's father in 1854. The later version seems certain to have been a
direct transcription of the original letter, whereas the earlier David Russell
would be writing from memory since the letters would still be in the
possession of his parents in Scotland. The sentimental style of writing

adopted by the earlier David Russell, and his obvious desire to pull at the heartstrings of potential donors to his Waterloo widows and orphans fund, suggest that he embroidered fairly freely, although it is possible that he was drawing on tales told by his father.

16. David Russell, Soldiers' Wives, *Sydney Morning Herald.*

Chapter Three

1. James Pagan, *Sketches of the History of Glasgow* (Glasgow, 1847), p. 105.
2. Quoted in C. A. Oakley, *Our Illustrious Forbears* (Glasgow, 1980), p. 33.
3. Quoted in JBR, *Public Health Administration in Glasgow* (Glasgow, 1905), pp. 106–107.
4. Letter from James Bryce, The High School of Glasgow, July 20, 1863, WIL Ms. 5143/20. About 100 letters received by Russell, including correspondence from Kelvin and Lister, are in this collection in the Western Manuscripts section of the Wellcome Institute Library.
5. Harry A. Ashmall, *The High School of Glasgow* (Edinburgh, 1976), pp. 75, 82–3.
6. Letter from James Bryce, WIL.
7. A peak in the Rockies is named after him. His accomplishments as a mountaineer and conservationist are described by Rennie McOwan in 'No Boundaries for Bryce,' *The Scots Magazine*, December, 1993, pp. 592–601.
8. H. A. L. Fisher, *James Bryce, Vol. 1* (London, 1927), p. 13. Fisher attributes the depressions partly to precociousness.
9. JBR, *Public Health* (Glasgow, 1905), p. xvi. Bryce's recollections of Russell are quoted in the editor's biographical note.
10. Edmund Ions, *James Bryce and American Democracy* (London, 1968), p. 16.
11. JBR, 'Miscellaneous Papers,' a scrapbook started in 1861, National Library of Scotland, ABS 3.80.20.
12. *Register of London Medical Society Missionaries*, no. 358, p. 40.

Chapter Four

1. University of Glasgow class registers and calendars 1854–5, 1855–6, 1856–7, 1857–8.
2. The descriptions of Russell's teachers and his student friends are based mainly on two contemporary sources, David Murray's *Memories of the Old College of Glasgow* (Glasgow, 1927) and the autobiographical fragment by Russell's friend Bryce quoted in full in H. A. L. Fisher's *James Bryce, Vol. 1* (London, 1927). pp. 13–35. Murray was a student contemporary of Russell's and knew him personally (see p. 78 of Murray's *Memories*). Other sources include James Coutts, *A History of the University of Glasgow* (Glasgow, 1909) and J. D. Mackie, *The University of Glasgow* (Glasgow, 1954).
3. Fisher, *Bryce*, p. 14.
4. Mackie, *University*, p. 280.

5. Fisher, *Bryce*, pp. 22–25.
6. JBR, *Public Health Administration in Glasgow* (Glasgow, 1905), editor's bigraphical note, p. xvi.
7. Fisher, *Bryce*, p. 23.
8. Robert D. Anderson, *Education and Opportunity in Victorian Scotland: Schools and Universities*, 2nd edition (Edinburgh, 1989), p. 308; Anne Crowther and Marguerite Dupree, 'The Invisible General Practitioner: the Careers of Scottish Medical Students in the Late Nineteenth Century,' *Bulletin of the History of Medicine*, 1996, 70, pp. 387–413.
9. 'Men You Know' no. 101, *The Bailie*, September 23, 1874 pp. 1–2 and 'The Late Rev. David Macrae', *Who's Who in Glasgow, 1909*, pp. 135–137.
10. Dated December 6, 1854 and now in the family archives.
11. Compiled between 1853 and 1860 and now in the family archives. Copy in GCA TD1434/2.
12. JBR, *Public Health*, editor's biographical note, p. xvi.
13. JBR, 'Miscellaneous Papers', a scrapbook starting in 1861, National Library of Scotland, ABS 3.80.20.
14. JBR, *Public Health*, p. xvi.
15. David B. Wilson, 'The Educational Matrix: Physics Education at early Victorian Cambridge, Edinburgh, and Glasgow Universities', in P. M Harman (ed.) *Wranglers and Physicists: Studies on Cambridge Physics in the Nineteenth Century* (Manchester, 1985), p. 34. Secondary education later supplanted the ministry as the most popular career choice among Thomson's top students, as Wilson shows in *Kelvin and Stokes: a Comparative Study in Victorian Physics* (Bristol, 1987), p. 60.
16. Murray, *Memories*, pp. 119–124 and 136.
17. Coutts, *History*, p. 386.
18. Murray, *Memories*, pp. 140–1.
19. Letter from D. M. McFarlane to JBR, February 28, 1862, WIL Ms. 5143/14.
20. Hector Cameron, Obituary of James Burn Russell, *GMJ*, December, 1904.

Chapter Five

1. David B. Wilson, *Kelvin and Stokes: a Comparative Study in Victorian Physics* (Bristol, 1987) p. 60.
2. JBR, *Atlantic Cable Journal*, 1858, GCA TD1434/1. Except where otherwise indicated the journal is the source of the information in this chapter.
3. Crosbie Smith and M. Wise Norton, *Energy and Empire: a Biographical Study of Lord Kelvin* (Cambridge, 1989), p. 669.
4. 'Atlantic Cable: Leaves from the Journal of an Amateur Telegrapher', *The West of Scotland Magazine*, new series no. 59, August, 1859, pp. 312–314. The Irish idyll is described in the second article in a three-part series contributed anonymously.
5. Smith and Norton, *Energy and Empire*, pp. 649–652.

6. Quoted in Silvanus P. Thompson, *The Life of William Thomson, Baron Kelvin of Largs, Vol. 1* (London, 1910), pp. 389–390.

Chapter Six

1. Quoted in Margaret Lamb, 'The Medical Profession', in Olive Checkland and Margaret Lamb (eds.), *Health Care as Social History: the Glasgow Case* (Aberdeen, 1982), p. 17.
2. Recorded in Russell's expedition journal.
3. G. E. Davie, *The Democratic Intellect: Scotland and her Universities in the Nineteenth Century* (Edinburgh, 1961), pp. 41–75. Davie maintains that the 1858 legislation was a social and cultural turning-point because of its failure to underpin the traditional broadly based first degree by complementing it with Continental models of specialist postgraduate study. He also argues that Scottish values were undermined by the new English-style examination system. This view has been challenged by, among others, R. D. Anderson in *Education and Opportunity in Victorian Scotland: Schools and Universities*, 2nd edition (Edinburgh, 1989), which argues that there was no real widening of the base of popular education, but Davie's thesis has been reaffirmed by Andrew Lockhart Walker in *The Revival of the Democratic Intellect* (Edinburgh, 1994), which states that Scots 'did not want intellectual mechanics, but liberally educated men able to reflect on the basis of knowledge.' For the effects of the Medical Act on the new university ordinances on medical education, see James Bradley, Anne Crowther, and Marguerite Dupree, 'Mobility and Selection in Scottish Medical Education, 1858–1886', in *Medical History*, 1996, 40, pp. 1–24. The authors show that the high failure rate of medical students was a deliberate attempt to get rid of the less able.
4. Davie, *Democratic Intellect*, p. 101; James Scotland, *The History of Scottish Education* (London, 1969), vol. 2, pp. 141–146. Scotland describes the 1870s as the last years of the old regime; the critical divide for him was the Universities Act of 1889, which set the pattern of Scottish university education for the twentieth century.
5. Letter from JBR to James Bryce, March 26, 1860, 'The Papers of James Bryce, 1838–1922,' Bodleian Library Mss. 1–528, folio 150.
6. M. Anne Crowther and Brenda M. White, *On Soul and Conscience: The Medical Expert and Crime* (Aberdeen, 1988), pp. 13–2.
7. Minutes of the Proceedings of the Select Committee of the House of Lords on the Glasgow Police (Amendment) Bill, 1890, GCA A3/1/130, p. 66. In his evidence to the committee JBR mentions having been a student in Edinburgh.
8. WTG, 'Memories of College Life', in *The Book of the Jubilee: in Commemoration of the Ninth Jubilee of the University of Glasgow* (Glasgow, 1901), p. 45.
9. Descriptions of Russell's teachers are based on David Murray, *Memories*

of the Old College of Glasgow (Glasgow, 1927); WTG, Memories; James Finlayson, 'Biographical Outline of Sir William T. Gairdner' (unpublished typescript), RCPSG 1/11/112; James Coutts, *A History of the University of Glasgow* (Glasgow, 1909); and J. D. Mackie, *The University of Glasgow* (Glasgow, 1954). Russell's teachers' opinions of Russell are contained in 'Testimonials in Favour of Dr James B. Russell' (RCPSG, Testimonials, vol. 1).

10. Rickman J. Godlee, *Lord Lister* (London, 1917), pp. 90–91; W. Henry Dobbie, 'Reminiscences of "The Chief"', in A. Logan Turner (ed.), *Joseph, Baron Lister, Centenary Volume, 1827–1927* (Edinburgh, 1927), p. 143.

11. Godlee, *Lister*, p. 90.

12. Letter of recommendation from Joseph Lister, Glasgow, April 27, 1863, WIL Ms. 5143/18.

13. Obituary of James Burn Russell, *GMJ*, December, 1904, p. 432. The address was also an expression of support for Lister's application for the post of surgeon at Glasgow Royal Infirmary.

14. JBR, *Public Health Administration in Glasgow* (Glasgow, 1905), editor's biographical note, p. xvii.

15. A lengthy extract from the *Sydney Morning Herald* article is quoted by Sylvanus P. Thompson in *The Life of William Thompson, Baron Kelvin of Largs* (London, 1910), Vol. 1., pp. 360–364, but is attributed merely to 'a junior member of the electrical staff' on the expedition.

16. Letters from the editor of *Recreative Science* to JBR, Stoke Newington, May 16, 1861 and November 21, 1861, WIL Ms. 5143/10 and 13.

17. Letters from W. Sykes to JBR, London, July 19 and August 5, 1859, WIL Ms. 5143/4 and 5.

18. Harold I. Sharlin, *Lord Kelvin: the Dynamic Victorian* (London, 1979), p. 83.

19. Letter from JBR to James Bryce, March 26, 1860, Bryce Papers.

20. Letter from JBR to James Bryce, March 26, 1860, Bryce Papers.

21. Letter from James Bryce to JBR, December 7, 1862, WIL Ms. 5143/16.

22. Murray, *Memories*, p. 343.

23. The nature of the disease is not mentioned in Russell's correspondence, but the *GH* obituary of Russell on October 24, 1904, states that he contracted enteric fever at the Royal Infirmary.

24. Letter from Donald McFarlane to Russell, Glasgow College, February 28, 1862, WIL Ms. 5143/14.

25. Letter from James Bryce to JBR, Oxford, March 13, 1862, WIL Ms. 5143/15.

Chapter Seven

1. Jacqueline Jenkinson, Michael Moss, and Iain Russell, *The Royal: The History of Glasgow Royal Infirmary, 1794–1994* (Glasgow, 1994), pp. 113, 133.

2. T. G. Naysmith, 'The Profession and the Public Health Service,' *SJ*, October, 1896, pp. 422–431.

3. JBR, *Public Health Administration in Glasgow* (Glasgow, 1905), p. 465.

4. Obituary of JBR in *The Scotsman*, October 24, 1904, p. 7.

5. *Glasgow, 1858: Shadow's Midnight Scenes and Social Photographs* (Glasgow, 1976).

6. Olive Checkland, 'Local Government and the Health Environment', in Olive Checkland and Margaret Lamb, *Health Care as Social History: the Glasgow Case* (Aberdeen, 1982), p. 10.

7. Checkland, 'Local Government', p. 7.

8. John Fergus, 'The Medical Institutions of Glasgow', in the British Medical Association's *The Book of Glasgow* (Glasgow, 1922), p. 105.

9. John Patrick, 'The Glasgow School of Medicine', in BMA *Book of Glasgow*, pp. 253–254.

10. George Alexander Gibson, *Life of Sir William Tennant Gairdner* (Glasgow, 1912), p. 106; A. Freeland Fergus, *The Origin and Development of the Glasgow School of Medicine* (Glasgow, 1911), pp. 22–23; James Finlayson, 'A Biographical Outline of Sir William T. Gairdner' (unpublished type-script), RCPSG 1/11/112.

11. Gibson, *Gairdner*, p. 317.

12. Gibson, *Gairdner*, pp. 318–9.

13. Report of the Medical Officer of Health for Glasgow to the Board of Police, April and July 1863, GCA LP1.1.

14. 'Testimonials in favour of Dr James B. Russell, 1864' (RCPSG Testimonials, vol. 1), pp. 5 and 11.

15. Fiona A. Macdonald, 'The Infirmary of Glasgow Town's Hospital, 1733–1800: a case for voluntarism?', *Bulletin of the History of Medicine*, Spring, 1999, vol. 73, No. 1 (forthcoming).

16. Minutes of the City Parochial Board, February 2, 1864, GCA D-HEW 1.1.

17. Margaret Lamb, 'The Medical Profession', in Checkland and Lamb, *Health Care*, pp. 27–28; David Hamilton, *The Healers: A History of Medicine in Scotland* (Edinburgh, 1981), p. 231.

18. Letter from William Mackenzie to JBR, January 1, 1864, WIL Ms. 5143/23.

19. Rona Gaffney, 'Poor Law Hospitals, 1845–1914', in Checkland and Lamb, *Health Care*, p. 46.

20. Alex Robertson, 'Town's Hospital or City Poorhouse', in James Christie, *The Medical Institutions of Glasgow: a Handbook Prepared for the Annual Meeting of the British Medical Association held in Glasgow, August 1888*, p. 77.

21. Quoted in Gaffney, 'Poor Law Hospitals', p. 49.

22. Jenkinson, Moss, and Russell, *The Royal*, p. 117.

23. Obituary, *GH*, October 24, 1904.

24. JBR, 'Analysis of Three Hundred Cases of Typhus', in *GMJ*, July 1864, pp. 142–173.

25. Nathaniel Hawthorne, who visited Glasgow a few years earlier, noted the same phenomenon. 'The children,' he wrote, 'seem to have been unwashed from birth, and perhaps they go on gathering a thicker and thicker coating of dirt till their dying days.' Quoted in Simon Berry and Hamish Whyte (eds.), *Glasgow Observed* (Edinburgh, 1987), p. 107.
26. JBR, *Public Health*, p. 20.
27. JBR, *Public Health*, p. 21.
28. JBR Testimonials, RCPSG; *GH*, April 26, 1865.

Chapter Eight

1. Minutes of the Magistrates' Committee of Glasgow Police Board, March 6, 1865, GCA E.1 6A.
2. WTG, Appreciation of JBR, *The Scotsman*, October 24, 1904, p. 7.
3. John Brownlee, 'Biographical Sketch of the late James B. Russell', in *Transactions of the Philosophical Society of Glasgow*, February, 1905, p. 87.
4. JBR, City of Glasgow Fever Hospital Report, 1865–6, p. 7, GGHB 23/1/2.
5. JBR, Fever Report, 1865–6, pp. 11 and 40.
6. JBR, Fever Report, 1865–6, p. 61.
7. F. B. Smith, *The People's Health, 1830–1910* (London, 1979), pp. 260–261. Russell, however, may have been influenced by moves in Edinburgh, where a Society for the Training of Sick Nurses had been started in 1861. Gairdner had played a leading role in improving conditions for nurses at Edinburgh Royal Infirmary in the early 1860s.
8. JBR, Fever Report, 1865–6, pp. 12–19 and JBR, *Public Health Administration in Glasgow* (Glasgow, 1905), pp. 45–46.
9. JBR, *Public Health*, p. 464.
10. Russell pasted a newspaper report of the speech, which was addressed to Edinburgh University students, into his commonplace book.
11. JBR, Fever Report, 1865–6, p. 10.
12. JBR, Fever Report, 1865–6, pp. 20–22.
13. Reprinted in JBR, *Public Health*, pp. 444–465.
14. Smith, *People's Health*, p. 243.
15. JBR, Fever Report, 1865–6, pp. 65–66.
16. JBR, Fever Report, 1865–6, p. 23.
17. JBR, *Public Health*, p. 84.
18. JBR, Fever Report, 1867–8, p. 14.
19. WTG, 'On Certain Arrangements made in the City of Glasgow, 1866, with a View to the Prevention of Epidemic Cholera'. Reprinted from the *Transactions of the Association of American Physicians*, 1891, p. 7.
20. JBR, Fever Report, 1866–7, pp. 7–14.
21. WTG, 'Cholera Arrangements', pp. 5–7. WTG, Report to the Superintendents and Visitors of Sections in the Recent Sanitary Visitation Movement, 1867, GCA LP1/18.2, pp. 15–47.
22. JBR, Fever Report, 1866–7, pp. 32, 35.

23. JBR, Fever Report, 1866–7, pp. 31–32.
24. JBR, Fever Report, 1866–7, pp. 35–36.
25. Letter from James Bryce to JBR, undated, WIL Ms. 5143/77.
26. Letter from JBR to James Bryce, June 16, 1865, The Papers of James Bryce, 1838–1922, Bodleian Library Mss. 1–528 Folio 152.

Chapter Nine

1. 'A sketch of the introduction of private nursing in Edinburgh, *The Pelican and Nurses' League Journal*, Royal Infirmary of Edinburgh, 1946, pp. 11–12, Lothian Health Board 1/109/36.
2. JBR, Commonplace book, GCA TD1434/2.
3. Letter from Dr John Brown to JBR, undated, WIL Ms. 5143/83.
4. *History of the Congregations of the United Presbyterian Church, 1733–1900* (Edinburgh, 1904), p. 472.
5. Glasgow Police Board minutes, April 27, 1868, GCA E1 3.5.
6. WTG, Appreciation of JBR, *The Scotsman*, October 24, 1904, p. 7.
7. City of Glasgow Fever Hospital Report, 1868–69, p. 17, GGHB 23/1.
8. *GMJ* Committee Minutes, 1868–1929, Royal College of Physicians and Surgeons of Glasgow, 6/1/3; 'The *GMJ* and its Editors', *GMJ* Centenary No., February, 1928, pp. 73–101.
9. *Glasgow Medical Examiner*, April 1870, p. 214.
10. Fever Report, 1869–70, pp. 24–5.
11. *GMJ*, November 1870, p. 138.
12. Fever Report, 1868–9, pp. 10-11.
13. Fever Report, 1870–2, p. 5.
14. Fever Report, 1870–2, pp. 8–10.
15. JBR, 'City of Glasgow Fever and Smallpox Hospitals', in James Christie, *The Medical Institutions of Glasgow* (Glasgow, 1888), pp. 82–97.
16. Marguerite W. Dupree, 'Family Care and Hospital Care: the Sick Poor in Nineteenth-Century Glasgow', *Social History of Medicine*, 6 (1993), pp. 195–211.
17. Fever Report, 1870–2, pp. 19–20.
18. A. K. Bowman, *Sir William Macewen* (London, 1942), p. 14.

Chapter Ten

1. WTG's preface to JBR, *Public Health Administration in Glasgow* (Glasgow, 1905), p. v.
2. Sir John Brotherston, 'Scottish Health Services in the Nineteenth Century', in Gordon McLachlan (ed.), *Improving the Commonweal: Aspects of Scottish Health Services, 1900–1984* (Edinburgh, 1987), pp. 5–6; T. C. Smout, 'Scotland 1850–1950', in *The Cambridge Social History of Britain, 1750–1950, Vol. 1* (Cambridge, 1990), p. 248.

3. David Hamilton, *The Healers: A History of Medicine in Scotland* (Edinburgh, 1981), p. 202.

4. R. J. Morris, 'Urbanisation and Scotland', in W. Hamish Fraser and R. J. Morris (eds.), *People and Society in Scotland, Vol. 2, 1830–1914* (Edinburgh, 1990), p. 87. Morris argues that the gap between Scottish and English practice was not as great as might appear because the early English Acts were not as effective as their supporters claimed.

5. Brenda White, 'Medical Police, Politics and Police: the Fate of John B. Roberton,' *Medical History*, 27 (1983), pp. 407–422.

6. C. I. Pennington, 'Mortality, Public Health, and Medical Improvements in Glasgow, 1855–1911' (Stirling University thesis, 1977), pp. 63–64; T. M. Devine, 'Urbanisation and the Civic Response: Glasgow, 1800–30', in A. J. G. Cummings and T. M. Devine (eds.), *Industry, Business and Society in Scotland since 1700* (Edinburgh, 1994), pp. 185–192. The Police Board was abolished in 1846 and a police committee set up under the Town Council, but in 1862 the committee was reconstituted as the Police Board. In 1877 the Town Council became the Commissioners of Police, but it was not until 1895 that it dealt with police and public health matters at its ordinary meetings. Until then a separate staffing and accounting system was retained.

7. JBR, *Public Health*, p. 17.

8. JBR, *Public Health*, pp. 5–7.

9. JBR, *Public Health*, p. 7.

10. JBR, *Public Health*, p. 16.

11. Ure's contribution to the developing sanitary service is assessed in Stephanie M. Blackden, 'The Development of Public Health Administration in Glasgow, 1842–1872' (Edinburgh University thesis, 1976), p. 108; and Pennington, 'Mortality', pp. 68–69. Contemporary accounts of his work include *The Bailie*, November 25, 1874, pp. 1–2.

12. George Alexander Gibson, *Life of Sir William Tennant Gairdner* (Glasgow, 1912), p. 94.

13. JBR, *Public Health*, p. 23.

14. JBR, *Public Health*, p. 26; Irene Maver, 'Glasgow's Civic Government', in W. Hamish Fraser and Irene Maver (eds.), *Glasgow, Vol. 2, 1830–1912* (Manchester, 1996), p. 460.

15. *Medical Examiner*, April, 1869, pp. 3–8.

16. *GH*, February 27, 1872, p. 4.

17. Police Board Minutes, January 3, 1870, GCA E1 3.7; *BMJ*, April, 1872, p. 454.

18. *GH*, May 21, 1872, p. 6.

19. *GMJ*, May, 1872, pp. 424–30.

20. Police Board Minutes for October 21 and November 4, 1872, GCA E1 3.9.

21. *GH*, October 22, 1872, p. 3; *North British Daily Mail*, October 22, 1872, p. 5.

22. *BMJ*, October 26, 1872, p. 476.

23. Letter from John Archibald Russell to JBR, November 5, 1872, WIL Ms. 514/27.
24. Police Board Minutes, December 2, 1872, GCA E1 3.9.

Chapter Eleven

1. William West Watson, *Report upon the Vital, Social, and Economic Statistics of Glasgow for 1872* (Glasgow, 1873), p. 78.
2. Brenda White, 'James Burn Russell, MOH, Glasgow, 1872–1898', in *Proceedings of the Scottish Society of the History of Medicine*, 1895–6, pp. 1–9.
3. Letter to the Editor from Professor John Glaister, *GH*, June 8, 1997, p. 3.
4. Obituary of Kenneth Macleod, *GH*, September 7, 1885, p. 6.
4. Police Board debate, *GH*, October 20, 1885, p. 3.
5. JBR, *Public Health Administration in Glasgow* (Glasgow, 1905), p. 88.
6. Police Board debate, *GH*.
7. JBR, *An Address Acnowledging a Presentation from the Staff of the Sanitary Department* (Glasgow, 1899), pp. 7–10.
8. JBR, *Public Health*, p. 91.
9. Health minutes, September 22, 1879, GCA E1 20.5, pp. 48–49.
10. Health minutes, January 18, 1875, GCA E1 20.2, p. 165.
11. JBR, *Public Health*, p. 342.
12. MOH's report for 1872, p. 9, GCA D-TC 14 2.37.
13. Medical Officer's Remarks on Glasgow Mortality Tables, 1873, pp. 1–2, GCA DT-C 14 2.39.
14. MOH reports, 1872–80, GCA D-TC 14 2.37–41. See also the statistics and graphs in JBR, *The Evolution of the Function of Public Health Administration* (Glasgow, 1895). I am grateful to Dr T. Scott Wilson for pointing out the importance of the use of logarithmic graph paper.
15. Letter from Dr Farr to JBR, April, 1875, WIL Ms. 5143/29.
16. *GH*, September 26, 1874, p. 4.
17. Health minutes, May 7, 1877, GCA E1 20.3, p. 212.
18. Health minutes, March 29, 1875, GCA E1 20.2, p. 202.
19. MOH reports, 1872–80.
20. JBR, *Public Health*, p. 93.
21. Health minutes, August 12, 1878, GCA E1 20.3, p. 141.
22. JBR, *Public Health*, pp. 93–94 and 342–343; Health minutes, October 23, 1878, pp. 190–191.
23. JBR, Letter to the Editor, *Lancet*, 1877, 11, p. 143. The failure of the measles policy is discussed in Anne Hardy's *The Epidemic Streets* (Oxford, 1993), p. 49.
24. JBR, *The Vital Statistics of the City of Glasgow* (Glasgow, 1886), Part 3, pp. 19–22, GCA DT-C14 2.41; JBR, *Public Health*, p. 343; Health minutes, November 4, 1878, GCA E1 20.4, p. 195 and November 17, 1879, GCA E1 20.5, pp. 80–81; and *GH*, September 22, 1874, p. 4.

25. *GMJ*, October, 1974, pp. 562–567.

26. Health minutes, August 14, 1876, GCA E1 20.3, p. 80.

27. JBR, *Lectures on the Theory and General Prevention and Control of Infectious Diseases* (Glasgow, 1878), pp. 92–96.

28. *GH*, November 17, 1874, p. 5.

29. Health minutes, March 29, 1875, GRA E1 20.2, p. 201.

30. Medical Officer's remarks on mortality tables, p. 6; JBR, *Public Health*, pp. 502–504.

31. *GMJ*, July, 1876, pp. 390–396.

32. Health minutes, March 13, 1876, GCA E1 20.3, pp. 2–3 and February 7, 1881, GCA E1 20.6, p. 16.

33. JBR, 'Report concerning a Remarkable Local Prevalence of Enteric Fever in January, 1873,' *GMJ*, August, 1873, pp. 475–481.

34. JBR, 'On Certain Epidemic Outbreaks of Enteric Fever in April, 1880, Traced to Contamination of Milk,' *SJ*, September 1880, pp. 193–213.

35. JBR, *On the Comparative Prevalence of Filth Diseases in Town and Country* (Glasgow, 1877), pp. 10–12 and 26.

36. Health minutes, January 17, 1876, GCA E1 20.2, p. 360.

37. Health minutes, March 15, 1875, GCA E1 20.2, p. 202.

38. 'Medical Ethics and the Sanitary Local Authority of Mearns,' *SJ*, December 1878, p. 318.

39. Health minutes, April 8, 1878, GCA E1 20.4, p. 46.

40. Health minutes, March 29, 1875, GCA E1 20.2, pp. 202–203.

41. Health minutes, January 28, 1878, GCA E1 20.3, p. 371.

42. Health minutes, April 7, 1879, GCA E1 20.4, pp. 311–313; *GH*, April 15, 1879, p. 7.

43. Health minutes, February 11, 1878, GCA E1 20.4, p. 6.

44. Health minutes, June 30, 1879, GCA E1 20.4, p. 370.

45. Health minutes, February 14, 1876, GCA E1 20.2, pp. 372–374.

46. Health minutes, December 18, 1876, GCA E1 20.3 p 138–140; Hardy, *Epidemic Streets*, pp. 137–142; JBR, *Evolution*, pp. 66–67.

47. Health minutes, April 23, 1877, GCA E1 20.3, p. 207.

48. Health minutes, September 24, 1877, GCA E1 20.3, p. 295–296.

49. JBR, *Public Health*, pp. 89–90; Hardy, *Epidemic Streets*, p. 127.

50. JBR, *Public Health*, pp. 334–335. In the following decade a 'female attendant' was appointed to wash children's arms before vaccination. See MOH's report for fortnight ending January 12, 1889, GCA E1 6A. 17, pp. 83–84.

51. Health minutes, February 12, 1877, GCA E1 20.3, pp. 169–70.

52. Health minutes, September 13 and November 8, 1875, GCA E1 20.2, pp. 283–285, 318–320; *GH*, September 21, 1875, p. 3; JBR, *Public Health*, p. 70.

53. Health minutes, November 8 and 24, 1875, GCA E1 20.2, pp. 322, 332.

54. JBR, *Public Health*, p. 85.

55. JBR, *Public Health*, p. 71.

56. Health minutes, March 24, 1879, GCA E1 20.4, p. 298.

57. Brenda White, 'James Burn Russell, MOH, 1872–1898', in *Scottish Society of the History of Medicine, proceedings, 1985–6*, p. 5.
58. Brian Edwards, 'Glasgow Improvements, 1866–1901', in Peter Reed (ed.), *Glasgow: the Forming of the City* (Edinburgh, 1993), pp. 88–89.
59. *GH*, October 6, 1874, p. 3.
60. *GH*, October 8, 1874, p. 3.
61. JBR, *Public Health*, pp. 96–102, 115–120.
62. JBR, *Public Health*, pp. 135–138.
63. JBR, *Public Health*, pp. 115, 132–133, 162.
64. JBR, *Public Health*, p. 133.
65. Health minutes, March 25, 1878, GCA E1 20.4, p. 38.
66. JBR, *Public Health*, pp. 138–140, 170–174.
67. Health minutes, October 25, 1875, GCA E1 20.2, p. 306.
68. Health minutes, January 17, 1887, GCA E1 20.10, pp. 285–286 and February 5, 1883, E1 20.7, p. 183.
69. JBR, *The Policy and Practice of Glasgow in the Management of Epidemic Diseases* (Glasgow, 1883), GCA LP/18.12, p. 29; Health minutes, June 21, 1875, GCA E1 20.2, pp. 245–246.
70. JBR, *Public Health*, pp. 185–186, 110–113.
71. Health minutes, December 17, 1877, GCA E1 20.3, pp. 340–341.
72. Health minutes, June 4, 1877. GCA E1 20.3, pp. 232–233 and June 18, 1877, p. 243.
73. Health minutes, July 31, 1876, GCA E1 20.3, p. 70.
74. Health minutes, September 10, 1877, GCA E1 20.3, p. 288.
75. JBR, 'The Local Authority v. Young,' *SJ*, January, 1880, pp. 329–333 and editorial, p. 364. For the criticism of Russell's policy, see *SJ*, February 1880, p. 391.
76. JBR, *Evolution*, p. 131. Russell includes a table showing Glasgow's birth and death rates.
77. JBR, *Vital Statistics*, part 111, p. 17.
78. JBR, *Vital Statistics*, part 1, pp. 7, 26–28.
79. JBR, *Vital Statistics*, part 1, p. 34.
80. MOH report for 1879, p. 5, GCA DTC 14 2.40.
81. John Glaister, 'The Epidemic History of Glasgow during the Century 1783–1883,' *Transactions of the Royal Philosophical Society of Glasgow*, April, 1886, p. 33.
82. *GH*, September 25, 1874, p. 5.
83. *GH*, September 30, 1879, p. 3.
84. *GH*, November 14, 1876, pp. 2 and 5, and November 28, p. 2.
85. Health minutes, November 18, 1878, GCA E1 20.4 pp. 213–216.
86. *GH*, 29 December, 1879, p. 3 and January 2, 1980, p. 4.
87. *GH*, January 6, 1980, p. 7.

Chapter Twelve

1. Petition to Sheriff to grant order for admission, certified insane, GGHB, 13/7/83.
2. GGHB 13/5/102.
3. Mr Sam Galbraith, MP, former neuro-surgeon at the Southern General Hospital, Glasgow, raised this possibility and supplied information on the disease. Dr Iain Smith, Consultant Psychiatrist at Gartnavel Royal Hospital, who also read the case notes, thought that the symptoms were consistent with a range of organic diseases.
4. Jonathan Andrews and Iain Smith (eds.), *'Let There Be Light Again': A History of Gartnavel Royal Hospital from its Beginnings to the Present Day* (Glasgow, 1993), pp. 63–64.
5. Register of deaths, GGHB13/6/95.
6. Gillian Small, 'Origins and Development of Dowanhill', unpublished typescript, Glasgow University Archives, UGD92/126, 1989.
7. Health minutes, June 14, 1880 and October 4, 1880, GCA E1 20.5, pp. 224, 297.
8. Alistair A. Clark, *Just a Minute or Two: the History of the Western Medical Club, 1845–1902* (Glasgow, 1994), p. 153.
9. John Dougall, *Historical Sketch of the Glasgow Southern Medical Society* (Glasgow, 1888), pp. 40–42.
10. Letter from JBR to Mrs Georgina Coats, January 24, 1899, quoted in *Dr and Mrs Joseph Coats: a book of remembrance compiled by their daughters* (Glasgow, 1929), p. 156. The book describes Russell as 'one of Dr Coats's most valued friends'.
11. *Dr and Mrs Coats*, p. 217.
12. 'The Late James Christie', *SJ*, January 19, 1892, pp. 437–441; 'Tribute by Dr Russell', *SJ*, January 19, 1892, pp. 443–444.
13. *Proceedings of the Royal Philosophical Society of Glasgow*, Vol. IX, pp. 73–5.
14. Henry E. Clark (ed.), *Memorials of Elgin Place Congregational Church, Glasgow: A Centenary Volume* (Glasgow, 1904), pp. 121–122.
15. M. Anne Crowther and Brenda White, *On Soul and Conscience: the Medical Expert and Crime* (Aberdeen, 1988), p. 26.
16. The Rev. Ambrose Shepherd, *In Memoriam James Burn Russell* (Glasgow, 1905).
17. Nicholas J. Morgan, 'Building the City', in W. Hamish Fraser and Irene Maver (eds.), *Glasgow, Vol. 2, 1830–1910*, pp. 49–50.

Chapter Thirteen

1. JBR, *Public Health Administration in Glasgow* (Glasgow, 1905), p. 141.
2. JBR, 'The First Principles of Cleanliness as regards Earth, Air, and Water: lecture to Airdrie and Flowerhill parishes' Young Men's Society, November, 1878', *SJ* January 1, 1879, pp. 340–341.

3. JBR, 'First Principles', p. 341.

4. JBR, 'First Principles', p. 342.

5. Health minutes, January 24, 1881, GCA E1 20.6, p. 4.

6. JBR, 'First Principles', p. 341.

7. JBR, *Public Health*, pp. 371–2.

8. JBR, *Public Health*, p. 155.

9. Health minutes, March 27, 1876, GCA E1 20.3, pp. 10–11.

10. *GH*, August 9, 1888, p. 9; 'First Principles', p. 388.

11. Health minutes, August 21, 1882, GCA E1 20.7, pp. 50–51.

12. Health minutes, January 22, 1883, GCA E1 20.7, pp. 165–172.

13. JBR, *Public Health*, pp. 412–443.

14. S. G. Checkland, *The Upas Tree: Glasgow 1875–1975* (Glasgow, 1976), p. 13; Allan Massie, *Glasgow: Portraits of a City* (London, 1989), p. 44.

15. Health minutes, March 5, 1883. GCA E1 20.7, pp. 199, 213–214. August 4, 1884, GCA E1 20.8, pp. 231–232.

16. Health minutes, October 2, 1882, GCA E1 20.7, pp. 78–80.

17. Health minutes, May 2, 1881, GCA E1 20.6, p. 90.

18. Health minutes, March 2 and May 21, 1888, GCA E1 20.11, pp. 237, 311.

19. Health minutes, March 12 and 26, 1888, GCA E1 20.11, pp. 252–257, 276–280. Russell's full account of the outbreak can be found in his *Public Health*, pp. 375–405.

20. JBR, Obituary of W. R. W. Smith, *Proceedings of the Philosophical Society of Glasgow, 1892–3*, pp. 206–210.

21. *The Bailie*, June 21, 1876, pp. 1–2.

22. JBR, Smith obituary.

23. *The Bailie*, May 2, 1888, pp. 1–2. *GH* obituary of Crawford, 1899, in Glasgow Corporation 'Doomsday Book' of press cuttings, GCA; Irene Sweeney, 'The Municipal Administration of Glasgow, 1833–1912' (Strathclyde University thesis, 1990), pp. 430–431.

24. *GH*, March 1, 1881, p. 7.

25. *GH*, December 6, 1881, p. 3.

26. JBR, *Public Health*, p. 226; *GH*, November 8, 1881, p. 3.

27. Health minutes, December 31, 1888, GCA E1 20.12, pp. 11–13.

28. *GH*, December 5, 1882, p. 3.

29. *GH*, November 7, 1882, p. 3.

30. Health minutes, November 24, 1875, GCA E1 20.2, p. 332.

31. *GH*, January 16, 1883, p. 3.

32. JBR, Public Health, pp. 209–210.

33. Health minutes, October 21, 1889, GCA E1 20.12, p. 108.

34. *GH*, January 19, 1892, p. 4; February 2, 1892, pp. 3, 6; and February 16, 1892, p. 3.

35. Health minutes, August 12, 1889, GCA E1 20.12, p. 84; *GH*, June 9, 1889, p. 3.

36. The debate is fully reported in *GH*, October 20, 1885, p. 3.

37. *GH*, May 19, 1885, p. 7.

38. *GH*, August 29, 1882, p. 3.

39. *GH*, March 22, 1887, p. 3.

40. *GH*, October 21, 1885, p. 11.

41. MOH's memorandum on the Local Government (Scotland) Bills, 1889, GCA E1 6A. 17, pp. 269–271, 289–290.

42. JBR, 'Errors in the Diagnosis of Infectious Diseases', *GMJ*, vol. 34, 1890, pp. 1–10.

43. 'Discussion on Errors in the Diagnosis of Infectious Diseases', *GMJ*, vol. 34, 1890, pp. 147–160.

44. *Lancet*, August 9, 1890, p. 291.

45. JBR, 'Report upon Uncertificated Deaths in Glasgow' (1876), GCA LP1/18–8, p. 67; Olive Checkland, *Philanthropy in Victorian Scotland* (Edinburgh, 1980), pp. 204–205.

46. S. D. Slater and D. A. Dow, *The Victoria Infirmary of Glasgow, 1890–1990: a Centenary History* (Glasgow, 1989), p. 1; JBR, *Public Health*, p. 207.

47. JBR, *Public Health*, pp. 405–411.

48. Reprinted in *SJ*, June 18, 1887, pp. 97–101.

49. Letter from WTG to JBR, December 20, 1877, WIL Ms. 5143/34.

50. JBR, *Public Health*, pp. 189–190.

51. JBR, *Public Health*, pp. 147–148 (editor's note).

52. JBR, 'First Principles', p. 345.

53. JBR, *Public Health*, pp. 196–197.

54. JBR, *Public Health*, pp. 301–323.

55. Michael Flinn, *Scottish Population History from the 17th Century to the 1930s* (Cambridge, 1977), p. 383.

56. JBR, *The Vital Statistics of the City of Glasgow* (Glasgow, 1886), p. 40, GCA DT-C14 2.41.

57. JBR, 'On the Distribution of Enteric Fever in Glasgow', *GMJ*, 1869, Vol. 1, pp. 59–66; House of Commons Minutes of Evidence taken before the Select Committee on Police and Sanitary Regulations in the Glasgow Police Bill, Thursday 12 January, 1890, GCA A/3/1/129, pp. 26–27; Stephanie M. Blackden, 'The Development of Public Health Administration in Glasgow, 1842–1872' (Edinburgh University thesis, 1976), p. 168; C. I. Pennington, 'Mortality, Public Health, and Medical Improvements in Glasgow, 1855–1911' (Stirling University thesis, 1977), p. 358.

58. Royal Commission on the Housing of the Working Classes, 1885, Vol. 5: Scotland (C4409–1), p. 49.

59. JBR, *Public Health*, pp. 260–262.

Chapter Fourteen

1. George Alexander Gibson, *Life of Sir William Tennant Gairdner* (Glasgow, 1912), p. 240.

2. John F. McCaffrey, 'The origins of Liberal Unionism in the West of Scotland', *Scottish Historical Review*, Vol. 50, 1971, pp. 47–51; John F. McCaffrey, 'Political Issues and Developments', in W. Hamish Fraser and

Irene Maver (eds.), *Glasgow, Vol. 2, 1830–1912* (Manchester, 1996), pp. 204–221; Irene Maver, 'Politics and Power in the Scottish City: Glasgow Town Council in the Nineteenth Century', in T. M. Devine (ed.), *Scottish Elites: Proceedings of the Scottish Historical Studies Seminar, University of Strathclyde, 1991–2* (Edinburgh, 1994).

3. JBR, Obituary of W. R. W. Smith, *Proceedings of the Philosophical Society of Glasgow*, 1892–93, p. 206.

4. Crosbie Smith and M. Wise Norton, *Energy and Empire: a Biographical study of Lord Kelvin* (Cambridge, 1989), p. 804.

5. I am grateful to Dr John McCaffrey for this information, and for valuable help on the subject of Liberal Unionism.

6. Gibson, *Gairdner*, p. 240.

7. Annotations in JBR's commonplace book, GCA TD1434/2.

8. McCaffrey, *Liberal Unionism*, p. 68.

9. Smith and Norton, *Kelvin*, pp. 805–806.

10. JBR, *Public Health Administration in Glasgow* (Glasgow, 1905), p. 274.

11. JBR, *Public Health*, p. 189.

12. JBR, *Public Health*, p. 110.

13. JBR, *Public Health*, p. 292.

14. JBR, *Public Health*, p. 283.

15. JBR, *Public Health*, p. 297. See also I. G. C. Hutchison, 'Glasgow Working-class Politics', in R. A. Cage (ed.), *The Working Class in Glasgow, 1750–1914* (London, 1987), p. 113.

16. JBR, *Public Health*, pp. 249–259.

17. JBR, *Public Health*, p. 296.

18. I. G. C. Hutchison, *A Political History of Scotland, 1832–1924* (Edinburgh, 1986), p. 205.

19. McCaffrey, *Liberal Unionism*, p. 69.

20. McCaffrey, *Liberal Unionism*, pp. 69–70.

Chapter Fifteen

1. Bernard Aspinwall, 'Glasgow Trams and American Politics, 1894–1914', *Scottish Historical Review*, Vol. 56, pp. 64–84.

2. *GH*, June 26, 1895, p. 9.

3. Bernard Aspinwall, *Portable Utopia: Glasgow and the United States, 1820–1920* (Aberdeen, 1984), p. 164.

4. Letter from James Bryce to JBR, undated, WIL Ms. 5143/79.

5. Albert Shaw, *Municipal Government in Great Britain* (London 1995), pp. 80–81.

6. JBR, *Public Health Administration in Glasgow* (Glasgow, 1905), pp. 225–226.

7. Irene A. Sweeney, 'The Municipal Administration of Glasgow, 1833–1912' (Strathclyde University thesis, 1990), pp. 428–429.

8. JBR, *Public Health*, introduction, p. xxii.

9. *GH*, July 25, 1896, p. 7.

10. *GH*, December 15, 1896, p. 11.

11. *GH*, July 25, 1896, p. 7

12. Sir James Bell and James Paton, *Glasgow—its Municipal Organisation and Administration* (Glasgow, 1896), p. 197.

13. Health minutes, June 27, 1892, GCA E1 20.13, p. 181.

14. Health minutes, January 25, 1892, GCA E1 20.13, p. 60; Bell and Paton, *Municipal Organisation*, p. 139.

15. *GH*, July 18, 1893, p. 2.

16. *GH*, January 20, 1891, p. 3.

17. Health minutes, November 2, 1891, GCA E1 20.12, p. 381.

18. Health minutes, December 14, 1891, GCA E1 20.13, p. 28.

19. MOH's report on 1891 census, GCA LP/22 pp. 26–27.

20. Health minutes, November 16, 1891, GCA E1 20.13, p. 11.

21. *GH*, October 27, 1891, p. 3; Health minutes, December 14, 1891, GCA E1 20.13, pp. 27–28

22. AKC pamphlets, GCA LP1/90.

23. Report by the Deputation Appointed by the Magistrates and Council of Glasgow to Inquire into the Treatment of Sewage in Various Towns in England, October, 1888, GCA LP 2/32,p. 30.

24. *GH*, December 6, 1892, p. 3.

25. Health minutes, August 29, 1892, GCA E1 20.13, p. 236.

26. Bell and Paton, *Glasgow*, p. 140.

27. Health minutes, May 14, 1894, GCA E1 20.15, p. 85.

28. Health minutes, May 28, 1894 and June 11, 1894, GCA E1 20.15, pp. 109–115, 135 and 169.

29. Neil McFarlane, 'Tuberculosis in Scotland, 1870–1960' (Glasgow University thesis, 1990), p. 45.

30. JBR *Public Health*, pp. 568–570.

31. JBR, *Public Health*, p. 530.

32. Anne Hardy, *The Epidemic Streets: Infectious Disease and the Rise of Preventive Medicine* (Oxford, 1993), p. 133. The author states that 'it is clear that medical officers, philanthropists, and interested sanitarians were promoting measures designed to reduce tuberculosis mortality from the 1860s onwards.'

33. JBR, *Public Health*, p. 165.

34. JBR, *Public Health*, p. 563.

35. Health minutes, April 4 and 17, 1893, GCA E1 20.14 pp. 106, 118–121.

36. *SJ*, November, 1891.

37. JBR, *Public Health*, p. 556.

38. JBR, *Public Health*, p. 593.

39. JBR, *Public Health*, p. 595.

40. JBR, *Public Health*, pp. 405–411.

41. Health minutes, August 10, 1891, GCA E1 20.12, p. 344.

42. Health minutes, May 14 and November 26, 1894, GCA E1 20.15, pp. 87–88 and 349.

43. JBR, *Public Health*, pp. 529–570.

44. JBR, *Public Health*, p. 369.
45. McFarlane, 'Tuberculosis' p. 3. The author argues that the strong public health tradition of the Scottish cities helps to explain the exceptional progress made in Glasgow. Female mortality fell faster than male, suggesting the importance of domestic and personal hygiene. Carolyn Pennington, on the other hand, gives greater weight to nutrition in her chapter on tuberculosis in Olive Checkland and Margaret Lamb (eds.), *Health Care as Social History* (Aberdeen, 1982), pp. 86–99. This is in line with the thesis advanced in Thomas McKeown, *Medicine in Modern Society* (London, 1965). McKeown's conclusions have been challenged by, among others, Simon Szreter in 'The importance of social intervention in Britain's mortality decline c. 1850–1914: a reinterpretation of the role of public health', *Social History of Medicine*, 1 (1988), pp. 1–37.
46. Michael E. Teller, *The Tuberculosis Movement: a Public Health Campaign in the Progressive Era* (New York, 1988), p. 3. Teller describes Massachussets in that period as 'a State that was conservative in politics but advanced in public health and social welfare.'
47. JBR, *Public Health*, p. 328.
48. *GH*, July 18, 1893, p. 2.
49. Health minutes, August 29, 1892, GCA E1 20.13, p. 234.
50. JBR, *Public Health*, p. 333; Health minutes, October 2, 1893, GCA E1 20.14, p. 264.
51. JBR, *Public Health*, p. 371.
52. JBR, *Public Health*, p. 366.
53. JBR, *Public Health*, pp. 344–356; AKC, *The Health of Glasgow, 1818–1925*, pp. 323–324. The improvement in Glasgow was not detectable when measured in five-year periods.
54. AKC, *Health*, pp. 283–286.
55. Health minutes, June 22, 1896, GCA E. 1 20.17, pp. 34–35.
56. JBR, *Public Health*, p. 362.
57. AKC, *Health*, pp. 288–289.
58. AKC, *Health*, pp. 194–195.
59. *GMJ*, October, 1874, pp. 562–567.
60. AKC, *Health*, p. 203. Chalmers pointed out that many breast-fed babies were also failing to thrive. The large proportion of deaths taking place in the first few weeks of life led to greater attention to the diet of nursing mothers.
61. John Glaister, *Forensic Medicine and Public Health in the University of Glasgow, its Position and Wants* (Glasgow, 1900), pp. 31–35.

Chapter Sixteen

1. Mary Russell, 'Diary of my First Tour of the Continent' (family archives).
2. JBR, *An Address acknowledging a Presentation from the Staff of the Sanitary Department and Fever Hospitals of Glasgow* (Glasgow 1898), pp. 4–5.

3. Health minutes, October 1, 1894, GCA E1 20.15, pp. 273–275.

4. Press Association report, *GH*, September 6, 1894, p. 4. For a discussion of Seaton's conference paper and other issues arising at this important congress, see Anne Hardy, *The Epidemic Streets: Infectious Diseases and the Rise of Preventive Medicine* (Oxford, 1993), pp. 87–88.

5. *GH*, September 11, 1894, p. 7.

6. *GH* June 26, 1895, p. 9.

7. JBR, *The Evolution of the Function of Health Administration in Glasgow in the Nineteenth Century* (Glasgow, 1895).

8. Health minutes, October 14, 1895, GCA E1 20.16, p. 208.

9. Letter from JBR to Lord Kelvin, June 16, 1896, Kelvin letters, Cambridge University Library, 7342, Jb192.

10. *GH*, July 24, 1896, p. 9.

11. *GH*, July 25, 1896, p. 7.

12. Health minutes, July 9, 1894, GCA E1 20.15, pp. 203, 206 and April 29, 1895, GCA E1 20.16, p. 81.

13. Health minutes, April 13, 1896, GCA E1 20.16, p. 367.

14. *GH*, August 13, 1895, p. 7.

15. *GH*, February 13, 1894, p. 3.

16. *GH*, June 30, 1896, p. 7.

17. The municipal politics of the period are analysed in Irene A. Sweeney (aka Maver), 'The Municipal Administration of Glasgow, 1833–1912' (Strathclyde University thesis, 1990), and Irene Maver, 'Politics and Power in the Scottish City: Glasgow Town Council in the Nineteenth Century', in T. M. Devine (ed.), *Scottish Elites: Proceedings of the Scottish Historical Studies Seminar, University of Strathclyde 1991–2* (Edinburgh, 1994), pp. 98–124.

18. Health minutes, December 17, 1888 and March 11, 1889, GCA E1 20.12, pp. 2 and 34–35.

19. *GH*, September 4, 1888, p. 3.

20. *GH*, November 12, 1889, p. 9.

21. Royal Commission on the Housing of the Working Classes, 1885, vol. 5: Scotland (C4409), p. 49.

22. Brian Edwards, 'Glasgow Improvements, 1866–1901', in Peter Reed (ed.), *Glasgow: the Forming of the City* (Edinburgh, 1893), p. 97.

23. *GH*, October 18, 1887, p. 6.

24. *GH*, November 12, 1889, p. 9.

25. Sweeney, 'Municipal Administration', pp. 633–636, 338.

26. Health minutes, February 18, 1895, GCA E1 20.16, p. 18. MOH's Memorandum on the Acts (general and local) dealing with uninhabitable houses and areas, Glasgow Police Department Minutes, January, 1895, GCA E1 6A. 21, pp. 260–265.

27. Health minutes, October 12, 1896, E1 20.17, pp. 128–131; *GH*, October 20, 1896, p. 7..

28. JBR's letter to the Town Clerk, Health minutes, October 12, 1896, E1 20.17, pp. 132–135.

29. The debate was reported in *GH*, October 20, 1896, p. 7.
30. *GH*, October 20, 1896, p. 4.
31. *The Lord Provosts of Glasgow, 1833–1902* (Glasgow, 1902), p. 564.
32. *GH*, October 24, 1896, p. 8, October 27, 1896, p. 7, and October 30, 1896, p. 8.
33. Sweeney, 'Municipal Administration', pp. 436–439.
34. See Ian Levitt, *Poverty and Welfare in Scotland, 1890–1948* (Edinburgh, 1988), p. 24.
35. Obituary, *Lancet*, November 12, 1904, p. 1274.
36. Letter from John Skelton to JBR, September 17, 1894, WIL Ms. 5143/49.
37. *The Bailie*, October 5, 1898, p. 5.
38. *SJ*, October, 1898, pp. 420–423.
39. *SJ*, February, 1898, pp. 638–640 and March, 1898, pp. 65–66.
40. Health minutes, October 10, 1898, GCA E1 20.19, pp. 79–80.
41. Letter from Lord Balfour to JBR, August 31, 1898, WIL Ms. 5143/49.
42. *GH*, December 28, 1898, p. 7.
43. *GH*, November 2, 1898, p. 23.
44. JBR, *Address Acknowledging Presentation from the Sanitary Department.*

Chapter Seventeen

1. Ian Levitt, *Poverty and Welfare in Scotland* (Edinburgh, 1988), p. 24.
2. Report on the Sanitary Association of Scotland's Deputation to the Scottish Secretary, *SJ*, March, 1893, p. 25–26.
3. *SJ*, October, 1894, pp. 422–424.
4. JBR, 'On the Existing Sanitary Regulation of the Milk Trade,' *SJ*, March, 1881, pp. 1–12.
5. JBR, 'Public Health and Pauperism,' *SJ*, July, 1884, pp. 129–134.
6. Levitt, *Poverty and Welfare*, p. 46.
7. *SJ*, May, 1901, pp. 122–123.
8. LGBS, 1900 (Cd. 701), p. xliv.
9. LGBS, 1900 (Cd. 701), p. xxxviii.
10. LGBS, 1903 (Cd. 2001), p. 81.
11. LGBS, 1902 (Cd. 1521), p. 65.
12. LGBS, 1900 (Cd. 701), p. lii.
13. LGBS, 1900 (Cd. 701), p. xliv.
14. LGBS, 1900 (Cd. 701), p. l.
15. LGBS, 1901 (Cd. 1051), p. xxxxix.
16. LGBS, 1902 (Cd. 1521), p. xxxi.
17. *SJ*, May, 1901, p. 122.
18. LGBS, 1900 (Cd. 701), p. xliv and 1903 (Cd. 2001), p. xlv.
19. LGBS, 1899 (Cd. 182), pp. 23–24.
20. LGBS, 1902 (Cd. 1521), p. xxxviii.
21. LGBS, 1902 (Cd. 1521), p. xxxviii.
22. LGBS, 1900 (Cd. 701), pp. xxx1x, xxxix–xxxix.

23. LGBS, 1901 (Cd. 1051), p. xlvi and 1902 (Cd. 1520), p. xlv.
24. LGBS, 1902 (Cd. 1521), pp. xxxv–xxxvii.
25. AKC, *The Health of Glasgow, 1818–1925* (Glasgow, 1930), pp. 103–104.
26. LGBS, 1900 (Cd. 701), pp. xxxv–xxxvii.
27. *GH*, November 1, 1901, p. 6. See also Brenda White, 'Plague and Boats and Trains: bubonic plague and the formation of a port health authority for Glasgow, 1900–1903', paper delivered at the annual conference of the Society for the Social History of Medicine, Liverpool, September 6, 1997.
28. Dr Myron Echenberg, of McGill University, who is writing a book on the 1901 plague, drew my attention to this contrast.
29. Mackenzie wrote a glowing view of JBR's *Evolution of Public Health*, which he described as 'an exposition of singular richness and potency of conviction.' He described Russell as Glasgow's prophet and declared that the city had at last come 'in the full consciousness of her powers, to pursue a policy designed and defined by a genuine social insight.' The review was published in *SJ*, December 1895, pp. 508–514.
30. *SJ*, May, 1901, pp. 122–123.

Chapter Eighteen

1. Letter from Malcolm McNeill to JBR, June 13, 1904, WIL Ms. 5143/73.
2. Letter from WTG to JBR, April 29, 1902, WIL Ms. 5143/62.
3. *Dr and Mrs Joseph Coats: a Book of Remembrance Compiled by their Daughters* (Glasgow, 1929), p. 156.
4. Letter from JBR to James Bryce, August 23, 1903, The Papers of James Bryce, 1838–1922, No. 129, Folio 155 (Bodleian Library).
5. Letter from James Bryce to JBR, September 3, 1903, WIL Ms. 5143/70.
6. Letter from WTG to JBR, June 20, 1904, WIl Ms. 5143/74.
7. Letter from Malcolm McNeill to JBR, June 13, 1904, WIL Ms. 5143/73.
8. LGBS, 1904 (Cd. 2514), p. liv.
9. Letter from Lord Balfour to JBR, September 16, 1898, WIL Ms. 5143/56.
10. Letter from WTG to JBR, February 22, 1897, WIL Ms. 5143/52.
11. Letter from J. Patten MacDougall to David Russell, January 17, 1905, WIL Ms. 5143/101.
12. Hector Clare Cameron, Obituary of JBR, *GMJ*, December, 1904, p. 436.
13. Obituary, *Lancet*, November 12, 1904, p. 1387.

Chapter Nineteen

1. Letter from Matthew Hay to Malcolm McNeill, WIL ms. 5143/98.
2. Appreciation, *The Scotsman*, October 24, 1904, p. 7.
3. *Lancet*, November 12, 1904, p. 1387.
4. AKC, *The Health of Glasgow, 1818–1925* (Glasgow, 1930), p. 59.
5. Thomas McKeown, *Medicine in Modern Society* (London, 1965).
6. Russell, who made a notable contribution to rising standards of food

purity, was interested in nutrition throughout his career. He had deplored the trend towards white bread and tea as early as the 1860s, when he was responsible for patients' diets at Glasgow Fever Hospital. He was not alone in suggesting that the Scottish diet was in some respects deteriorating in quality towards the end of the nineteenth century. See Rory Williamson, 'Medical, economic and population factors in areas of high mortality: the case of Glasgow', in *Sociology of Health and Illness*, vol. 16 no. 2, 1994, pp. 165–166; also W. Hamish Fraser and Irene Maver, 'The Social Problems of the City', in Fraser and Maver (eds.), *Glasgow, vol. 2, 1830–1912* (Manchester, 1996), p. 362.

7. Thomas McKeown's arguments in favour of the primacy of nutrition were challenged by Simon Szreter, 'The importance of social intervention in Britain's mortality decline c. 1850–1914: a reinterpretation of the role of public health', *Social History of Medicine*, 1 (1988), pp. 1–37. Szreter demonstrates the importance of sanitation and hygiene—for example in reducing mortality from tuberculosis. Anne Hardy, in *The Epidemic Streets: Infectious Diseases and the Rise of Preventive Medicine* (Oxford, 1993) warns of the dangers of making historical extrapolations from recent research on the relationship between malnutrition and disease in developing countries: the indications are, she points out (pp. 280–281), that malnutrition has to be severe before it aggravates infection. Her study of local epidemiological trends in England reinforces the argument that preventive measures were significant.

8. Neil Munro McFarlane, 'Tuberculosis in Scotland, 1870–1960' (Glasgow University thesis, 1990), p. 2.

9. C. I. Pennington, 'Mortality, Public Health, and Medical Improvements in Glasgow, 1855–1911' (Stirling University thesis, 1977), pp. 381–385.

10. Pennington, in 'Mortality in Glasgow' (p. 409), concludes that the main explanation for the fall in mortality lies in public health improvements such as better sanitation and a slight improvement in housing and density as well as better standards of food purity. Williamson, in 'Medical Factors' (p. 175), though emphasising economic and industrial influences, maintains that 'much of the credit must lie with public health measures.' Sanitary reform and housing improvements are also emphasised as explanations of the mortality decline by Charles Withers in 'The Demographic History of the City', in Fraser and Maver (eds.), *Glasgow*, p. 158. It is generally agreed nowadays that advances in medical science played only a small part in the mortality decline.

11. JBR, *The Evolution of the Function of Public Health Administration* (Glasgow, 1895), p. 53.

12. *SJ*, March, 1893, p. 26; JBR, 'Sanitary Reform in the Rural Districts of Scotland A Necessity in the Interests of Populous Places', *SJ*, May 4, 1883, pp. 64–70.

13. JBR, *Public Health Administration in Glasgow* (Glasgow, 1905), p. 183; JBR, 'Common Lodging Houses', *SJ*, April 17, 1889, pp. 33–38.

14. JBR, *Public Health*, p. 241.

15. JBR, *Public Health*, p. 248.
16. JBR, *Public Health*, p. 274.
17. JBR, *Public Health*, p. 195.
18. *GH*, December 29, 1879, p. 3.
19. *SJ*, March, 1898, pp. 67–68. The article quotes a letter from Russell to the *Birmingham Mail*, which had asked for his opinion. He touched on the same topic in his evidence to the Royal Commission on the Housing of the Working Classes in 1885 (Vol. v: Scotland, C4409 -I, p. 47).
20. Nor, for that matter, did Dr William Horne, the MOH at the time, but he was overruled. Russell's opinion of the London flats is given in JBR, *Public Health*, pp. 141–142.
21. R. A. Cage, 'Infant Mortality Rates and Housing: Twentieth-century Glasgow', in *Scottish Economic and Social History*, Vol. 14, 1994, pp. 77–92.
22. See chart of death rates in Glasgow sanitary districts in AKC, *The Health of Glasgow, 1818–1925* (Glasgow, 1930), facing p. 76. Glasgow Corporation annual report of MOH for 1898, GCA LP1/19, pp. 14–19.
23. S. G. Checkland, *The Upas Tree* (Glasgow, 1976), p. 18; Michael Pacione, *Glasgow: The Socio-spatial Development of the City* (Chichester, 1995), p. 397.
24. JBR, *Public Health*, p. 285.
25. JBR, *An Address Acknowledging a Presentation from the Staff of the Sanitary Department* (Glasgow, 1899), pp. 13–14.

Family Footnote

1. Margaret A. Ormsby, *Coldstream Nulli Secondus: a History of the Corporation of the District of Coldstream* (Manitoba, 1990).

Index